THE
SPEED
OF
SOUND

THE SPEED OF SOUND

BREAKING THE BARRIER BETWEEN MUSIC AND TECHNOLOGY

THOMAS DOLBY

**FLATIRON
BOOKS**
New York

AUTHOR'S NOTE

This is an entirely true story, though some names and details have been changed and time frames compressed. I should also make it clear to the reader that I am not associated in any way with Dolby Laboratories, Inc., maker of Dolby noise reduction systems, nor am I related to its founder, Ray Dolby, or to his son the writer Tom Dolby.

www.flatironbooks.com

Designed by Jonathan Bennett

The Library of Congress Cataloging-in-Publication Data is available upon request.

ISBN 978-1-250-07184-2 (hardcover)
ISBN 978-1-250-07191-0 (e-book)

Our books may be purchased in bulk for promotional, educational, or business use. Please contact your local bookseller or the Macmillan Corporate and Premium Sales Department at 1-800-221-7945, extension 5442, or by e-mail at MacmillanSpecialMarkets@macmillan.com.

First Edition: October 2016

10 9 8 7 6 5 4 3 2 1

For Harper, Talia, and Graham, who once asked me,
"Daddy, how come you're not a multimillionaire?"

CONTENTS

CONTENTS

PROLOGUE

Dan the driver opened the pneumatic door of the tour bus and I stumbled out, blinking in the Nevada sun. I had my arms full of electronic equipment: a Philips cassette machine, my Radio Shack portable computer, assorted cables, and those weird rubber acoustic cups that you push the phone receiver into to send and receive files. The pockets of my corduroy trousers were bulging with quarters.

I'd made Dan pull off the highway at a run-down gas station a million miles from anywhere. This pissed him right off, but I needed to use the phone booth. He brought the bus to a stop in a cloud of its own dust. There was a beaten-up wooden shack with a porch and—I kid you not—an old guy in a rocker with a pipe.

The sun was getting high now and the desert landscape was dull, featureless. Wrecked cars, the odd cactus. Somewhere off in the distance a glistening metropolis called Las Vegas rose out of the desert. It would be the middle of the morning by the time our forty-five-foot silver Prevost tour bus rolled up the Strip, still less than halfway to our destination, Salt Lake City.

Dan the bus driver was from Texas. He had his little tin of amphetamines open on the dash and he was determined to make it all the way to Salt Lake by midafternoon. By law his limit was ten straight hours of driving. But he wanted that overdrive bonus bad, so he'd waved away the idea of bringing a relief driver; and he still reckoned we would arrive at the venue just in time for sound check. Barring unscheduled stops.

It was all because of Michael Jackson. He'd been on the guest list for our gig at the Greek Theatre and afterwards he came backstage. I'd just finished my encores and I was cooling off in this big tent they'd set up as a green room. His entourage outnumbered my band and crew, which was awkward, but he beckoned me off into a corner and we stood facing the canvas wall and talked as the backstage freeloaders kept their distance, pretending not to look.

I hadn't seen Michael since that rainy night at his house in Encino the previous February. His skin was translucent, like a lithe black vampire's. He was evolving.

He spoke in a whisper, but I think he said he really liked the show. He knew the names of the individual songs, and was impressed that I had a Fairlight up there onstage, a fragile $90,000 computer music instrument. Was it better than his Synclavier, which cost twice as much? I gave him my views on both. I spouted bit rates and azimuth. This calmed me down. I was nervous because he was a showbiz genius, possessor of a God-given talent. He could have gotten up there and moonwalked circles around me any day of the week, singing his lungs out, and we both knew it. So I thought, I might as well blind him with science.

We talked like that for ten minutes before he told me he had to get back to the Record Plant, where he and his brothers were supposed to be recording a new album. It was chaos and they were way behind schedule. Each of the Jackson brothers had come in with his own demos, and everybody wanted a songwriting or production credit. But most of the songs, Michael admitted, were "lame." His brothers wanted a piece of the action because his new solo album *Thriller* was selling millions, smashing all *Billboard* chart records. The smallest songwriting credit on a multiplatinum album was worth a fortune. He was worried the brothers' squabbling was going to escalate into full-scale war unless they could find some decent tunes pronto.

I told him I had some great ideas I'd been working on in the back of the tour bus. "You mean like 'Hyperactive!'?" he asked, "I love the groove on that." "Yes!" I said, enthusiastically. "As it happens I have one *just* like 'Hyperactive!' and another that's as good."

Michael wanted to hear demos. I told him I could send him some later on that night or the next day. "We're leaving town right after the party. Oh, but I can send them to you from my portable computer." He said, "You've got a computer on your tour bus? *Cooool.*" I told him about my Radio Shack TRS-80, state of the art. It could even send files over a telephone line.

I was thinking to myself, I'll stay up all night if I have to and write the damn songs.

I skipped the afterparty, and by the time the bus was ready to roll out of L.A. at about 3 a.m. I was already hard at work on the demos. Dan the Texan bus driver walked the length of the bus to check everyone was on board before he hit the road. My backing band was still in a partying mood, and in the main lounge the booze and drugs were flowing. Someone had been chopping out lines of cocaine on the steel countertop. Lyndon, my six-foot-two keyboard player, was still wearing the wedding frock and blond wig that he favored for important gigs. Justin, a chain-smoking drummer with the airs of an English aristocrat, sat up front with Dan trading bawdy jokes. Matthew and Lesley seemed to be deeply involved in a game of mental chess. Our diminutive Colombian guitarist Chucho, hair greased back, looking like a freedom fighter in his shades and army fatigues, was trying to sweet-talk a waitress from Orange County into staying on board for the overnight trip to the next gig.

In the twilight of the rear lounge I was rocking out by myself, my face all lit up by LEDs. I had my battery-powered Roland TR-606 drum machine and TB-303 Bassline fired up through some Akai headphones. I was punching in melodies on the miniature keys and jotting down random lyric ideas on a yellow pad. My number-one white linen suit and shirt, still damp with sweat from my onstage gyrations at the Greek, were hung up to dry next to me on a mirror. I was wriggling around on the bench seat as I fiddled with my shiny silver boxes, my sopping stage clothes dripping onto the Naugahyde. Dan stuck his head through the curtain and scowled. "Gayest damn bus *AH* ever drove," he muttered.

The sun came up somewhere around Barstow. The band had passed out in their coffinlike bunk beds. I was nearing completion of my two demos and getting ready to put down a rough vocal. I was pleased with the first, called "Interference." It had an irresistible, elastic groove. Okay, so it was a touch reminiscent of "Wanna Be Startin' Somethin'," from Michael's *Off the Wall* album; but only a touch. He was bound to go for it. I felt he might like the second even better, though it was more restrained, more like a Prince power ballad. But I knew I'd better not mention that. Michael didn't approve of the Purple One. "Prince is too dirty," he had told me once. "You can't sing songs about sleeping with your sister!"

So there I was, in the middle of the Nevada desert, head stuffed into a phone booth in the rising heat, trying to hook up my acoustic couplers. I'd called ahead to Michael's sound engineer, Bill Bottrell, who had another TRS-80 at the Record Plant ready to receive the digital files. But I'd tried three times and I was not getting a dial tone. My stash of quarters wouldn't last forever. I called Bill back and he said, "Michael just walked in, I'm going to put him on." Michael came on the phone and I apologized for my tech problems and told him where I was. "Oh," he said. "Why don't you just sing it down the phone, like in the old days?"

Crap. How did I land myself in this one?

I took a deep breath, stared out across the desert, and started tapping out a beat, one-handed, on the metal chassis of the phone box. I cleared my throat and began to sing, in the time-honored fashion of He Who Has Not Yet Written the Lyrics:

"*Interference* / on my TV / freak-a-dum-dum / upside of me . . . /
Interference / da-dum-dum-you / such a loser / you blew your cool . . ."

"What does it mean?" interjected Michael.

I tried to stamp out a trail of fire ants getting ready to crawl up the leg of my brown corduroy trousers.

"What does it *mean?*"

"Yeah, you know, is it like, *running* interference, for a quarterback—or is it television interference, the little dots on your TV screen?"

"Yes, yes, more like that," I said, a little breathless. "Like digital snow. No signal. Garbled . . . radio waves and static . . . er, electrostatic wavelengths."

Silence on the other end.

Eventually Michael said, "What's the other song called?"

"Um, it's a kind of power ballad," I said. "It's only a groove, really, but I'm calling it 'Iron Curtain.'"

"What's an iron curtain?" Michael said. It sounded odd in his high falsetto.

"It's a quote from Winston Churchill," I said. I cupped my hand over my mouth and put on my best radio imitation. "*'An iron curtain has deshended over Europe.'*"

More silence. A tumbleweed rolled by.

"Look," I said, "it'll be easier for me to send you the actual demos when I get to my hotel tonight . . . Hello? Hello, Michael? *Hello?* God damn it." I slammed down the receiver.

You could hear the wind whistling in the telegraph poles.

Thirty yards down the road, Dan the driver gave a honk on his horn, and the pneumatic door swung open. I turned and stumbled back towards the bus, juggling wires and cables. "Electrostatic wavelengths. What a fucking idiot."

I just blew my one shot at writing songs with the New King of Pop. And now I wanted to be many thousands of miles away from this infernal desert heat. I wanted my old life back. I wanted to be back in my bed-sitter in drab South London, in 1978, in the Winter of Discontent.

PART 1

CHAPTER 1
THE WINTER
OF DISCONTENT

Mr. Ron Grigson said the door of his fruit and vegetable shop had to stay open all day so customers would walk in off the street. This was February, so it was as bloody freezing inside as it was out. Customers were a rarity anyway—Kensington Church Street with its art galleries and high-end leather handbag boutiques is a stupid place to have a fruit-and-veg shop. When I got there at ten every morning to work the lunchtime shift, Grigson would trot over the road to the pub and drink till it closed at three. Brian Jones and I used to stay warm with a periodic game of turnip football. (General guidelines for turnip football: It has to be a small one. You boot it around the floor using the legs of the fruit stands as goals. The average turnip lasts about ten minutes, then it's too bruised and beaten up, so into the gutter it goes and you swap it for a fresh one.) I was beating Brian 11–8, but we had to stop because a posh lady came in for a pound of Fuji apples.

Grigson got back a little after three, completely sloshed. He went right to the till and checked the cash. Seemed he'd bumped into the apple lady and she complained that the boys in his shop were messing around. Grigson was constantly grumbling that his shop didn't make a profit, and always looking for someone to blame. He usually took it out on Brian, because he thought Brian was a bit dense. Brian was nineteen, a year older than me, and had spiky black hair, like Sid Vicious in the Pistols. He'd left school at fifteen. He worked long hours with Grigson, riding the van to market early in the morning to load in the day's stock. He knew I read the *NME* and had a music O-level, and he was curious to pick my brains. Brian wanted to learn the bass guitar, because he said Sid was "rubbish," and he reckoned he could do a better job. I told him I could show him the basics, but he was going to have to think up a better stage name, as "Brian Jones" was taken. He failed to see the significance of this. Anyway, Grigson was back now and he went off on a drunken rant about young people today, and Brian and I grinned and made faces at each other behind his back. When I asked Grigson for my wages he muttered something under his breath about honest staff; he zeroed out the till again and grudgingly handed me my £3.50. That was my daily wage. Some days I would also take home a bag of discount veggies, but not today, as I knew the bastard would charge me top whack.

The only good thing about my job at the shop was that I could go in late and leave early, avoiding the rush-hour traffic. I caught the number 28 bus to Wandsworth, got off near the Young's brewery, and walked home to Putney from there. There was a wicked wind coming off the Thames, but I chose to walk along the river anyway. There were a few interesting little one-story shops down there, and I liked to peer in the windows. One was EMS Synthesisers. Why they had their workshop in my little backwater of London I have no idea. In their window there were a couple of their machines displayed at odd angles on a piece of cloth. They made amazing synths, like the one Pink Floyd used all over *Dark Side of the Moon*. EMS made a synth that was built into a suitcase, with a matrix of little pins on it like a game of cribbage. It cost £2,500. I can't imagine they sold many to passersby. If you peered into the back of the shop you could see people fiddling around at workbenches. It was like something out of Dickens, but in a weird twisted time warp. On the walk up the hill I mused on the coincidences. Funny how the little street their shop was on was called Florian Road. One of my favorite synth players was Florian from Kraftwerk. He and his band barely ever left Germany. But they wrote a track called "Franz Schubert." And I lived on Schubert Road.

I knew Brian Eno had an EMS, too, and he'd used it on *Low* by David

Bowie, one of the best albums ever. The first side had actual pop hit singles on it like "Sound and Vision," but many of the songs were made entirely with electronic instruments, not your typical guitars and drums. The whole of side two had hardly got any vocals on it at all! Bowie had balls to take a risk like that. Big wobbly elephant balls of steel.

Later on I met up with Brian from work to go and see a band at the Railway Arms in Putney. He'd read in the *Record Mirror* that they were punk rockers from Newcastle, and he was mad for anything punk. They were called the Police. They were pretty good, but nobody really understood what punk was. As far as I could tell, any band that didn't have long hair or flared trousers was a punk rock band.

Afterwards we took some cans back to Brian's basement and I showed him how to tune his crappy electric bass. He'd bought it out of the back of *Exchange and Mart* for a tenner. It was a Japanese copy, and the roundwound strings were rusty and wouldn't stay in tune. I don't think Brian really noticed. I taught him the notes for "Pretty Vacant" by the Sex Pistols, and he was well pleased with that. He took his shirt off and gazed at himself in the mirror, £10 bass guitar slung down below his hips.

The next day I got fired from the shop.

Grigson came back early from the pub and caught me climbing into the cellar of the antique shop next door. Down in the basement where he kept his old orange crates there was this wooden shutter. I was waiting for the kettle to boil to make tea and I got curious and lifted the shutter off its hinges. There was a high-up window opening, and in the half-light beyond I could see this musty cellar, full of curious shapes. I called to Brian to come and see. We talked in a hush. "Are you going in then, or am I?" said Brian, grinning. "Yeah, all right," I said. It wasn't like me. I suppose it was the thrill of it, the dare. I'd never stolen anything in my life, and wasn't about to. Brian gave me a leg-up to the narrow entrance, and I dropped down onto the stone floor, kicking up a cloud of dust sliced through by rays of sunlight from the grate. There were stacks of oil paintings in gilt frames, old clocks, chests of drawers half covered in canvas, and brass knickknacks. Brian was watching from the window opening, but suddenly he said, "Shh!" He had this

11

terrified look on his face and his head spun around. Grigson was clomping about in the shop above, shouting angrily down at us. Brian went haring upstairs, and I could hear them arguing. But I couldn't get back through the window easily, there was no foothold. I heard Grigson's heavy boots coming down the wooden steps. He caught me on my stomach, half in, half out of the opening, covered in cobwebs and rat droppings. I looked at him guiltily, expecting a drunken onslaught. Instead he just turned slowly around and walked back up the stairs. Once I'd brushed myself off, I took a deep breath and followed him up to the shop. He had his back to me, sorting avocados in a rack.

"Did you take anything?" he said quietly.

"No."

"Then get out."

"Don't suppose there's much point in asking for my . . . um . . ." Silence. I caught Brian's eye as I left the shop. He gave a faint helpless shrug.

"Been down the riots, then?" asked one of the two lanky skinheads wedged next to me in the front seat. I hopped aboard when they slid open the door of their Ford Transit as it slowed for the traffic light at North End Road.

"Riots?"

"Yeah, we been down Lewisham all day, chucking bricks at the coppers, kicking heads in. We're off 'ome for our tea now, back down Lewisham again later." It was nice of them to give me a lift, but now I eyed them suspiciously and wondered if they were National Front. And whether they thought I was, too. I jumped out near Hammersmith tube station just as it was starting to turn from a drizzle to a proper downpour. Hustling down the steps into the underpass, I felt the heavy raindrops mixed with pigeon shit from the rooftops, dripping down the collar of my ex-army greatcoat. Maybe that's why they picked me up. It must have been quite hard to tell us apart from behind in those days. It was Saturday afternoon and London was crawling with punks, skinheads, mods, football thugs, and electro boys like me. Cropped hair, torn trousers, tattoos, standing around on street corners chugging Tennent's Lager or picking at kebabs in greasy paper.

I just had enough for the bus fare to Putney Bridge. That was the last of my cash. Back at my bedsit, I decided the only thing to do was to telephone the Aged Parents from the phone box on the landing. I wanted to know if they could lend me some money, as I'd lost my job. Didn't tell them why I'd lost it, of course. Not much sympathy there: "Look, we told you if you're definitely not going to go to university you've just got to support yourself! Look for another job, for heaven's sake."

I left high school at the age of sixteen. I was two years ahead of the rest of my class at Abingdon, but I had zero interest in studying and no desire to go to university. My only ambition was to make it in music, and London was beckoning. They never said so, but I knew my parents had half wanted me to follow in their footsteps and become an academic. My dad was an expert in classical archaeology, and a Cambridge professor, like his dad and his grandfather before him. My mother taught algebra for years. No one in our family had ever met anybody connected with show business. Not surprisingly, they were dubious when I talked about my plans to make a living as a musician. I loved my family, but they had never even heard me play or sing, so why would they believe me?

My parents told me they'd cover me if I got desperate, but to try and make do. Then they hung up. I was a bit gutted, as I'd been planning to go and see Elvis Costello at the Nashville Rooms in West Ken. People were not quite sure if he was a punk rocker either, but he was starting to get lots of play on John Peel's late-night radio show. So I decided to go down to the Nashville in the late afternoon. If I helped the roadies hump gear maybe I could get on the guest list. I hung around the stage door pushing flight cases up the ramp, and in the end a bloke called Simon agreed to get me in. "Just tell that ugly bouncer at the front Jake Riviera said it was okay."

Elvis Costello was brilliant. The band was sharp as hell, with Elvis on his Telecaster, a guy on a tinny Vox Continental organ, and a reggae-ish rhythm section. After a couple of tracks people knew from the radio he said he was going to play some brand-new songs, and launched into this amazing thing called "Watching the Detectives," then another one just as good. My mates Mike Fairbairn and Wyn, a couple of West London lads I'd known since our early teens, were in the crowd and they bought me a pint. We watched in awe from the bar. They grinned when Elvis sang the phrase "get your kicks at sixty-six." Mike explained that it was a reference to No. 66 King's Road, where there was a posh squat—an empty house that a bunch of rich kids had occupied, so they could live for free and throw wild drug parties every night. The beat was great and Elvis had this way of stressing every syllable. "They call her Natasha when she looks like Elsie / I don't want to go to Chelsea."

I rather *did* want to go to Chelsea and meet someone called Natasha in a squat, actually. I didn't mention this to Mike, whose sister Lesley Fairbairn had been my sort of on-off girlfriend ever since we were at school. I'd been inside a few fancy squats before. It was all over the papers: the London wealthy were abandoning their property in the capital, or even leaving Britain altogether, to escape the high taxes imposed by Jim Callaghan's socialist government. There were some beautiful houses in the nice areas of London that had been left unoccupied, and many had been broken into and made into collective homes by marginalized young people. The pubs and venues in Fulham, Chelsea, and Islington were teeming with semi-broke, unemployed youths looking for a great night out.

In the mid-seventies England was poised on the verge of a cultural revolution. You could see it in the politics of the time, with the accumulated blunders of successive Labour governments playing right into the hands of Margaret Thatcher and her union-busting Tories. You could feel it on the streets, in the radical fashions, the polarized attitudes, and the chaotic musical melting pots of Brixton, Camden Town, and Notting Hill Gate. For years my circle of friends had been listening to bands like Supertramp and Genesis and Yes. But progressive rock had nowhere to progress to except up its own backside. Summer open-air festivals in the UK featured the likes of the Allman Brothers and Little Feat. Chartered accountants were buying subscriptions to *Rolling Stone* magazine. Whether you were seventeen or thirty-five, your hair was long and shaggy, and your trousers were flared. This left little room for angry youths to annoy their parents and make their presence felt.

I distinctly remember the afternoon when a group of us were skiving off from school. We were in a café in Strutton Ground, smoking and sipping tea, when in walked Sean MacGowan. (Years later he was to change the spelling of his name to Shane and become the frontman of the Pogues.) Sean used to sit next to me in the back row of English lit class. At sixteen he was already the gnarliest, skinniest, most unappetizing human being I'd ever laid eyes on; yet when called upon to analyze a verse of Chaucer or a paragraph of Jane Austen he was surprisingly astute. The rest of us always looked up to him when it came to matters of coolness and taste, because Sean knew everything there was to know about modern music. On this particular afternoon, we had been debating the merits of the newly released Pink Floyd album *Wish You Were Here*. Shane sat down at the table and lit a Woodbine. We asked him what he thought of it.

"It's all crap," he mumbled through the stumps of his nicotine-stained teeth. "Floyd, the Beatles, the Stones—all rubbish. Their music is just old and stale, and so are they. They ought to be put to death."

A collective gasp went around the table. We were so shocked we had to loosen our wonky school ties. How could Sean say such things about our most revered musical heroes? When my blood pressure had finally lowered, I asked him: "Well, what *should* we be listening to, Sean?"

He proceeded to spew out the names of bands I'd never heard of, presumably American. "MC5 . . . Iggy Pop . . . the Ramones . . . the New York Dolls . . . Johnny Thunders and the Heartbreakers. It's the future, man. Sod all that corporate rock pap!"

The first time *New Musical Express* reviewed a Sex Pistols gig, at the Marquee in early 1976, their reporter was similarly scandalized. "The lead singer, one Johnny Rotten," wrote the *NME* scribe, "snarled and swore at the audience, spat on the stage, then walked off in a huff after only twenty-five minutes. His band could barely tune their instruments. Who exactly do these Sex Pistols think they are?" Within a few months, of course, the *NME* were the shining champions of punk rock and everything it stood for. I spent much of my eighteenth year scanning its pages, while grumbling about the out-of-touch Labour government and the stifling summer heat. I hung out on the King's Road and in Camden Market, waiting to discover that, exciting as it was to dress like a punk, punk rock was really not for me.

After yet another night of scrounged pints at the Red Cow, I walked all the way home to Putney and got up to the house on Schubert Road just before midnight. I squeezed past the prams and bicycles lining the corridor that smelled of curry. Up six flights of stairs to my attic bedsit. The usual crap from the neighbors, coming through the walls. On one side, Charlie Potts the big-band jazz fan, playing Benny Goodman at high volume while he clapped and bumped around his room, scatting along to the brass section. On the other side, Melanie. She was seriously anorexic and rarely came out of her room. She groaned and sobbed whenever Charlie's music was too loud. "Shuuuuuut . . . *UP!*" she kept wailing, over and over again. My room was wedged between them, separated by thin plaster walls.

I put 50p in the meter to turn on the gas fire and opened up the wardrobe, which housed a single-burner electric ring, to make myself some baked beans on toast. The place was fucking miserable, but at £12 a week you got what you paid for. The only way to block out the din from the neighbors was to switch on my music, put on my Koss headphones, close my eyes, and sink into the grotty armchair. I was broke, but at least I still had my music rig, a hefty ghetto blaster with a built-in cassette. I'd recorded last night's John Peel show off the BBC. Richard Hell and the Voidoids' "Who Says?"; "Janie Jones" by the Clash; and a live version of "Roadrunner" by Jonathan Richman and the Modern Lovers. I rolled a joint and stayed up till about 2 a.m. jamming along on my Wurlitzer electric piano with its puny built-in speakers, wishing I had something with a bit more poke.

I've still got that cassette, and the date scrawled on it is October 11, 1977—a few days before my nineteenth birthday, which is a day I remember well. It got off to a bad start, but ended up being the best birthday ever.

In the morning I had to report down at the Labour Exchange. It was my third appointment, and they told me there were still no jobs listed in recording studios or road crews. Not that I expected otherwise. They pressured me to go for an interview at the pesticides division of Shell Oil. With my two A-levels, they assured me, I'd be a great fit for a job selling dog flea collars to

Dubai. I kept telling the clerk it was a bad fit, I didn't even like dogs. He said okay, but don't expect the dole checks to keep rolling in forever.

On the way home I took a shortcut along the river and swung by the back of the EMS shop. There was a garbage dumpster outside in the street. No one was around, so I heaved myself up and had a gander inside. A bunch of flattened cardboard boxes, an old fridge, and . . . hold on: a black metal box with lots of knobs. The guts were hanging out of it, but I could see the words TRANSCENDENT 2000 printed on the front. Somebody from the work-shop must have thrown it in the dumpster. I thought, I'm having that! So I scooped the whole lot out and took it home. I found an AC cable, and, to my amazement, the box turned right on. I didn't really know what it did, so I called Trevor, a bloke who worked at a shop called Macari's Music in the West End. Trevor always let me fool around in the keyboard room at the back, and he knew all there was to know about music gear.

"It's a synth module, you wally," he said. "A kit synth, DIY job. They print the plans in *Popular Mechanics*. You'll need a keyboard to play it though, and some eight-volt-per-octave connectors. Unless you just want to make noises."

Just making noises was fine by me. I got out my soldering iron, opened up the Wurlitzer piano lid, and hooked the Transcendent to the Wurly's speak-ers with a bastardized guitar lead. At first there was no sound, so I got its back off and had a fiddle around with the circuit board. Sometime in the early hours of the morning I figured it out. Because there was no keyboard, you had to fake out the gate by shorting out the "-12V" and "+12V" pins on the keyboard five-pin connector. I melted a blob of solder in there, and to my delight, out of the speakers came the drone of a sine wave. I instantly went for the knobs on the front panel: *yesss!* Pitch, filter, wave form, white noise, and sample+hold, all working. I had an actual living synthesizer under my sweaty fingertips, and it was mine, all mine, mwooah-ha-ha-haaa! Finders keepers. I was up half the night, making all manner of bleeps and blips, until around 6 a.m., when Melanie woke up and started groaning "Shuuuuuut . . . *UP!*"

I barely left my room for several days. It was a call from Micky Potts, an Irish singer that Brian knew, that finally persuaded me to take a break from doodling with my new synth module. He tipped me off about this amazing band that were playing in a basement club in Ladbroke Grove: Throbbing Gristle, with a support called Clock DVA. The place was packed out with spotty-looking blokes in anoraks. Tending the bar was an ancient Rastafarian with thickly matted dreadlocks, his gold teeth glinting in the light from the beer pumps. There were a few punks milling around at the front, and the air was thick with body odor and cigarette smoke. The canned music cut off as Throbbing Gristle took to the stage. Their manic frontman had a little dictaphone tape recorder loaded with weird chaotic noises and he held it up to his mic, cupping his hands like a harmonica player. Projected behind them on the whitewashed brick walls were 8mm film images of bombed-out European cityscapes and vivisection experiments. I felt like I'd found my people!

I recognized the guy that was mixing their sound. It was Simon, who had got me into the Nashville Rooms to see Elvis Costello. I stood by him for most of the night watching what he was doing with the knobs and faders. Between bands I told him about how I'd found a Transcendent 2000 and got it working. Afterwards I helped him coil a few cables and asked if he ever needed an assistant on a gig. He said to write down my phone number on a beer mat.

But the evening ended up very sadly. Outside the club I bumped into Micky, Brian's singer friend from Dublin, who had missed the gig. He told me Brian had been crossing Marylebone Road when he was hit by a lorry. He was dead by the time they got him to the hospital.

I sulked in my room for days. Brian was a lovely, kindhearted bloke, and I realized how much I would miss our turnip football tournaments and late-night electric bass sessions. I knew Brian was an only child, and somewhere his parents were grieving far, far more deeply. I'd never given much thought to whether my own parents worried about me, living in a bedsit all alone in London.

A week later I pulled myself together and went out to see Television and Talking Heads at the Roundhouse. They were over from New York. At first I thought they were one band, not two, because talking heads are on TV . . . ? Never mind. They were both utterly, utterly brilliant. Talking Heads came on first, and the singer looked like some sort of nervous exotic bird, twitching his head approximately in time to the music, playing an edgy rhythm guitar, and singing in a jagged, paranoid squeak. They had a blond girl bass player who never took her eyes off the drummer for an instant, and the two of them were tighter than a duck's arse. Then Television came on, and in the chorus of the first song it sounded like they were chanting "Television, don't go to my head." Clever to have a song with the same name as your band, like the Monkees. They had dueling guitar soloists, one of them very fluent and melodic, the other kind of raw and simplistic like Neil Young but completely spellbinding. This is nothing like punk rock, I thought, thank God, but it does have some of the same intensity and passion.

I got home feeling totally inspired. I spent the whole night playing my keyboards, trying to piece my own songs together. I had some great bits, but they were just bits. Intros, verses, instrumental themes. Fragments, really. It was fun, but frustrating as hell.

In memory of Brian I bought a packet of orange hair dye and a tube of gel from Boots and gave myself a spiky punk do.

Over the next few months I began helping Simon do a few sound-mixing gigs, driving all over London in his beaten-up Ford Transit loaded with PA gear. He only paid £5 a night, but it was a good laugh, and he usually let me work the faders for a bit while he went to the bar to try to pick up girls. Which sometimes worked, if he could convince them to stick around while we packed up the gear. Usually they just wanted to know where the band members were going after the gig. There was this fleapit of a hotel in Chalk Farm called the Cipriani that all the out-of-town bands ended up staying at. So long as you kept bribing the night porter he would serve you vodka and gin miniatures in the lounge, and endless packets of potato chips.

One night I was at a gig at the Greyhound in Fulham Palace Road for a band from Swindon called XTC. They were absolutely effing brilliant. They came on with this manic punk energy and played at a thousand miles an hour, but with actual chord sequences and interweaving riffs and melodies, and insane lyrics about "Cross Wires," "The Atom Age," and song titles like "I Set Myself on Fire." The lead singer hopped around the stage on one foot like a demented Chuck Berry, while his bass-playing sidekick with the

Beatle hairdo spun out these amazingly funky minimalist bass parts. At one point they went into a slow menacing song called "I'm Bugged." On cue, half the crowd put on their sunglasses and writhed around in a termite-like mass. "I'm bugged / you all look like insects / in your brand new sun specs . . ."

They had an organist too, and God, did I want him dead. It's not that he was bad—actually he was great in a deranged, atonal sort of way—but I had a waking fantasy that he would go into cardiac arrest right there onstage, and XTC would have to ask for a volunteer out of the audience to take over on the keyboards. Me! Me! Me!

Simon got himself what he called "a bit of posh totty" up in Hampstead Village. This girl, Becky, wanted him to go to her daddy's house in the country while her parents were away in Sardinia for the weekend, and he was thinking about letting me do a gig at Dingwalls for a band called the Members on Saturday night, on my own. I was not insured to drive the Transit, but I said I was willing to risk it. I definitely felt ready to set up the PA and mix a gig myself—it was only a punk band and I reckoned it'd be a piece of cake.

Rash words! The gig was almost a complete disaster. The headline band came onstage and announced they'd just been signed to Stiff Records, *and* it was their two-year birthday party. The crowd was a mixture of the band's close friends, North London teddy boys, and football yobs in town for the Ipswich Town vs. Arsenal cup final—an explosive combo. Halfway through the set the singer Nicky Tesco's girlfriend brought on a huge rectangular chocolate birthday cake she'd baked herself, lemon with raspberry jam filling and a chocolate icing, with the band's name in huge pink icing letters. Nicky Tesco propped it up on the bass cab so the crowd could see it, and the band launched into their hit song "The Sound of the Suburbs." This of course was the cue for one of the oiks down the front to bum-rush the stage and grab a handful of birthday cake, which he proceeded to hurl out into the crowd, triggering a general stampede onto the stage. In a few moments the scene was like a custard pie fight from a Three Stooges movie. As I watched powerless from my mixing desk on the mezzanine I could see cake splattering all over my—or rather Simon's—PA stacks. Once all the cake was all gone the band launched into their last song, finished with a crash, left the stage, and were wafted off into the night by a mob of jubilant Ipswich Town supporters, leaving me alone to clean up the mess. To my disgust, the grilles of the onstage wedge monitor speakers were matted with desiccated coconut and chocolate icing. I cleaned them up as best I could, but the pub manager, who had no one else to take it out on, kicked me and my PA out before midnight. On the drive home I had to keep a keen eye out for police cars. Not being insured, I didn't dare to risk leaving the PA in the van overnight, so I had to hump all the cabinets into the front hall corridor and stack them up to the ceiling, waking the baby in the ground-floor flat. Cue a torrent of abuse in Punjabi. I finally collapsed into bed and got up early to spend most of Sunday sponging the squashed birthday cake out of the speaker grilles.

Simon never had to find out about it, and when he got back from his steamy weekend in the country he seemed pleased that I had pulled the gig off on my own. He said he was willing to let me do more of them using his PA and van, and we would split the money—he charged £100 a night, so that was fifty a pop for me. But he advised me to declare it to the dole office and go legit. Which would mean no more weekly social security checks to cash; and I'd have to get proper insurance to drive the van. Still, if I could do three or four gigs a week I might be able to save some decent money and buy new synth gear.

On a balmy Saturday afternoon in July 1978 I bought my first proper synthesizer. It was a one-year-old Micromoog, £650 in a sale at Selmer's. I had to get it on hire purchase, but my mum agreed to cosign for me. It was quite small and light, so I was able to get it home on the District Line, wrapped in brown paper and string. The pitch bend ribbon was a bit worn; other than that it was in perfect condition. It was the first time I'd owned a keyboard with pitch bend, so I was able to start to imitate Chick Corea, who could solo like a lead guitarist. It sat on top of my other keyboard, a Solina String Synthesizer—which, two years later, the Musicians Union voted to ban because it was taking jobs away from "real" string players. I also learned to double parts on two keyboards at the same time like the guy from Weather Report.

As my chops improved, I eyed the back pages of the *Melody Maker* for bands looking for synth players. I replied to a couple of ads. It was a hassle to get around with my gear, because I couldn't always count on Simon letting me use the van, but I did go to one audition for a band called the Warm Jets, who said they were punks, though to me they sounded more art-school glam rock, like Roxy Music. It was in the back of a pub at the other end of London, and despite the very expensive two-way taxi ride I didn't get the job. They said I "knew too many chords." The fact was, the punk rock floodgates were open, and keyboard players were too posh. Most bands would have been more into me if I'd said I was willing to trash my Wurlitzer onstage.

They had a point. Years earlier I'd seen Roxy perform on the BBC's late-night stoner music show *The Old Grey Whistle Test*. Their singer was a lithe and sexy crooner in a sharp suit, but their heavily made-up synth player just stood at the back in his seven-inch-heeled, knee-length lizard skin platform boots, arms folded, looking thoroughly bored. Every now and then he would lazily reach out a gloved hand to tweak a knob on his Moog, which was apparently playing itself. His name was Brian Eno. I thought to myself at the time, If all you have to do is pose around and twiddle a few knobs, and meet girls and make bags of money, that's the career for me!

CHAPTER 2
SKIN TENSION UNDER LEATHERETTE

I was doing three or four mixing gigs a week by now, and in some decent venues, too. In the first two months of 1978 I did sound for the Fall, Gang of Four, and Blancmange. But watching all those musicians onstage really made me desperate to get in a band in my own right. On a night off I went to Alexandra Palace to see Siouxsie and the Banshees. I completely loved them. I had recorded a four-song John Peel session they did, and I'd been making up synth parts for their songs. I was hoping to get a cassette to them before or after the gig. They had a great doomy sound and a new look, all dripping in monochrome. Punks were usually so colorful with their tartan trousers and green Mohawks. Bands like Siouxsie and the Cure were going the other way altogether, like tragic heroes out of a German silent horror movie. I gave my cassette to one of their roadies, but I never heard anything back. Over the following weeks I did away with my orange spikes and cultivated a lank, raven hairdo with a center parting.

Eventually I decided to place a *Melody Maker* ad of my own, saying I was a synth player looking for a band, and listing influences like Cabaret Voltaire, Throbbing Gristle, Pere Ubu, and the Normal. The paper came out on a Thursday, and by the weekend I'd had a few calls. Most were duds, but one guy that called seemed pretty interesting, and he lived close to me.

I spent a few afternoons with him at his flat in East Sheen, and I was deeply impressed. His name was Bruce Woolley, a great singer and fluent rhythm guitarist with a real craft for writing catchy pop songs. I would see him stitch them together, and it was like watching someone really good do the *Times* crossword. It was not totally my kind of music, but I knew I could learn a lot from Bruce. Though he was intrigued with the underground electronic scene, he didn't see a commercial future in it. None of those bands seemed to be getting signed up by major labels, whereas Bruce had an actual record contract with CBS, and they wanted him to go out on the road. He seemed to like my keyboard playing. So I joined his band and set about helping him put the rest of the band together.

Richard Wernham was our drummer. He'd been in the Motors, who had a UK chart hit with a song called "Airport." His girlfriend was a bass player who looked like Tina Weymouth. The lead guitarist, Dave Birch, was a childhood friend of Bruce's who idolized Mick Ronson from Bowie's band, grinding on the low end of an amped-up Les Paul and playing loud melodic solos with lots of vibrato.

Bruce's songs were poppy and accessible, and his vocals were quite high and androgynous, a bit like Sparks, a good contrast to the grittiness of the band. I detected a rather twisted, perverse undercurrent. There was a hint of a disturbed childhood in songs like "English Garden" and "Get Away William." My job was to add subtle textures with my synths and make the chords more peculiar. I saw a way to blend in some of the darker Germanic leanings of early electronic music with the irreverent energy of punk and goth.

Bruce's managers insisted his name had to be featured up front, so we became Bruce Woolley and the Camera Club. We met four nights a week in a sweaty rehearsal joint under a railway arch in Tooting Bec. Bruce had received an advance from his deal with CBS Records, and his managers were advising him to invest in his future, so they put us each on a retainer of forty quid a week. I felt like a professional musician, and was able to start turning down sound-mixing gigs when they clashed with rehearsals. We went over and over the songs, stopping and starting, fine-tuning our parts, reworking intro riffs and breakdown sections, practicing vocal harmonies. During breaks we went to the pub and got into heated debates about whether or not it was poofy to wear eyeliner onstage. We had a debut gig booked at the Marquee Club in Soho, a showcase for CBS's European convention. Some bigwigs from the USA were going to be there. Our drummer thought we should try to look hard, like the Clash or the Pistols; but Dave Birch said the English punk groups were all rip-offs of the New York Dolls and the MC5 anyway, and those guys were no strangers to the cosmetics counter.

Wedged behind my keyboards at the back of the stage, it didn't really matter how I dressed. If I spiked my hair and dyed it green or left it lank and greasy, I still looked like a weedy little public-school boy who'd crossed the tracks, which is exactly what I was. So I just lost myself in the music. I loved my Micromoog. It could only play one note at a time and had a single oscillator and filter, but cranked up through a beaten-up Ampeg SVG bass amp it sounded effing great. I learned to squeeze every last drop of expression out of it, which was not a lot. I was also practicing a wide-astride leg stance so I could rock mechanically side to side like John Foxx from Ultravox. Stances are everything to a synth player. I saw Bowie do a cameo with Iggy Pop at the Hammersmith Odeon once playing a four-voice Oberheim (oh what I'd have given to get my hands on one of those beauties!) and he had this great variation, with one leg forward and one back. See what he did there?

My only innovation in the fashion stakes was my National Health glasses with the sticking plaster round the bridge. My dad was always breaking his specs and repairing them with Elastoplast. Mine weren't broken, but I thought it was a cool look.

The record label gave us the budget to have our own stage clothes made. We each got to design our own outfit with a seamstress in a workshop above Oxford Street. It was the end of the 1970s, and the punk street look seemed to be waning a little; startling new bands like Spandau Ballet and Devo were more fashion conscious and sci-fi. After a lot of soul-searching, I opted for a one-piece space cadet suit with plenty of zips. Bruce Woolley himself cut a fine figure at the microphone in a sort of *Star Wars* tunic, like an officer from the Death Star. We piled into the reclining aircraft seats of a splitter van and took off on tour around the provinces. We honed our sound in towns like Torbay and Milton Keynes and Aberystwyth. We checked into crummy suburban bed-and-breakfasts with our guitar cases and garment bags, feeling very much like pop stars.

We even played a handful of gigs opening for XTC, by now signed to Richard Branson's label, Virgin Records. Virgin believed they could turn one of the UK's most challenging new wave bands into a commercial success. Barry Andrews had left the band, but instead of replacing him with another keyboard player they had brought in a second guitarist. The manic songs of theirs that I'd admired in the early punk days still worked pretty well, but I noticed a brand-new number in their set called "Making Plans for Nigel" that sounded to me like an instant classic. Bassist Colin Moulding was singing the lead, and with Dave Gregory's guitar layered on top of Andy Partridge's, they'd settled on a more accessible midtempo sound that seemed a sure bet for the charts. When the record became a breakthrough hit for them a few months later I was thrilled. There was something special about walking into Woolworth's and seeing the name of a band I'd once followed around the London pub circuit now listed in the Top 20. I still had Andy Partridge's home number in my phone book. I went to visit Colin Moulding and his girlfriend in a trendy pad in Chelsea that he'd actually paid for with money he made from pop music. Somehow the glass ceiling of pop stardom was shattered. It no longer seemed impossible that a band I was in could actually make the big time as well.

Bruce Woolley had cowritten a catchy song called "Video Killed the Radio Star" with his friends Trevor Horn and Geoff Downes, but they had their own band, the Buggles, and there was a race on to see who could get it released first. Our version was rockier, but lacking the refinement and finesse of Trevor's ingenious production; it stalled out in the lower UK charts, while the Buggles' version got massive radio play and went straight to #1 all over Europe. I now had the sensation of being tantalizingly close to a bona fide hit record. Though the Buggles' success meant a massive publishing windfall for Bruce, losing out to his old mates was a bitter pill to swallow, and it threw CBS Records and his management into a tailspin.

When you have a hit, everyone slaps each other on the back and no one stops to analyze what went right. When your record dies a death, there's inevitably a postmortem, and fingers begin to wag. The word was that Bruce Woolley and the Camera Club were not poppy enough for the mainstream UK charts, yet we weren't hip enough to be darlings of the indie music press either.

There was only one thing for it: pack us off to America.

During the winter of 1980 I toured the USA playing synth with Bruce Woolley and the Camera Club. We played clubs and small theaters. It was the beginning of a new British Invasion, and the audiences went crazy. We were flown around from city to city, staying in rock-and-roll hotels like the Gramercy Park and attending frequent parties laid on by CBS Records. There was probably a huge shortfall to the tour accounts, but nobody questioned it. The cost would be reflected in Bruce's next royalty statement.

It was all a little overwhelming for me. And at times I felt homesick. I would make expensive long-distance calls back to England and spend hours chatting with Lesley Fairbairn. Lesley was always so good at grounding me. We'd become boyfriend and girlfriend in our mid-teens—too young, really. Over the years we went through phases of being a couple followed by spells as friends. Though we came of age together, deep down I don't think either of us believed it was a match made in heaven. But she was always my biggest supporter, organizing my stuff and contributing occasional silky backing vocals to some of my songs. I would call her from my U.S. hotel rooms in the early hours, when it was morning back in England. She listened patiently to my war stories from the road and was sympathetic up to a point. But when I complained about this and that, the endless waiting around in airport lounges or the annoying fans clamoring for photos, she said, "Oh, Tom, get a grip. You're a lucky man. Enjoy yourself!"

There were girls everywhere. There were girls in the dressing rooms, outside the stage door, and in the hotel lobbies. At one hotel we stayed at—the Tropicana, in Hollywood—there were girls living as full-time nonpaying residents, lying around the pool all day, just waiting for the next rock-and-roll band to check in. This was 1979, after all—post-Pill, but pre-HIV. I think you get the picture.

Many of our U.S. dates were in larger venues playing as a warm-up for Lene Lovich. Lene was a UK-based Detroit transplant whose brilliant, quirky songs and whirling-dervish stage antics had got her signed to Stiff Records. Her single "Lucky Number" reached the UK Top 5 and was now making waves in the U.S. dance and college charts.

I watched Lene from the wings each night, cooing and yelping her way through her fast-paced new wave set full of epic, heroic songs. She spun circles around the stage like Edith Piaf on crystal meth. The intro to her final song was almost mystical: she stood motionless at the microphone in a narrow revolving beam of light, fixing the audience with a mesmerizing stare while a string of unearthly bird trills emanated from deep inside her throat, echoing around the hall. Lurking close by in the shadows was her partner and cowriter, Les Chappell. While Lene was all frills—thick stage makeup, outlandish home-sewn outfits, lace gloves, braided hair extensions, a mysterious mid-Atlantic accent—Les was just the opposite, with a black tracksuit, shaved head, and no eyebrows. He just stood there looking fit and taut, like a hip bouncer outside the Mudd Club. I was in awe of them both. One night after a show in Seattle I happened to find myself in the same hotel elevator as them, and I was overcome with shyness. As the lift doors opened at their floor Les turned to me and said quietly, "We caught Bruce's set tonight. Great synth parts. Lene thinks you're a star."

That night I had a dream. Lene and I were apartment hunting together in what felt like Paris or New York. We were viewing a large apartment, empty aside from a few cardboard boxes. It had grand high ceilings and two massive symmetrical rooms, each with a picture window facing the street at opposite ends. In the center was a partition with open double doors. Lene was walking back and forth through the doorway from one room to the other, gazing around, looking quizzical. "I only see two rooms. But I sense there is another. There is a third room here, Thomas, but we can only see two."

I set about writing Lene a song. It's easy for guitarists to write on the road, perched on the edge of a hotel bed with a steel-string like Jagger and Richards. It's harder for a keyboard player, because we need a lot more gear. You have this image of Joni Mitchell or Kate Bush finding her way into a darkened hotel ballroom and pulling the canvas off an antique Bösendorfer. But there were no Bösendorfers at the shitholes we stayed at, like the Cipriani and the Tropicana.

Tascam had just come out with a new recording device called a Portastudio. It recorded on double-speed cassette tapes, using all four tracks so that you could keep overdubbing new parts. So I saved up my gig fees and twenty-dollar per diems and bought myself a Tascam Portastudio. After shows I had to wheel my keyboard flight case up to my hotel room. The rest of the band was usually down in the bar, or taxiing off to some nightclub to pick up girls. But I would stay up late with my headphones on, working over song ideas. I had a little Boss Dr. Rhythm drum machine, and I would program simple grooves and play or sing all the rest of the parts. After many nights of learning and experimentation I was ready for Lene to hear my song. It was called "New Toy." I slipped a rough mix to Les in an envelope at the breakfast buffet one day, along with a letter to Lene describing my dream. He thanked me for the tape, but he said Lene was in bed sick with laryngitis and a fever. Later that day I found out that the last few dates of the tour had been canceled, and we were all taking an early flight back to England.

Weeks passed before I heard from them. I tried to put it out of my mind. Then Lene called me and said they wanted to meet. She never mentioned my dream. But she and Les loved the song and she invited me to their rehearsal room in Kentish Town to try routining it with her band. They already had a piano and organ player, but there was a second keyboard rig set up, so I jammed with them on several of her songs, which of course I knew by heart. It felt good, really good. Especially "New Toy," which, after all, I'd tailored to suit Lene's voice and the players in her band. When Lene and Les asked me to join the band, it felt like my career had just shifted up a gear. That evening I called Bruce and told him I was leaving the Camera Club. He was sad and disappointed, but he wished me all the best. Bruce was always a good friend and boss, though I probably didn't acknowledge how much he had influenced me until many years later.

We recorded and mixed "New Toy" in a single long day at a sixteen-track studio in Kentish Town. Les took it in to Stiff Records the next day, and they immediately picked it as Lene's next single. A mere two months later the record was released, and the same week it was added to BBC Radio 1's A-list. I began to hear my song coming from upstairs balconies and out of cars stopped in traffic jams. I wanted to lean my head in the car window and tell them, I wrote that!

My mum bought twenty copies of the single in her local record shop. Over the years, she bought at least twenty copies of each single I released, believing it would make a difference to the chart positions. The record shop assistants used to have a stack of them behind the counter ready for Mrs. Robertson when she walked in. "My son's going to be a pop star, you know!" she told them. Sure enough, in May 1981 "New Toy" entered the lower reaches of the charts, and Lene and her band were invited to perform on Britain's main music TV show, *Top of the Pops*. It was the first time my family had ever seen me perform.

I have three brothers and two sisters, all older. I am the youngest by six years. My mother and father both had respectable and successful teaching careers, but they loved children. The elder siblings were very academic, like their parents, the younger ones less so. I was the only one in the family to pursue a career in entertainment. Though we all appreciated music, there wasn't much participation in our household when I was growing up. My sister Lucy played the clarinet, and my brother Dominick was in a rock band when he was about seventeen. He had a Hammond B-3 organ, and I remember sneaking into his room and firing it up when he wasn't around. I taught myself the intro to "A Whiter Shade of Pale." I think my parents were initially quite disappointed that, though I was evidently bright like my siblings, I never really applied myself at school. They were relieved when I discovered that making music was something to sink my teeth into, and probably imagined when the phase passed I would settle down to a normal job. Then, once my name started to show up in the papers and on the radio, my parents dined out on it. Among the Cambridge dons and their spouses at the Trinity College "high table," they would successively recount the scholastic achievements of their older children, adding with a chortle, ". . . and young Tom's going to be on *Top of the Pops* this week!"

I was elated about my upcoming *TOTP* debut and called all my friends to let them know to be sure and tune in at 7:25 p.m. that Thursday evening. I decided this called for a brand-new look. No more dour goth. No more New Romantic space cadet in eyeliner. I duly hit the local Oxfam thrift shop and picked out a nifty tan leisure suit, white shirt, and dark tie, and accessorized it with a crocodile belt and my National Health glasses.

While *TOTP* was the only "live" UK pop music show, music videos were just coming into vogue. If you had a video, your single could get more exposure via kids' TV and breakfast talk shows. So Stiff Records agreed to make a low-budget video for "New Toy." To save money, Stiff Records' founder Dave Robinson decided to direct it himself. We had a single day to shoot it at a ritzy address in Regent's Park.

On the morning of the shoot I stepped out of a taxi with my garment bag, and as I reached the top of the stairs my jaw dropped. It was the apartment from my dream. I had never been to a house as grand as this in London, which is why I'd assumed we were in Paris or New York. It was a chilly morning and you could see your breath. The crew was busy setting up cameras and lights. In the middle of the space they were rigging a huge white tube made of parachute silk, brightly lit and blown open by giant fans, through which Lene and the band were going to move while singing the song. This ethereal tunnel was the third room Lene had sensed in my dream, six months earlier.

I've never had a supernatural experience, before or since. I'm not that sort of person, and I don't possess those kinds of powers. Lene clearly did. In time I came to believe that this extraordinary dream had not come from my own subconscious—it came from Lene's.

I believed that for years, actually, right up until I wrote it down for this book. Now I realize the truth is obvious. Lene picked out that location *because* it matched the one in my dream. *Duh!*

"New Toy" was not a huge hit in the UK, but it made enough of an impact within the industry to get me noticed. And now that I'd pulled it off once, songwriting and recording didn't seem so intimidating. So I decided to use the little money I had left over from gigging to buy studio time and make a record under my own name. As a long shot, I put in a call to Andy Partridge from XTC to ask if he would help. To my amazement he offered to take a train to London and coproduce my two new songs, "Urges" and "Leipzig." A couple of weeks later we completed them in a pokey eight-track studio in a back street near Goodge Street Station. Andy played bass drum and tambourine on the recordings, and twiddled the knobs, but he refused to let me pay him.

The studio owner introduced me to a music business lawyer called Tony Simons. He was a diminutive man with a bald pate, whose dad had been a record industry big shot. He listened to my tapes and said he was fully confident he could get me a solo record deal. I was running really short of money again, but Tony offered to forgo his fees for three months while he circulated the tapes to his contacts in the music industry. I agreed that if he was able to get me a record deal I would either pay his fees or appoint him my full-time manager at 15 percent commission. We took the tapes to a few meetings at labels. Most turned us down, but A&M Records showed a lot of interest. This American-owned company, Tony assured me, was the perfect home for me because they were known to be especially supportive of developing artists like the Police—the band I'd seen that night at the Railway Arms in Putney, who were now filling sports arenas.

While Tony went back and forth on terms with A&M, I decided it was time to move out of my loathsome Putney bedsit and get a place north of the Thames. I moved into a small ground-floor flat on the Hammersmith-Fulham border, paying a weekly rent on a rent-to-buy basis, so that with my record deal signed and the advance money in the bank I could maybe put down a deposit to buy the lease outright.

I seemed to have a cozy rapport with my new record label friends. I would ride my bicycle every day the short distance to the A&M offices in Parsons Green to discuss plans for the release of "Urges"/"Leipzig" and the recording of my first solo album. It seemed to be taking an age for the contract to get done, but eventually Tony brought me the final draft and a date was set on April 20, 1981, for a signing ceremony at A&M, complete with press, photographers, and a lunchtime celebration.

On the evening of April 19 I got an angry call at home from a vice president of A&M. "We refuse to be mugged!" he said. "The deal is off. For good." There was no further explanation, and before I had a chance to ask questions he hung up on me.

There was no word from Tony Simons for several days. It finally came in the form of a hand-delivered envelope under my front door. Inside was a typed invoice for £4,500 in respect of the deferred hours he'd spent working on my record deal. I immediately called Tony's voice mail and told him he was a fucking crook and he knew where he could stuff his invoice. This turned out to be a bad move, because the next letter I got, a week later, was from a collection agency, threatening legal action if I didn't pay up. They suggested I sell my keyboards and recording equipment to cover it. In the meantime, they informed me, Tony had possession of my multitrack tapes for "Urges" and "Leipzig," and I should consider myself prohibited from trying to offer the masters elsewhere.

I couldn't believe I'd been betrayed like that, and I desperately wanted A&M to know that I had nothing to do with whatever it was Tony Simons was trying to put over on them. Or perhaps they had just decided not to sign me after all, and used Tony as a smoke screen? It made little difference either way. The fact was, I was twenty-two years old and flat broke. I'd overextended myself on the new place, and I had no idea where the next rent check was going to come from.

The small grubby boys playing in the street outside my house had seen me on TV and ran after me squealing, "Pop star! Pop star!" It felt like a taunt.

Within a few days, I came to a decision. I would sublet my Fulham flat to my friend Matthew Seligman, bass player with the Soft Boys, and get the heck out of London. In early May I hitched a ride in a refrigerated chicken lorry and took the ferry across the English Channel, arriving late at night in Paris with nothing but a small backpack and Jo Kerr's address on a scrap of paper.

CHAPTER 3
NEEDLE DROP

When Jo was about seventeen he was the epitome of coolness at our school. He drew subversive cartoons of the teachers. His hair length pushed the boundaries, and his boots had three-inch heels. He played guitar. He had connections to shady characters at Kensington Market who could sell us Moroccan hashish.

I was a couple of years younger, closer in age to his brother Tim. The Kerr brothers had a group called Amberband that played occasionally at end-of-term concerts or at the neighboring girls' school, and I was proud to be their roadie. Jo was a social magnet, with a powerful ego. His lyrics and chord progressions showed a prodigious talent. He went on from school to Oxford, but he rejected the obvious career path, which would have been into the law, following his father, a high court judge. After graduating he disappeared to the Mediterranean, where, while living like a hobo in a makeshift tent on a beach, he'd apparently had a vision. I was never clear what this vision was, but when I met up with him in Paris, the ego was gone, evaporated. He'd shed a skin and left it there on that beach amid the driftwood.

Jo was crashing on a couch in a small apartment in Ménilmontant, in the eleventh arrondissement in northeastern Paris. I turned up on his doorstep and followed him up a stairwell that reeked of urine and disinfectant as he punched the rubberized light switches on the landings. He showed me his room and made a space for me to lay out a sleeping bag. We sat at the kitchen table and caught up over a plastic bottle of supermarket red wine. Our experiences since the Amberband days couldn't have been more different. While the lead singer was working in Paris as a street musician, his former roadie had been tasting the rock-and-roll lifestyle in the USA; yet now here I was, showing up at his hovel with my tail between my legs.

Jo explained how the busking thing worked. You could just about manage to scrape a living provided you played by the rules. You needed to be up at the crack of dawn and set up in one of the central Metro stations. If you weren't there by 7 a.m. you might not find a "pitch." The French commuters didn't pay much, but around midmorning the tourists would start flowing through in big numbers, and they were a lot more generous. He said if he could find me a guitar we could work out some songs as duets and we might make decent money. So the next day we borrowed one off his neighbor Francis and went about putting together a set. Paul Simon songs worked well— Jo sang the lead and I filled in gently with the Garfunkel harmonies. My guitar playing was (and still is) pretty rudimentary, but I knew bar chords and could strum my way through most things, plus I had a good ear. We sat up all night working out standards by Bob Dylan, the Stones, Lennon and McCartney. First thing the next morning we headed out to see if we could sing for our breakfast.

We took a shortcut through the vast cemetery of Père Lachaise with our guitar cases on our backs. The sun was just coming up, and scrawny cats and their feral kittens darted away among mossy headstones. Jo pointed out the famous tombs, inscribed with names like Molière, Chopin, Colette. There were graffiti arrows pointing to the shrines of "Jim" and "Oscar." There's one supine statue whose sculptor carved the deceased exactly as he was in death. The arousal evident under the subject's tunic led to him acquiring a reputation among childless Parisian women as something of a fertility symbol. He's mostly drab and green, but his crotch, as well as his nose and toes, are worn to a shiny bronze.

In the Metro station at Odéon we looked for a suitable spot to pitch up.

Jo talked me through his routine: we picked a straight section of tunnel with a sharp bend at the end, giving us a good thirty seconds of earshot with the oncoming pedestrians. We laid out a rug and two folding footstools to sit on, with a guitar case open in front, and a few of our own coins and notes to get it started. We tuned up and launched into "The Boxer." I was pretty tentative at first, but I soon found my voice. After a while the coins started clattering into the case. We rotated through our short set. You didn't really need an extensive song list. The biggest earner by far was "Stairway to Heaven"—especially popular with the Japanese, who would take endless photos with their Canons and Yashicas. I commented that we would probably have made the most money just looping "Stairway to Heaven" over and over, but Jo said he liked to keep it fresh. There was a limit to how much you had to suffer for your music.

Busking was a great lesson in how to balance art and commerce. The equation was simple: if they didn't like what you sang, you went hungry. Sometime towards midday Jo said we'd made enough, and we should pack up and go get some lunch.

This became the pattern of our days. We'd keep an eye on the coins and notes dropping into the guitar case; on a good day we could afford to stop around midmorning, whereas on a slow day we wouldn't get to eat till early afternoon. This was in the days before buskers were properly licensed, and sometimes the police would come and move us on. *Les flics* were known for their belligerence, and Jo said one policeman had broken a friend's guitar over his knee when he tried to sneak back to the same spot.

A little old lady loaded with shopping baskets stopped to listen to us, smiling and tapping her foot along to "Maggie Mae." When the song ended she said, *"Les jeunesses, je l'aime bien, votre chanson. J'ai pas d'argent, mais tenez ce chou-fleur."* And she lumped a large cauliflower into Jo's guitar case.

One time we were harangued by a gang of neo-Nazis from the National Front. It looked serious for a moment, but we placated them with a high-speed version of "Anarchy in the UK" and they pranced around in their jackboots before streaking off down the platform.

Provided we'd made enough money, our lunchtimes and afternoons were spent drinking and smoking in a bar on the Rue de Rivoli where all the busk-ers used to hang out. We met some real characters there, from all over the world. English was the lingua franca, but many only spoke it by stringing together song lyrics. Some of the buskers were legendary. There was a sixty-year-old Peruvian hippie called Pablo who was reputedly the first to "play the trains." Musicians were banned on the national rail system, but Pablo figured out that you could bribe this one ticket conductor at the Gare de Lyon, board the Marseilles express, work your way along the train a couple of carriages behind him, then lock yourself in the toilets for a few minutes before hopping on the return, arriving back in Paris by nightfall with three or four hundred bucks in your pocket.

I gradually built up the courage to play solo without Jo's guidance, and spent several months living this curious half-life among the Paris buskers. Sometimes I would sleep late and go out to busk in the evenings, in a restau-rant called Le Tournabour on the Boulevard Saint-Michel. It was there that I met Elizabeth Aumont. She was twenty-one and eating dinner with her father, a rich banker. I stood at their table and began to sing a ballad; I think it was "Nights in White Satin." The father waved me away, but Elizabeth said, *"Non, Papa! Il est mignon!"* as she grabbed my elbow and told me to carry on. A few songs later I had made my way to the other side of the restaurant, but I couldn't keep my eyes off Elizabeth. Her father paid the bill and got up to leave, but she wrote down her number on a matchbook and came over and stuffed it into the bridge of my guitar.

We met the following afternoon for coffee. She was studying textile de-sign at the Sorbonne. Her hair was short and tomboyish, but she had a beau-tiful wide smile and a lovely figure, and she spoke the most ridiculously bad English, with a cartoon accent. Of course, I was completely smitten. We spent the last few nights of that humid summer under the sheets of Elizabeth's bed with a flashlight, making up fantastical children's stories in broken Franglais. But sadly, our love affair was not to last.

I received a postcard from Matthew back in London, saying that Mick Jones had been calling incessantly and wanted to book me for a keyboard ses-sion. I got pretty excited, thinking this was the guy from the Clash, one of my favorite bands. I'd followed them from the early punk days as they became one of the top rock acts in the world, and I had very happy memories of seeing them play a secret free concert on Christmas morning under the Westway overpass in West London, when they tossed out all their leftover posters and T-shirts to the astonished crowd of a mere eighty or ninety fans.

It wasn't *that* Mick Jones. It was the other one, the guitarist from Foreigner, whom I thought of as an American AOR rock group. Actually the founders were Brits, living in the USA, hence the name. I barely knew their music—didn't they have a hit called "Cold Blooded"?—but apparently their producer, Robert "Mutt" Lange, had been sent my demo tape of "Urges" and "Leipzig" by his South African business partners in a tenacious UK-based music publishing company called Zomba. Mutt had immediately taken note of the keyboard playing and sounds, and told Zomba to track me down. Their inquiries had led them to my flat-sitter, Matthew, and Matthew contacted me at my forwarding address in Paris.

On a long-distance call from New York, where Foreigner were in the studio close to finishing their new album, Mutt said he wanted to try me out on their album, and asked how soon I could be on a plane to the USA at their expense. He wondered whether $500 a day would work for me for a session fee. I flashed a quick glance at Elizabeth, who was down at the bottom of the bed, innocently sucking my toes. I thought about the paltry smattering of francs and centimes in the flap of my guitar case. And I told Mutt that once I'd wrapped a few things up in Paris I could be there by oh, say, Thursday?

I told Elizabeth I was sure I'd be back in a few days. "*Ça, je crois que non,*" she said. "But one day, we weel be ze Pirate Twins again." She was quoting from one of our made-up children's stories.

When I touched down at JFK there was a limo driver from the record company holding up a sign with my name on it. It was the first time this had ever happened to me. He drove me directly to Electric Lady Studios in Greenwich Village and said he would take the bags on to my hotel on Central Park South. Feeling pretty spaced out, I was shown into the control room and introduced to Mutt Lange and Mick Jones. I had been in a couple of first-class studios before, but only as an observer; this time I was there as a hired musician. When Mick invited me out into the studio to jam with him a bit, my natural shyness overcame me and I completely froze. He'd had his guitar stack set up and a Fender Rhodes for me, but I could barely play a note. I could see Mutt listening in on us in the control room. They probably wondered what they'd let themselves in for.

Mutt played me rough mixes of a few of the new songs. They were under the gun to get the vocals done so they could mix the album and deliver it to Atlantic, but Mutt said he was unhappy with the keyboard player they'd hired. He liked the synth sounds on my demos and he wanted to try out something similar on the Foreigner tracks. Mutt asked me what I envisaged for synth parts, and pulled out a laminated equipment list from Studio Instrument Rentals that looked just like a takeout food menu. He said he especially liked my song that went "Urges! Urges!" So I selected the synth I'd used on it, a Roland JP4, and when it showed up barely a half hour later the roadies set it up in the control room and I went about programming the same soft slidey sound I'd used on my own song. With Mutt working the faders, I laid the first part down, and it sounded great. Mick Jones bobbed around snapping Polaroids of my bespectacled reflection in the chrome side panels of vintage tube compressors. A little later Lou Gramm showed up, ready to lay down a lead vocal. Mutt suggested I must be tired, and why didn't I go get some shut-eye. I could return to the studio in a few hours when they wrapped up the vocals. I said that would be around . . . 3 or 4 a.m.? He said yes, there would be a relief sound engineer who would tell me how many tracks I could fill up, and I could rent any keyboard on the list. S.I.R. was open all night. They would be back in the morning to listen to what I'd done. As I left I heard Lou start to warm up for his lead vocal. The chorus sounded a little familiar: "Urgent! Urgent!" Hmm . . .

That night I was like a kid in a candy store. The best studio I'd been able to afford to date was a semiprofessional eight-track demo joint. Now I was alone in the control room of a world-class professional studio, in the very seat where Jimi Hendrix must have sat to record his immortal solos on *Electric Ladyland*. It had a beautiful Neve 8078 mixing desk with automated faders.

And there against the back wall were not one but *two* Studer A80 twenty-four-track tape machines! Smacking my lips, I picked up the phone to S.I.R. and ordered up a brand-new Prophet-5 synth and a vintage Minimoog. I told the engineer to load up the ballad Mutt had played me called "Waiting for a Girl Like You." He had asked me to program and rerecord the descending ostinato line that opened the song. It wasn't sitting well with the rest of the song, and the previous keyboard player just hadn't nailed it. It took me an hour to find some richer and much more evocative sounds, and replace all the original keyboard parts. But then I had this idea I'd always wanted to try out . . .

There's a classic electric keyboard called the Mellotron, made famous by the Beatles, who got into it during their drug-inspired period and used it all over songs like "Strawberry Fields Forever." Each key you press on the Mellotron's keyboard triggers a tape of a single note, recorded from a classical instrument such as flute or cello. I'd never gotten my hands on a Mellotron personally, but I had this theory that you could emulate its psychedelic effect by recording single notes of a synthesizer on consecutive tracks of a multitrack tape, then "playing" the faders on a mixing console to create chords and harmonies. So I went through about ten tracks of the multitrack, recording a sustained note on each using the rented Minimoog, in the scale of A minor. I then ran the multitrack, using my fingers to slide faders up and down in waves, recording the combined output to a stereo tape machine. The result was ethereal and very spacey. I had the engineer add around thirty seconds of blank tape to the start of "Waiting for a Girl Like You," and we laid in my new intro. When the downbeat hit, my intro segued perfectly into the ostinato, and the overall effect was unbelievable.

Mutt and Mick showed up around 11 a.m., this time with the rest of the band and their manager, Bud Prager, in tow. They were eager to hear what I'd done with the intro to the ballad. We darkened the lights and I proudly signaled the engineer to roll the song, up as far as the vocal entry. The master fader was pulled down, and there was a long pause. Finally the bassist, Rick Wills, said, "What would you call that, stylistically?" Dennis Elliott, the band's Cockney drummer, said, "It's sort of like . . . massage music, innit?"

"Cor, I could really use a massage, actually," said Rick. "Hey, Bud, can we get some Asian girls in?"

Mick and Mutt were really into my "massage music," though, and—the occasional *Spinal Tap* moment aside—I spent a very productive month working with them to put my synths all over their album, leading Mutt to give me a new nickname: Booker T. Boffin. (The first part was a reference to the great Hammond player Booker T. Jones, who scored a massive jukebox hit with "Green Onions" with his band the MGs. The *T* was for Thomas. And a boffin, in the UK, is a geek who tinkers around and invents things.) I gained the utmost respect for Mick Jones, a thoroughly decent bloke, as well as for Mutt Lange's amazing production skills. Mutt had already had a lot of commercial success producing bands like Graham Parker and the Rumour, the Boomtown Rats, and AC/DC. I've never worked with a more fastidious producer. He would make me go over and over my parts, adjusting the inflections on every single note until it was exactly perfect. Some simple strings of notes took hours and hours to record. Yet when he brought in sax legend Junior Walker for a solo on "Urgent" and recorded at least a dozen versions, Mutt had the wisdom to recognize that the very first solo Junior blew, rough edges and all, was The Take. He could spend hours hunched over the faders making microscopic adjustments to a background sound in the middle eight; then sit back and listen to the song from the top as if it were the very first time he'd ever heard it. He could transform himself, at will, into a fanboy.

I was sharing a hotel suite with Mutt, and often he'd get up and leave before me in the morning to work a twenty-hour shift in the studio, not arriving back until after I'd gone to bed. He would then sit cross-legged on his bed with an acoustic guitar, singing his own songs, in a high shaky voice with Van Morrison–like inflections. He worked every single day during the month I was in New York, aside from one morning when he had to make an emergency visit to the dentist to deal with a toothache that prevented him from working. On one occasion, halfway through a mix, he suddenly looked up and said, "What the fuck are we doing indoors on a beautiful day like this?" He ordered up a big stretch limo, and we piled into it to head off to Central Park, stopping only at FAO Schwarz to buy a selection of Frisbees. We ran around for a few moments tossing Frisbees, but after less than five minutes Mutt said, "What the fuck are we doing at the park? We've got an album to mix!" And we all piled back into the limo.

Late one night as I was working on my keyboard parts, there was a strange banging noise from behind the speakers. Suddenly an axe came smashing through the studio wall, followed by a troupe of the campiest Greenwich Village firemen you've ever seen, decked out in their protective suits, boots, and yellow helmets. It turned out that at the weekly midnight screening of *The Rocky Horror Picture Show* at the Eighth Street Cinema, next door to Electric Lady, an audience member had accidentally set a seat cushion on fire during a lighter-waving sing-along anthem. It had been smoldering for hours until someone on the street spotted smoke and summoned the fire department, who duly smashed though the shared wall in an effort to locate the source. I believe if you listen closely there's an interesting sound effect mixed into the background of "Juke Box Hero."

At our agreed daily rate, I ended up being owed $6,500 for my month's work with Foreigner. On the last day, Bud Prager sat me down in his office and asked if that was too much for a virtually unknown twenty-two-year-old to earn. Absolutely not, I said—if anything they were getting a bargain. He laughed and pulled a fat brown envelope out of his desk drawer with a wad of hundred-dollar bills in it. "It's all there," he said. "I trust you," I replied. And that night I flew back to the UK—in economy—determined to use the cash to make an album of my own.

It felt strange to be back in London after the experiences of Paris and New York. Nothing about the place had really changed, yet I felt as if I'd been away a lifetime. Matthew had the flat looking nice for me, and I collapsed into bed and slept for about fifteen hours. He woke me up with a cup of tea. Sitting on my bed, he told me that the independent label Armageddon, which had released his band the Soft Boys' records, was interested in releasing "Urges"/"Leipzig" as a single. I called the label boss, Richard Bishop, an amiable young businessman with a good ear for eclectic music. Later that day I rode my bicycle over to his office. Because Armageddon was a small label, he said, it could turn a single around very fast. If we could agree on a deal that week, he could have it pressed and in the shops within six. He showed me a form contract he'd used with another band, and said if it worked for me he would get a new one typed up. The advance was only £1,500, but the royalty rate was very fair, so if it did well I would see a decent return, and there were no renewal options. I was reluctant to use a lawyer because I didn't want anyone in the legal world to know about the deal, in case word of it got back to Tony Simons, who still reckoned he controlled the rights to my recordings.

The single came out in early 1981 and got great reviews from the usually snooty British music press. Several of the reviewers mentioned my work with Lene Lovich, and the one in the trade rag *Music Week* also plugged my work on the upcoming Foreigner album. My single made zero impact on the pop charts, but within the industry I was starting to make some serious waves.

Matthew had set aside a stack of mail for me. One letter was from Tony Simons, and it was surprisingly friendly. It took me a while to swallow my pride and call him. He was willing to overlook the unpaid invoice and felt we should sit down and plan a new strategy for getting me signed to a major record company. I was still feeling pretty pissed off, and I was cautious about approaching major labels after the A&M debacle, but I thought I should hear what he had to say.

I needed a lift home from the dentist's after an operation to take out my wisdom teeth. I knew I would be too dozy from the anesthetic to make it home on the Underground on my own. Tony offered to pick me up in his plush Bentley, and he treated me with kindness and consideration. I'd been planning to make him tell me what really happened on that last day before the A&M signing party, but I decided to let it go. I was thinking to myself, So what if Tony got too greedy and blew the deal? Everyone makes mistakes. And in a weird way, the whole Paris/New York episode might never have happened had A&M stuck to the plan. Perhaps it was the car, or perhaps it was the medication, but by the time he dropped me off at home in Fulham he'd persuaded me to give it another try with him.

We talked again the following day. While Tony felt the timing was now good to go straight to the major labels, I had a different suggestion. I said it was crazy to look for a deal before they'd really heard what I was capable of.

I could use the cash I'd made from Foreigner to record the album myself, and then approach the majors with a proposal for a distribution-only agreement, with me retaining ownership of the masters. The other advantage of doing it that way was, I could work on my live performances, play some clubs around London, and build up a grassroots following prior to the album coming out. Tony saw the wisdom in this, and I think he was impressed. We agreed that this time out there would be no per-hour fees, but that he would become my lawyer and manager for two years in return for a 15 percent commission on everything I earned during that period.

Mutt Lange's business partners in London were Clive Calder and Ralph Simon, a pair of South African expatriates who had set up a music publishing company called Zomba and a recording studio complex in the Northwest London backwater of Willesden. They invited me to tour their studios and talked to me about my songwriting. I didn't have the highest regard for most music publishers, who seemed to me to be lazy and lethargic, just sitting back reaping their share from statutory copyright royalties. But Clive and Ralph were different. On Clive's desk was a copy of the latest *Music Week* trade magazine, open to the charts page, and I noticed that every instance of the words *Copyright Control* was circled in marker. I asked what that meant, and Clive explained it was an indication that no publisher was assigned to that particular composition. He would make a point every week of tracking down the songwriters and making them an offer to administer their publishing at a much better rate than the so-called "majors." I suppose it was naïve of me to imagine that no one else had thought of this idea, but the impression I got from my songwriter friends was that most music publishers were pretty dense. Zomba was a rare exception. Clive and Ralph were keen to expand, and told me of their plans to release themed compilation records on their own label. The idea was to find a TV celebrity, such as the news anchor Angela Rippon, and persuade her to be on the front cover of an album of keep-fit tracks or soothing baby lullabies. Zomba would license one well-known hit song—e.g., "Let's Get Physical," by Olivia Newton-John—and fill in the rest of the album with generic original tracks written by their own staff writers and recorded in their studios. Clive and Ralph were also very excited about a new genre of music coming out of the New York club scene known as rap, and determined to put together a rap group themselves, forming a rap-oriented record label that they would run from their offices in London. Though Zomba's artistic aspirations were questionable, their business acumen was rock solid, and they'd picked up an understanding of the music of the streets at the house parties and highlife jam sessions in the Johannesburg projects. It was quite plain to me that these guys were way smarter than anyone else around, and the kind of people I needed in my corner. So Tony Simons negotiated a limited-term publishing agreement with Zomba, and this gave me additional cash and resources to launch my solo career.

My first project with Zomba was a rap/dance record called "Magic's Wand." I built up the groove and chord sequence in late-night sessions in their Willesden studios, and the backing tracks were sent to the USA, where a pair of black college graduates called Whodini added a rap. It became the first-ever release on Zomba's U.S.-based Jive Records label, and topped the Billboard DJ dance charts, becoming the first rap 12" ever to sell a million copies. The royalties from that one record repaid the entire advance Zomba had given me on signing the deal. Not bad going for an English geek and a bunch of South African cowboys.

Many years later Zomba exercised a buyout obligation in their contract with distributors BMG and sold them the Jive label for $2.74 billion, a sum arguably equal to the value of the entire record industry at that time.

I needed a new HQ. Somewhere I could be left alone to write songs for my own album, hone my one-man-band sound, and work up a killer live act. In late December I found it, in an old Victorian industrial estate just off the railway tracks near Earls Court. The rent was very cheap because you had to walk through a meatpacking plant to get to it. Once inside, you found yourself in a splendid top-floor loft, with brick walls and arched windows looking down on railway sidings covered in snow, like a scene from post–World War II Eastern Europe. As a bonus, the huge cast-iron gates of the estate were locked every night at 10 p.m., and if you were still inside at that time they wouldn't let you out until 8 the next morning. This would be the perfect isolation I was looking for, right in the heart of London.

I set up my gear in the loft and got right to work. In the early hours of the second night, I was startled by a knock at the door: I'd thought I was alone in the building. I cautiously opened the door, and found myself chest height to an enormous Canadian. He had long hair, a bushy beard, and a checked shirt, like a lumberjack. "Hi," came the booming friendly voice. "I'm Ivan." He looked a lot like Rasputin the mad monk.

Ivan was a hacker—though in those days the term had probably not yet been coined. He had one of the workshops down the hall from mine. It was full of welding equipment, partially dismantled shortwave radio sets, and the hulks of obsolete mainframe computers. He'd heard noises coming from my loft and came to see who or what was behind them. Ivan could take anything apart, that was sure. Whether or not he could put it back together remained to be seen. But I took him under my wing—or was it the other way around?— and over the next few months he became my roadie, computer boffin, and IT guy, rolled into one.

My songs started to take shape. I had no single theme in mind, but as I added more and more to my set, jotting lyrics down on random pieces of paper, coming up with improbable electronic grooves that incorporated the curious machinery Ivan soldered together for me, I seemed to be moving into a sort of postapocalyptic reverie, a parallel universe. I would look out over the snow-covered railway tracks and imagine how London might have turned out if one of the many threatened invasions of our island had been successful. I imagined living under a repressive regime, where free speech was prohibited and everything rationed. Would there be a resistance movement? A secret society of freethinking artists and writers, lurking in the ruins of abandoned factories? Of course there would, and I would be the one to write their anthems.

On January 19, 1981, I sketched a rough idea for the cover of my first album. The picture was of me at the bench of my workshop, tinkering with some mysterious invention. It was in the style of a *Boy's Own* comic, but the title was *Wireless Weekly.* This was the running order as listed on the backside:

1. Radio Silence
2. Flying North
3. Europa and the Pirate Twins
4. Pedestrian Walkway
5. Urges
6. Leipzig (Is Calling You)
7. Windpower
8. Airwaves
9. Weightless

If I'd stopped for a second to reflect on the fact that my obsessions with science fiction, ham radio, and the Cold War might prove a little unsuitable for the delicate pop sensibilities of the mass record-buying public, I'd have chosen a different path. I could have written catchy songs about jealousy and teenage angst. I might have joined the ranks of the smiley poster-boy singers of the early 1980s, got my hair cut at Antenna and bought my clothes on South Molton Street. But when I turned on BBC Radio 1, or watched *Top of the Pops*, there was nothing, absolutely zero that appealed to me. The idea of adding to the general chorus of syrupy pop chatter and unrequited love songs filled me with loathing. I was determined to go full-on with my own peculiar brand of dieselpunk music and visuals; and if I couldn't crack the big time, I would go down behind enemy lines in a blaze of glory.

London in 1981 was in a state of flux. After the violence of the anti-police riots in Brixton during the spring, the city streets were quickly cleaned and scrubbed to prepare for the wedding of Prince Charles to Diana Spencer. Their smiling faces were appearing on biscuit tins and knitted tea cozies. By the summer, there were flags and banners hanging out of every window. On the rare days when the sun came out, Londoners stopped whatever they were doing to go to sit in the park with a pint of beer, getting sunburned. It was as if the civil unrest had been swept under the carpet; but there was still a lingering sense of uneasiness. This was the backdrop to my first attempt at a live one-man show.

I had no reputation yet as a live act. Few people had heard of me, but Tony and I managed to get bookings at a handful of small London venues, including a couple where I had previously mixed sound for other bands. Performing onstage with my fragile electronic rig was precarious, even with Ivan on hand with his voltmeter and duct tape. The early performances were a mixed bag. Being the front man and center of attention was new to me. When everything went smoothly, I felt relaxed and sang well into my headset microphone, swapping hands between my Simmons percussion pads and the keyboards of two synths. The core of my setup was a PPG 340/380 Wave Computer of German origin that had originally been designed to control Tangerine Dream's light show. I had it hooked up to play my bass and drum grooves. It could only handle one song at a time, meaning there was an enforced gap between each number in the set. Starting a new song required me to insert a pair of microcassettes into the PPG and type "LOAD" on the command line of its green screen. The load time was exactly fifty-two seconds— after which there was about an even chance that the sequence would play. So I got pretty good at telling stories in chunks of fifty-two seconds. I would explain how the different bits of my equipment worked, or tell the audience the background to each song. Many of my lyrics were set in a kind of dystopian parallel universe, in ruined cities like Leipzig and Budapest. I created mythical heroic characters like Europa and Caroline 452. I began to notice that one or two people would be in the front row at every gig, dressed up like the characters in my songs.

The arrangements were very mathematical, blending the hypnotic, pulsing sequences of Kraftwerk and Edgar Froese with longer, soaring melodies and unusual jazzy harmonies. Behind me was a parabolic video screen showing montages of billowing cumulonimbus clouds, cells dividing in petri dishes, and cheerful factory workers building Spitfire fuselages. I'd say the audiences that stumbled into those small London pubs and clubs were a little perplexed. They knew they were seeing something wildly experimental and ahead of its time, but a Thomas Dolby gig wasn't exactly a toe-tapping night out.

What it did do was give me a chance to try out my songs on a real audience before going into the studio to record my first album. In an odd way, tucked away in the corners of those little clubs I felt I was busking again, singing for my supper. For an unknown audience to appreciate my unusual lyrics and melodies the first time around, I had to learn to project myself, to try and cast a spell and reel them in. As a performer, your consciousness is often in two places at once. Even before you get to the applause, you always have a sense of how your song is going over. Some parts don't work out the way you expect, so you make small changes the next time around until you get it right. One night I played a simple ambient piano improvisation at the end of "Airwaves" and randomly twiddled a knob on my Micromoog as if tuning a radio dial. It created an effect that was solemn and desolate, but somehow very beautiful. At the next night's gig that section duly became integrated as the intro to the song. The audience was mesmerized. When you make minor gains like that at concerts, you take them into the studio with you and it makes your album that much stronger.

I recorded most of *The Golden Age of Wireless* in a basement studio in Barnes belonging to a Greek South African named John Kongos. Lesley Fairbairn was now working as his studio manager, and I got a great discount on the hourly rate, enabling me to work there for two or three weeks. I brought in Lene Lovich's rhythm section and a brilliant guitarist named Kevin Armstrong to replace some of the electronic grooves with a more organic rock sound. We tried working with a producer called Wally Brill, but after a couple of days I think it was plain to both of us that I needed to be in control myself. Was I a bit of a diva? A brat? Maybe just a little, but it was really about knowing precisely what I wanted, being willing to strive for something unique and individualistic at the risk of making my own mistakes.

Once I had presentable rough mixes of half a dozen songs, Tony Simons started playing them to major West End record companies, on the understanding that what we were looking for was a distribution agreement for my new label, Venice in Peril. VIP was, at this point, nothing more than a logo on headed notepaper. I'd borrowed the name from a charitable organization run by the eminent British peer Sir Ashley Clarke. They agreed to let me use it provided I publicly supported their cause, which was to save the city of Venice from sinking by restricting tidal flows in its lagoon. There would be more acts on the label as soon as I had completed and released my own album. I now had the funds to hire Lesley Fairbairn myself and put her on the payroll as my personal assistant, which seemed to work out well for both of us.

At that time, it was an ambitious move for an artist with little or no commercial history to form his own label. CBS, Warners, Island, and Chrysalis all passed on the deal, but EMI were very keen. They were enjoying chart success with a young Birmingham band called Duran Duran whose debut single "Planet Earth" had stormed into the Top 20, and they'd just decided to turn down Culture Club, leaving a gap in their roster. So a massive eighty-page contract was drawn up, and Tony started to sift through it. He came down to the studio having barely slept for three days and showed me his marked-up copy, which was bristling with yellow sticky notes. He told me recording contracts are a nightmare to go through because they will try every trick in the book to set traps for artists so they end up owning you lock, stock, and barrel. I was grateful Tony had waived his hourly fees, which would have wiped me out.

EMI was offering pretty good money, which would not only cover all my recording costs, but enable me to live for a year or so while I promoted the album and maybe even put down a deposit to buy my Fulham flat. After several weeks of to-and-fro on the contract, Tony felt he had squeezed as many concessions out of EMI's lawyers as we were likely to get, and he presented me with a summarized page of bullet points.

I was somewhat appalled to read that from now on, every single note I sang or played on a recording would belong to EMI or its successors, in perpetuity. They had the option to remix my records, include them in cut-price compilations, give them away for promotion, discount them, or to decide not to release them at all (as was the case with Bruce Woolley when he presented CBS with his second album). They also had the option at any stage to drop me from their roster altogether. Each "album period" of the seven-album deal would be extended until I had delivered, and they had accepted, an album that they considered technically and artistically suitable for the current music marketplace. They would pay me around 11 percent (10 percent in the USA) of the sale price of my records, less "returns and breakages" that they themselves would dictate; these deductions varied between record contracts, and many were more heinous than mine. Todd Rundgren once told me he was required to pay for unsold copies of his albums to be shipped back to the factory and burned.

As for my own rights? Basically, I had none. I would have no opportunity to object to their marketing methods or to extract myself from the contract under any circumstances, regardless of EMI's performance level. The word *exploit* cropped up fifteen times in the summary alone.

It was a long way from the distribution-only contract we'd envisaged. What it did offer, which was very rare for new artists at that time, was complete artistic control. For as long as our relationship remained friendly, EMI would allow me to select my own photos, design my record covers, and pick directors for my music videos. They would leave me to my own devices in the studio. For some reason EMI seemed willing to trust my instincts.

"This," Tony assured me, "is a great contract. You should have seen the one the Beatles signed! Your royalty rate is ten times better."

There was something reassuring about the idea that I was going to make ten times as much as the Beatles. And of course, I was anxious about losing the deal in another A&M-style U-turn. So in spring 1981 I took a deep breath and signed a seven-album recording contract with EMI Records. Thirty-five years later, the EMI Corporation still owns every note I recorded during the entire first decade of my career. CEOs and employees have come and gone, the company has been bought and sold several times, but I still have those three little letters stamped on all my tapes. And, all things considered, I was one of the lucky ones.

EMI cautioned me that now they'd spent some time with Tony Simons, they were not overly impressed. Had I ever thought about changing my manager? Perhaps I needed someone more proactive than Tony, who was primarily a lawyer and lacked the experience to take an artist to the highest level.

I was expecting Tony to be awkward about it. Nobody likes being dumped. But he was gracious enough to step aside, and he even interviewed three managers who had acts on EMI and wrote me a memo. I met with them over the course of a few weeks, and the one I really liked was Andy Ferguson, who managed my new labelmates the Undertones. Andy knew the record business inside and out, and was instantly able to make significant improvements to the EMI contract, persuading them to up the advance on the basis that I needed money for equipment so I could go on tour and promote the record.

Then I found out that Tony Simons was terminally ill. He died several months later, leaving me wondering if I'd been kind enough to him while he was alive. Tony may have screwed up over the A&M situation, but I felt he'd made amends, and I was shocked and saddened to hear of his death. I had him to thank for the fact that the semiprofessional chapter of my career was over. Using the EMI money, I cleared up my studio bills, paid off what I still owed the backing musicians, and took out a mortgage to buy my flat. I set aside enough to cover two years' worth of living expenses. That still left me around £10,000 to play around with.

My first move was to get myself a Jaguar. Not a brand-new one, like the kind you see streaking down the carpool lanes or double-parked outside Knightsbridge bistros, but a petrol-guzzling, *gor blimey guv'nor* 1964 Mark IV—a proper getaway Jag suitable for pulling a bank job in the East End. "That's Mr. D, he's the brains of the outfit," fearful Shadwell chimney sweeps would mumble as I wound down my window with a stately wave.

I found just such a car in *Exchange and Mart* and took the bus down to Battersea to take her for a test drive. She had a gorgeous leather front bench seat with room for three and a dark maroon paint job. She belonged to a retired Argentinian pilot called Carlos, and as I drove the classic sedan around South London we got chatting. By coincidence I'd just finished reading *Alive*, the story of an Uruguayan rugby team whose plane went down in the Andes and who ended up eating each other. Carlos said he knew the pilot's cousin. The plane was a Fairchild. I wondered if it was the same company that made a highly prized piece of recording studio gear called the Fairchild EAR 660 Valve Limiter; Ivan had one in his workshop that only worked sporadically. I suddenly had this insane idea to bring Carlos up to my loft and record him doing Spanish radio distress calls through Ivan's valve limiter. Later on I added an instrumental piece behind his samples, and a new song, "The Wreck of the Fairchild," was born. It had a thumping ska beat, and was the final song to get added to *The Golden Age of Wireless*.

After that, I had little choice but to buy the Jag.

My first major-label single, "Europa and the Pirate Twins," came out in October 1981. It peaked at a lowly #48 in the UK charts, and in the ensuing months it reached roughly the same position in the U.S. and Canada. The upper reaches of the charts at that time were populated with the likes of Depeche Mode, Orchestral Manoeuvres in the Dark, the Human League, and Soft Cell, and I was confused. The song was about as catchy and atmospheric as I could make it, featuring a Bo Diddley–type groove, half a dozen synth hooks, some nifty harmonica by Andy Partridge of XTC, and a story line drawn from my brief Parisian romance with Elizabeth. The music press took quite kindly to what they saw as an exciting new mix of electronic and rock music; but the chart positions were disappointing, and the paucity of radio play did not bode well for the commercial prospects of the album. In April 1982, *The Golden Age of Wireless* was released in the UK and Europe, along with a second and third UK single, which also barely scraped the charts. It was to EMI's credit that they persevered with me, but it was clearly not the stellar career launchpad they expected for their new artists.

In those days I would drive to EMI's offices a couple of times a week. I spent my time in the conference rooms studying radio playlists and sales graphs, and asking tricky questions of the promotion and marketing folks in an effort to grow my feeble understanding of the complexities of the UK music business. This made the EMI staff visibly uncomfortable, and I think they rather dreaded my visits. Out of the corner of my eye I would often catch Simon Le Bon or John Taylor from Duran Duran perched on the corner of some pretty secretary's desk, looking dapper in a brand-new suit, with an armful of free albums under one arm and a long-distance phone call on hold to L.A. It took me way too long to realize that inquisitive artists aren't really welcome at record companies. The whole equation functions a lot better if the artist is a little bit cheeky, craving attention, making the ladies swoon and the men jealous. The Duran guys were always perfectly nice to me, but I couldn't help wondering how they'd got it right and I'd got it so wrong.

I tried to make friends with the employees. It wasn't easy to pin them down. There were certain EMI executives who would get in to work around 11 a.m. (having been out late at a showcase gig the night before), and around 1 p.m. they would head across the road to the pub, sinking several pints of beer and a ploughman's before putting in a couple of hours' work in the afternoon. The perks of their jobs included all-expenses-paid trips to European or U.S. conferences and media events, plenty of satin tour jackets, and all the NOT FOR SALE promotional copies of new releases they could carry— many of which would be bartered for favors and then mysteriously turn up FOR SALE in vinyl bargain bins a couple of days later. Of course this was not true of all of the employees. I had many supporters within the company from top to bottom. The managing director at the time was Cliff Busby, who always stuck by me and was a stalwart fan. I worked closely with my A&R executive Hugh Stanley-Clarke, a hard worker and great advocate of my music. But, like me, he was swimming against the tide.

On a two-day trip to Milan for a round of TV shows and press interviews, I was picked up at the airport by the local label rep, a very attractive Italian brunette in a low-cut blouse. I asked her how a company like EMI was to work for. She spoke reasonable English but with a strong accent. "Well, is fine but they no pay us enough," she said. "I have to find some other way to make a living, know what I mean?" I was waiting for her to tell me she was moonlighting as a lingerie model, but no: "Last week, I order copy masters of some new releases from Abbey Road, saying I need to give to a TV station here. Then I sell them to a man I know in Pakistan. I do this every couple of months. I think I do yours a few weeks back, just before it hit the stores."

Though I was deeply bothered by the implications of a conversation like this, it was soon forgotten. The effects of pop stardom were much more apparent in foreign countries where celebrity sightings were relatively rare. Later that day I appeared on the biggest Italian evening talk show, miming to my latest single. From the TV studios my rep drove me to a lovely restaurant

hidden away in the medieval streets of Trastevere, where we shared an excellent meal and several bottles of Chianti, and the manager, who had just
seen me on TV, refused to let us pay the bill. We moved on from there to a
neon-lit nightclub with a long line waiting outside the door. As I stepped out
of the car the bouncer held back the crowd and unclipped the velvet rope for
me. Inside I was shown to an elevated private seating area and a waitress
brought us a chilled bottle of champagne on the house. There was some sort
of modeling convention in town, and the spectacle on the dance floor kept
my mind off those copy masters in Karachi.

On another promotional trip I flew to Tokyo for a round of TV appearances
and interviews courtesy of EMI's Japanese subsidiary, Toshiba EMI. Also
on my plane were the band Spandau Ballet, who were enjoying international success with their first album. We shared a stretch limo from the
airport. Tokyo was all beautiful contradictions, with its neon alleyways and
cherry blossoms all in bloom. We drove into the city past the emperor's palace and down an avenue packed with discount electronics shops. An Elvis
impersonator waved from a Plymouth convertible. There were curious little
shrines billowing with hanging banners and incense, and cross-dressing punk
rockers with spiky hair. We were staying in a towering hotel with a giant
atrium lobby. Since news had leaked of Spandau's arrival, the hotel had under-
gone an infestation of teenage pop music fans, and in every corner of the
lobby there were pockets of giggling schoolgirls. To my surprise it wasn't just
Spandau sightings they were after—they had heard the name *Thomas Dolby*
on the radio and seen clips of me on TV. The instant I walked onto the lobby
floor I was surrounded by teenage girls, many still in their school uniforms,
smiling and cooing at me, with singles and albums for me to autograph.

Unlike any other country in the world, these Japanese fans also had something to give back: each had prepared a beautiful little handmade present.
By the time I made it to the elevator my arms and pockets were loaded up
with all the trinkets and charms I could carry—decorative paper doilies,
beads, papier-mâché animals, and a two-inch-high glass jar of microscopic
shells with a label that read "I WISH YOU TINY COSMOS." I found all this ut-

terly charming, but more than a little surreal. It was my first trip to Tokyo and I'd just flown for seventeen hours.

At the breakfast buffet the next morning I found myself sharing a table with Spandau Ballet's Gary Kemp, who cofounded the band with his brother Martin. He was friendly and down to earth, and we talked about the music we liked and laughed about the extraordinary Japanese music fans and their Zen-like presents, which he said were called *o-miyage*. Over the next few days I often found myself at the same TV station or nightclub as Gary and his band, and they were each as cheerful and debonair as the next—with one notable exception. Their front man and singer, Tony Hadley, declined to shake my hand, would not make eye contact, and turned away when I tried to talk to him. It was the strangest thing: I wondered if we had met somewhere or had prior history, or if he maybe just hated my record. When I mentioned this to Gary Kemp later in the elevator, he looked puzzled and said, "That's not like Tony at all."

Gary must have said something to Tony, because on our last day in Japan, as we were waiting around in the green room before an appearance on a live TV talk show, Tony took me aside.

"Look, Thomas, I'm sorry if I've been a bit unfriendly, mate. It's just that when we arrived in Japan I was wearing this new suit, right? Bespoke tailor in Golders Green, white as snow, beautiful piece of cloth. Two grand, it cost me. Two grand! So we got off the plane and there was all these little Japanese girls pushing up to get my autograph. I'm signing all their records, right, and they're like a bloody swarm of bees around me with their Magic Markers. So I get to the hotel room and hang up my suit, and—fuck me, I've got fucking Magic Marker all over the sleeves of my fucking brand-new suit! And I thought to myself, Fuck Japan, fuck the little Japanese girls. I'm fucking off back to London on the next plane."

Back in the UK, my single "Windpower" had got to #38 in the charts, and I was summoned to do my first solo *Top of the Pops* performance. Although I'd appeared on the show once before, as keyboard player with Lene Lovich, it was an incredible thrill to think that now I'd be doing it in my own name.

Top of the Pops had been a staple of British life since the 1960s. My contemporaries in the UK charts, bands like Culture Club, Simple Minds, Tears for Fears, and Wham!, had all grown up addicted to the show. At the height of its popularity it was viewed on a weekly basis by three-quarters of the population of our islands and exported by the BBC to over a hundred countries around the world. For an ambitious young pop star, being selected was a dream come true—but it was also a kind of rite of passage, because *Top of the Pops* embodied everything that was idiotic about the UK pop business.

A *TOTP* appearance was by far the biggest and most crucial factor in having a major chart hit. It was nigh on impossible to break into the charts without it, but if you were lucky enough to get picked, your record would jump ten or fifteen chart places the following week. The thirty-five-minute show was shot every Wednesday afternoon with a small live audience, and broadcast the following evening, with something like 82 percent of the nation's viewers tuning in. Filming was at the BBC's White City studios, a gargantuan circular building in West London.

The weekly *TOTP* routine sent the London music business into a flurry of activity. Although the show was mimed to playback, those backing tracks had to be rerecordings, not the originals, so that musicians would earn an additional fee of around £56 apiece. This was the result of a long-standing treaty of the BBC with the Musicians Union. But the treaty and the rerecording process were a complete scam, and everybody knew it. Records didn't get made in a few hours as they had in the Beatles' day. By 1982, most singles were taking days or even weeks to record. You couldn't possibly hope to re-create your record in three hours. (Trevor Horn famously spent over £70,000 recording Frankie Goes to Hollywood's single "Relax" after entirely scrapping two earlier versions, all of which his label, ZTT, charged back to the band.) The simple thing would have been to just pay the musicians an extra residual fee and be done with it. But that wouldn't fly with the Musicians Union.

The way it worked was this: On Tuesday morning the new singles chart for that week would be published, and from that the BBC would make its selection of the week's featured acts, and each record company summoned its artists. Half a dozen top London recording studios were prebooked for a three-hour session on Tuesday night. At 6 p.m. the band, producer, and reps from the BBC, the MU, and the record company would meet at the studio, where roadies had already set up the band's equipment and an engineer was in the process of getting a drum sound. After a brief hello, the record company chap would take the BBC and MU guys around the corner for a nice dinner and a few bottles of wine. Two hours later they would return to the studio to find the band gone, the roadies breaking down the gear, and a set of gleaming stereo master tapes of the new "rerecordings" sitting on the desk. The MU would sign off on these, and they'd be taken to White City to be used for playback the following day.

I knew the drill, having been through it all before with Lene Lovich, and I acted out the whole ludicrous pantomime with a polite smile on my face. The stakes, after all, were a high chart position for my song "Windpower," international fame, and plenty of money in record sales and performance fees. But it made me a little sick to the stomach to see the chumminess of the handful of BBC producers who dictated the weekly playlists with all the well-paid music business "intermediaries." Between them they were spoon-feeding the innocent British public an illusion of a pop chart based on popularity. Though the weekly chart was accurately calculated from actual over-the-counter sales, the TOTP and BBC playlists had such a profound effect on sales, the corporation might as well have been writing the chart themselves.

As well as *Top of the Pops*, the BBC's White City building was home to *Dr. Who* and *Monty Python's Flying Circus*. So the taping session for "Windpower" was pretty hilarious. I stepped out of a taxi and strode into the foyer with Lesley alongside me jotting notes on her clipboard. There was one continuous long circular corridor around the complex that contained the TOTP "star dressing rooms," along with the group changing rooms overflowing with gaggles of Vikings and Daleks. You could catch the whiff of Jimmy Savile's cigar smoke. I signed a couple of autographs, and with my suit bag over my arm I walked around the circular corridor until I spotted my name on a door, wedged right between Duran Duran and Spandau Ballet.

Though I was on good terms with members of both bands, they were at

59

the time deadly rivals for the crown of top British pop group, and the animosity was palpable. At showtime, when the knock came on the doors of our respective dressing rooms, one band would turn clockwise and the other counterclockwise, with their noses turned in the air. I couldn't help sniggering when two minutes later they came face-to-face again at the opposite point of the compass rose.

The *TOTP* production crew had pulled out all the stops for my performance. There were massive wind machines surrounding my small stage, bold monochromatic lighting, stroboscopes, and enough fog to cause a collision at sea. I sprang around between multiple keyboards and Simmons drum pads, spectacles askance, hair blowing in the wind, in a dapper fawn suit. Back in my dressing room I watched the playback on a monitor and felt quite pleased with the way it turned out. I was wiping off my makeup when there was a knock on the door. It was one of the BBC producers; I'll just call him Julian. He complimented me on my performance and said he loved the song. He asked whether it was getting lots of plays on Radio 1. I said it was getting a few odd plays here and there, but not nearly as much as I'd have liked. "Well," said Julian, "you're new on the scene and you probably need to get to know some of us a little better. Tell you what, I'm having a pool party with a bunch of guys at my house in Essex next weekend, you should come and join us. It'll be fun."

I suddenly remembered I had a prior engagement.

CHAPTER 4
POETRY IN MOTION

My stories may make it seem very trite, but the British music business in the early eighties was a juggernaut. It was the world's second biggest record market, and the five top companies manufactured over 85 percent of all records released. EMI UK had probably seventy acts on its roster at the time. A few were evergreen classic bands, such as the Beatles, Pink Floyd, and Queen. These bands could go for years without releasing a new record, and EMI's shareholder reports would be buoyed by their consistent long-term sales. Then they had maybe four or five "new and contemporary" bands who would string together hit singles and successful albums. In the first few months of my contract, I was on the cusp of this group, but I was also teetering close to the abyss—the pool of fifty or more acts that languished in EMI's catalog, erratically releasing records that failed to break even. The majority of bands on the roster were trapped in limbo, struggling to engage with the label or gain access to any part of its powerful marketing resources. The net loss generated by their poor sales would be offset by EMI's fabulous profit margins on the big hit records put out by their handful of successful acts.

The basic gist of my EMI royalty statements was this: "Good news! You've sold 185,000 albums worldwide. There's no check because we're using the

61

proceeds from your record to promote it, but we expect to sell loads more next quarter!" Like most artists signed to the major record companies, I bought in to the myth that I was investing in the longevity of my career, when in truth I was just adding to the years of my own servitude. If you don't want to take it from me, go ask George Michael, Prince, or Sheryl Crow.

I was determined not to become one of the forgotten artists in the nether reaches of EMI's roster, but my radio play and sales were simply not good enough. I needed a different way to break through.

When an artist was unable to appear live on *Top of the Pops* because of being on tour or out of the country, the BBC would show their music video instead. Music videos were fairly unsophisticated (typically featuring the singers onstage in a simulated concert setting with plenty of shots up the lead guitarist's trouser leg, or a band cruising down the Sunset Strip in an open-topped car covered in balloons), yet they still made a welcome change from the formulaic *TOTP* shooting format. EMI had already made three music videos—"Europa and the Pirate Twins," "Airwaves," and "Radio Silence"—that had never been shown on British prime-time TV, but demand for them was increasing in Europe, Japan, and the USA, where a new all-music cable channel had recently been launched. It was called MTV.

The more daring music video directors were starting to introduce narrative story lines into their clips, people like Kevin Godley and Lol Creme from 10cc. I saw these videos as short silent films with a soundtrack. I was a huge fan of the classic silent films of Buster Keaton, Harold Lloyd, and Charlie Chaplin, and could relate to their underdog heroism. In an era when my contemporaries were pinups like Sting and Adam Ant, I was never going to compete with the major pop stars of the day in the poster child stakes. But I came from a long line of university professors, so why not draw on that pedigree? I could be the dweeby nice guy who beats the odds and ends up winning the girl's heart. I began dreaming up a scenario for a music video set in a Home for Deranged Scientists, including a mad psychiatrist and his hot Japanese lab assistant. On a storyboard pad I started to sketch out the script. My character would arrive at the clinic astride a classic vintage motorbike with sidecar. After an initial session on the analyst's couch, I would be drugged and wheeled into the operating theater for some sort of corrective procedure. There followed a surreal dream involving sinister schoolboy twins and a waltz with the female lab assistant in a Magritte-style cello gown. I was to be put out to pasture with the other deranged scientists, but I escaped in a strait-jacket, and the psychiatrist got his comeuppance.

I scrawled a title at the top of my storyboard, *She Blinded Me with Science*, and took it in to the head of EMI's video department, Geoff Kempin, telling him I wanted this to be my next single. "It's cute," he said, "but where's the song?" "Um, I'll bring that in on Monday," I replied.

Over the weekend at the meatpacking loft I sat down to write the song. I got a great funky groove going on the PPG, with a tight Moog bass line and some luscious strings. Jo Kerr was back in town and stopped by to hear it. He wrote some of his own lyrics and sketched them on a piece of paper. By Sunday night I had a demo good enough to play the record company.

EMI had recently contracted to make two videos with a director called Steve Barron. They showed me some rough cuts and I was impressed with his work. I duly set up a time to meet him later that week at his production company, Limelight Films. When I arrived at their offices on Soho Square the receptionist looked embarrassed. She quickly disappeared into the back to find Steve's producer, his older sister Siobhan. As she walked up to me to shake hands, I couldn't help imagining casting her as the lab assistant in my video. She was a former *Vogue* model, immaculately dressed, with a disarming elegance. Her broad smile curled a little at the edges. Seated beside me on the sofa in a tiny screening room piled high with Betamax tapes, Siobhan explained to me that Steve was actually at that moment on a plane to Los Angeles, where Michael Jackson had summoned him to discuss the video for the first single from his new album, *Thriller*. Siobhan was sorry if I'd made a wasted trip, but said she would love to hear my concept for the new single.

I pulled out my storyboard and talked her through it. She laughed a lot and complimented me on the camera angles I'd drawn. When I asked how soon Steve might have an opening to direct the piece, she said, "Thomas, *you* should be the one to direct this, your ideas are so brilliant and you can make it quirky and original. Why not do it yourself?"

I was taken aback by this, and said I had no idea how it all worked on a film set. "Not a problem," said Siobhan. "We shoot videos all the time. We've got two on the go this week alone. Come down to the set and I'll explain how it all works. We've got an amazing crew. I'll introduce you to the right people. We will bring your ideas to life!"

I was concerned that EMI would not go for the idea of me directing my own video. "Oh, don't worry about them," Siobhan said. "I can take care of it. They're so cheap, when I tell them how much money they will save by not needing a director, they'll be all over it." (In actual fact it wouldn't have made much difference to EMI, as they recouped the video costs from my royalty statement, even though they retained full ownership of the video.)

I arranged to meet Siobhan for a night shoot at the huge and derelict Butler's Wharf, on the south bank of the Thames. It was close to midnight as I drove through the deserted alleyways, and I could see an area where the crumbling warehouses were all lit up by powerful film lights. There was a dolly track rigged across the cobblestones. Camera grips, wardrobe and makeup people were milling around, their breath visible in the cold night air. At the center of all the activity I could see Phil Oakey from the Human League flanked by two female backing singers, miming to playback on a small speaker. Siobhan was wrapped in a fur coat, and she turned and waved at me. At the end of the take she came over and gave me a kiss on the cheek. "Ooh, Thomas, let's get some Bovril and sit in your Jag." It seemed she had a deep fear of rats. She slid next to me on the leather bench seat and began pointing out equipment and members of the crew, explaining their roles.

Needless to say, I was smitten with this elegant woman and the enticing world of film and glamour that she represented. We became lovers, and for a few months I followed her around like a puppy dog as she breezed through London cocktail parties and gallery openings. The room would light up as she walked into the middle of a crowd; often she would get bored after five or ten minutes and announce she was leaving to go somewhere else, trailing half the partygoers with her.

EMI gave us the budget for a long single day's shoot on the "Science" video, and my call was at 5:15 a.m. The location was the Holme, a fabulous Georgian building and gardens in the middle of Regent's Park, and we were lucky with the weather. The lighting cameraman had a pretty good handle on how to compose the shots I'd described, so my job was to direct the actors, grab an occasional peek through the lens, yell "Action!" and jump into the frame. I'd hired Dr. Magnus Pyke, a well-known TV personality and scientist, to play the part of the mad psychiatrist. We didn't see eye to eye. Despite the fact that I'd sent him a copy of the storyboard, along with a check that wiped out a large chunk of our budget, Dr. Pyke was not comfortable with the idea of wearing a white lab coat on-screen, and he was refusing to come out of his trailer. An assistant director brought me the bad news, so I went to see him myself. "My public don't regard me that way," he complained, clearly on the verge of a tantrum. Siobhan told me I should let it drop and move on, hurrying me along so we could stay on schedule and get all the shots done without incurring overtime.

My father, Martin Robertson, was in the clip, playing a deranged inventor, gamely firing up his rocket-powered roller skates on the lawn. He was the only bona fide professor on the set, the rest having been hired from Central Casting. He introduced himself to Dr. Pyke, who by coincidence had formerly taught chemistry to two of my older brothers at prep school. Dr. Pyke's only response was to repeatedly ask Martin to check with me whether his car was going to be there for him at noon. He also expressed his dissatisfaction with the premise of the clip. "As a known scientist," he said, "it would be a bit surprising if the girl blinded *me* with science." In his defense, he was darned good at flapping his arms around and looking demented on cue.

I bumped into Dr. Pyke many years later, in Edinburgh at a conference. He'd just returned from a lecture tour of the USA. I asked him how it had gone. "Badly, Dolby," he spat back. "Every time I walked down the sidewalk someone would sneak up behind me and yell 'SCIENCE!' at the top of their lungs! It seems that bloody MTV video of yours is more widely recognized than my body of scientific work."

By lunchtime I was frantic with agitation and somewhat exhausted. I sat at a trestle table with my band, trying to eat half a sandwich. One of the musicians said, "Here Tom, take one of these," and handed me glass of water and a pink pill. I took it and downed it in one and then said, "What was that?" "Oh, just a Dexedrine 20," he said. "I get them on prescription. It'll keep you awake." "What the *f*—?" Within five minutes I felt a second wind coming on; but with it came a terrible case of itchy mouth. In the later shots from the clip you can see my tongue flailing around like a rabid dog's.

When we wrapped at the end of the day, Siobhan handed me a large box of Scotch whisky miniatures. "Give one of these to each of your brilliant crew," she said quietly. "They'll remember you for it." Siobhan was like that. She knew every crew member personally and took great care of them, but was humble enough to let the artist take the credit for her gifts.

Limelight hooked me up with an excellent editor called John Mister, and we spent five days cutting my film in an editing suite in Soho. I learned to my delight that John had worked on *Monty Python and the Holy Grail*, and had been roped into playing a bit part as the knight who got his throat ripped out by the homicidal rabbit, nearly drowning in the middle of Hampstead Heath when his helmet filled up with fake blood. It was fascinating to watch the physicality of John's editing process—the way he would pick a strip of celluloid from a long rack, wind it through on his Steenbeck editing machine, mark the perfect in and out points with a china pencil, apply a touch of glue, then use both hands to stamp the shot into the master reel. All of this can be completed these days with a few strokes on a QWERTY and undone in an instant. Back then, you had to be pretty confident that a cut was going to work. John could eyeball two pieces of film either side of a potential cut, knowing intuitively if it was going to flow. "See the way her hand comes up into frame right there? It's not going to work. And I've got nothing else to cut away to. You need to get more coverage, Thomas!"

In the editing suite next door was Steve Barron, who had just returned from Los Angeles, where he'd shot the video for Michael Jackson's "Billie Jean." Michael was planning a secret visit to London to sit in on the edit of his clip. Siobhan told me to keep it to myself, because he didn't want to attract any paparazzi attention. He worked with Steve in the adjacent suite over the course of several days. One afternoon we met at the watercooler.

Michael was wearing simple white jeans and a black leather jacket. I introduced myself and asked him if he was pleased with the progress on his video. I complimented him on the arrangement of "Billie Jean," and I wasn't lying when I said it was one of the best singles I'd ever heard in my life. He told me he really liked "She Blinded Me with Science," too. He said it was already getting some plays on "urban" radio and in dance clubs in the U.S., along with its B-side, "One of Our Submarines"; but he'd assumed I was a black guy. He showed me Steve Barron's work in progress on his video. Mostly it was successive takes of Michael strutting down an illuminated dance floor with his collar up. But he said that for the next singles from his album *Thriller*, he really wanted to try some narrative videos that had a real story line. Which was why he was interested in "She Blinded Me with Science." Michael gave me his number on a scrap of paper and said if I was ever in L.A. I should look him up. I wrote it in my Filofax, not really expecting I would ever get a chance to use it.

In America, EMI's acts were released on either Capitol or Harvest. I'd never met any of the U.S. executives, but Capitol vice president for A&R Bobby Colomby, the former drummer with Blood, Sweat & Tears, was so excited by the potential of a U.S. hit with "Science" that he flew to England to meet me in person. He told me that though radio play was still sparse, MTV were about to add the video into their rotation, and that many dance clubs were playing the 12" version. The *Billboard* chart was derived from a combination of sales and radio play. Now that MTV was available in the major cities, hip people were staying home on a Saturday night to watch videos instead of going out to concerts. As a result, MTV's rotation was beginning to influence radio programmers, which in turn had a direct effect on the charts. If we played our cards right, Bobby said, Capitol would put some serious might behind my record. I should be on alert to get myself on a plane at any moment.

An amazing new computer music instrument had recently become available, the Fairlight CMI. For the first time, real sounds could be digitally recorded, processed, and played back as notes and chords on a musical keyboard. It was, in effect, a digital Mellotron, but with a whole world of new possibilities. The genius of the Fairlight was that unlike most new instruments developed by musicians, its user interface was not based on a recognizable metaphor: it was a truly original instrument. You could use its electronic "light pen" to draw wave forms on the screen. Sounds were displayed in a three-dimensional perspective that looked like a mountain range—a look made famous by Joy Division's album cover design for *Unknown Pleasures*. The Fairlight was invented in Australia by a brilliant maverick engineer called Peter Vogel. He had only a fleeting interest in music, but created the Fairlight, he said, because he *could*. When asked to bring the instrument to Stevie Wonder's hotel suite for a demo during his stadium tour, he reportedly said, "Who's Stevie Wonder?" Over the years he's been credited with numerous controversial innovations, including a way to block ads from TV hard disk recordings and a method of turning Northern Australian scrub grass into renewable energy.

Although the Fairlight CMI cost nearly £30,000—more than the value of my London flat—I knew I had to have one, and I borrowed against future royalties to pay for it. I set it up in the meatpacking loft and locked myself in for several nights. I was not disappointed! After years of being limited to electronically synthesized sounds, it was a revelation to be able to work with the sounds of real strings, brass, ethnic instruments, and drum kits. In the first few days alone I programmed some amazing grooves into the Fairlight's Page R sequencer, and a couple of brand-new songs were emerging.

EMI were optimistic about the prospects of my new single "She Blinded Me with Science," which they were preparing to release in the UK and the United States, but they were insistent that I needed to be ready with a new album to back it up. I had a handful of complete new songs, plus some rough ideas that could be rapidly worked up into finished tracks. Andy Ferguson booked some cheap studio time with my band at a small studio in Brussels, and we rented an apartment in a poor Muslim immigrant suburb of the city. With the help of a crafty percussionist named Clif Brigden we began to weave Roland TR808 grooves and Fairlight sequences into my sound, adding fretless bass and upright piano, trumpet and trombone, producing an almost organic feel. In studio breaks, Matthew and I played football in the streets with the scruffy local Muslim kids. Kevin Armstrong had brought his car over on the ferry, a mean-looking Citroën sedan, and we would work all day on the tracks and then go clubbing in the scary Citroën. The soundtrack blaring out of his system on those hot nights was the new Marvin Gaye album, *Midnight Love*. I mentioned how much I loved the album to a *New Musical Express* photojournalist called Anton Corbijn who was in Brussels to do a piece on us, and he told me that his next assignment was in New York, where he was to photograph Marvin at a convention called the New Music Seminar. I knew that Siobhan was going to be in New York, where Limelight was looking into opening a U.S. office, and I thought it would be nice to surprise her. Andy managed to get me into the conference as a speaker on the same panel as Marvin. He said the timing was good, as we could wine and dine some of the independent radio programmers working on my record, which had just entered the *Billboard* charts. Actually, I was more interested in seeing my glamorous new girlfriend again and meeting the legendary Marvin Gaye.

That New York trip was a triple catastrophe. On the flight across the Atlantic I felt I was coming down with something (it turned out to be mononucleosis). Our luggage was delayed, and on account of some bad traffic I had to take the limo straight to a midtown restaurant to meet the promotions guys. I called ahead to Siobhan and asked her to meet us there. The guests of honor were Rick Carroll and Lee Abrams, supposedly two of the most influential rock radio promoters in the country. If these men got behind your record, I was told, you were almost guaranteed a big hit. They had been working my album from the start, and I was to be especially friendly and complimentary to them. Capitol Records had promised them a special treat that night. The plan was to present them each with a gold disk for my album *The Golden Age of Wireless*, which had just passed five hundred thousand sales. But Lee and Rick had arrived at the restaurant early and asked the maître d' for the Capitol Records table, and waiting there at the booth was a beautiful ex–*Vogue* model. Rick assumed that Siobhan was their special treat. So when I walked in from the street with my suitcases, the first thing I saw was Rick Carroll with his arm around Siobhan, whispering sweet nothings in her ear.

She looked at me in horror and tried unsuccessfully to slide away from him. I was more than a little confused, not least when the dinner got under way and Lee Abrams decided to launch into his famous Texan Air Traffic Controller routine. Cupping his hand over his mouth, he produced a torrent of airplane radio chatter in a deep southern accent, and of course the Capitol guys found this hysterically funny. It went on for about fifteen minutes.

Siobhan and I headed back to her hotel, and we had a huge row. Of course the Rick Carroll thing was hardly her fault, but she was unhappy that I'd sprung this surprise visit on her. She was not someone you could keep on a leash, she said. She had her own set of friends in New York, and I might not get on with them. She had important business meetings, and she didn't want to feel she had to entertain me as well. I was not her boyfriend, just someone she slept with every now and then.

I went back down to reception and booked myself a single room.

The next morning, still shell-shocked after Siobhan's outburst and feeling the onset of a cold that I thought I must have picked up on the plane, I hailed a taxi to head downtown to the music convention where I was to be a panelist. I found my place behind the long table on the stage as the audience took its seats, and snuck a peek at the name tag in front of the seat next to mine: Marvin Gaye! I was thrilled to finally meet one of my idols. The moderator said we'd get started in a few moments, but right as the lights dimmed, Marvin's name tag was removed and replaced with another. I nervously turned it around: Kevin Rowland. The front man of Dexys Midnight Runners. Mr. Gaye had canceled.

Rowland showed up a little drunk. He was unshaven and his armpits smelled. After introducing the panelists the moderator asked me for my comments on the state of the U.S. music business, but before I could answer, Rowland grabbed the desk mic off me and launched into a rant about how fucked up it was, and how you knew it had all gone to shit when all the radio played was crap like Thomas Dolby.

By now I was feeling feverish from the mono. The Rowland outburst had left me speechless. I was too shaky to do the usual postpanel schmooze, and

I asked for a cab to take me back to the hotel. When I got up to my room, the red light on my phone was blinking. Was it a message from Siobhan, begging me to make up with her? No. It was Andy Ferguson:

"The good news is, your single is #1 in Canada. The bad news is that you need to pack your bags again. Capitol urgently need you in L.A. They want to repackage *The Golden Age of Wireless* album with 'Science' and 'Submarines' on it, plus they want you on a live TV show—tonight."

A slot had opened up on *MV3* that very evening. The show had a big audience rating, and it could well affect the next week's chart position. If I checked out of the hotel right away I could catch the next flight from LaGuardia, and someone from the label would be there to pick me up at LAX and take me right to the studio.

Staring out of the window of a Pan Am jetliner somewhere high over Cleveland, my fever started to spike, and my mind turned to dark thoughts about the row with Siobhan. I had left New York without a word to her, but now I couldn't bear the thought of never seeing her again. Aside from my admiration of her style and grace, she was a fabulous video producer. She'd been such a powerful influence on me, getting me to take that first stride as a filmmaker. I pictured her floating among the warehouses on that cold night at Butler's Wharf, wrapped in fur, joking and encouraging the film crew, moving the shoot along, keeping the mood upbeat. Then I thought about her other "friends" in New York City, and wondered who she would be with tonight.

Siobhan was no stranger to drama. Only two years my senior, she had been married twice. Her first husband, she told me, was a mafioso who paid her for sex so she could buy drugs. She said he'd coerced her into marriage at nineteen to prevent her testifying against him; they divorced after she shot off his toe in a domestic squabble. She had then been married briefly to Stevie Wonder's sound engineer, before conceiving a love child with the cofounder of Virgin Records. Perhaps I had dodged a bullet? Looking back, my infatuation was unhealthy. But unhealthy infatuations are the lifeblood of songwriters. We are drawn in like moths to a flame. I pulled out a small notebook and began to write down disjointed words and lyrics. In time these evolved into a song called "Screen Kiss." It's possibly the best I've ever written.

Suddenly, as we crossed the Rocky Mountains, our plane dropped a thousand feet in the blink of an eye. We were skirting a massive electric storm, and the plane shook violently all the way to LAX. It was already getting dark, and as we came in to land the heavens opened.

CHAPTER 5
WONDERLAND

The thing about the music business is, the moment your record goes on the charts somewhere in the world, you drop whatever you're doing and hop on a plane. It's understood. Touching down in Los Angeles, on my way to record a TV show that could be the vital last push to break my single into the Top 20, you'd think I'd be feeling a bit like James Bond on a mission. But I was sick to my stomach, and it was a bad landing. The L.A. area was being battered by a tropical monsoon. You could hardly see the tarmac in the torrential downpour. Between the mononucleosis and the emotional distress of the bust-up, I was running a high fever. I'd been drenched in sweat since somewhere over the prairies. Agent 007 didn't enter into it. I threw up into the bag in my seat pocket.

At the gate I was met by a delegation from Capitol Records. They had two limos outside. They introduced themselves enthusiastically: each rep made sure I knew exactly what he did for me, along the lines of "Hi, I'm Bruce Wendell, I got you fifty-seven radio adds this week!" or "Hi, Thomas, Dean Cameron. I'm the guy that discovered you."

My luggage was sent on to the hotel, but my new entourage accompanied me to the *MV3* studios in Burbank. The show was fronted by legendary disk jockey Richard Blade, an expatriate Brit who looked like a surfer, and shot in front of a live audience. There was a packed crowd of bright-faced teen-agers, and the stage was set up with a two-tiered keyboard stand and a microphone—which were not really plugged in, because this was a "playback" show, meaning the artists mime the words. The kids all knew my new record "She Blinded Me with Science" from the radio and instantly jumped up to dance as it was piped through the wedge speakers.

There was only one problem: the version of the song that was getting played on the radio was the five-minute 12" mix. I had hurriedly reeled off that mix at 4 a.m., at the tail end of a fifteen-hour session during which I'd concentrated on the shorter album mix of the song. I can remember assuring my exhausted coproducer, Tim Friese-Greene, that it would only take us an hour or so to dash it off. We'd rapidly edited together instrumental passages, drums-only sections, and even restructured the vocals. In this extended version, the order of the verses was flipped.

I hadn't listened to the extended mix since the night we spliced it together three months earlier. So here I was on live TV, miming the *wrong* words, and missing some cues altogether. I was totally screwing it up. The adoring kids in the front row knew my record better than I did!

Backstage after the taping, my Capitol entourage poured into the dressing room, predictably full of praise for my performance. They told me about the fun evening they had lined up for me.

"We thought we'd go for tacos at Carlos and Charlie's, then take in a couple of cool bands at the Whisky a Go Go," enthused Dean Cameron. "Then maybe some late-night drinks in the VIP lounge at the Rainbow Room," added Bruce Wendell. "Whaddaya say, TD?"

"Actually, I promised I'd go and see some people tonight," I replied, not wishing to offend my new record label friends.

"Oh sure, we can drop you off wherever. Here, wanna use the phone?" Somebody handed me a clunky wireless receiver.

I rooted around in my shoulder bag and pulled out my leather-bound Filofax. Flipping through the pages, I was desperate to find any local number I could call. The humiliation of my lame TV appearance in front of all those screaming teenagers was sitting heavy on me; plus the mononucleosis and the jet lag were seriously kicking in.

There was only one Los Angeles number in my book, and it was Michael Jackson's. So I dialed it, not telling my Capitol buddies who I was calling. To my surprise, Michael himself answered. I said: "Hullo, it's Thomas, we met at an editing suite in London."

"You're really in L.A.? Where?"

I had to ask. "Er . . . I'm in Burbank, apparently. Is that anywhere close to you?"

"Yeah, it's close," said Michael. "I live in Encino. Want to come over?"

"That would be great," I said, relieved at the thought of getting the entourage off my back. He gave me his address, a number in the high thousands on Hayvenhurst Avenue.

The two limos headed out into the torrential downpour. In the back of ours, a crystal decanter of Scotch was doing the rounds, and the Capitol execs were in high spirits. Someone chopped out lines of cocaine on a mirrored side table. I was so spaced out already, the last thing I needed was chemical stimulation.

I gave the limo driver the address. It was pitch black now, and rain was still pelting down. The driver squinted at the house numbers. "Doesn't Michael Jackson live on this street?" he said over his shoulder.

"Yes. Actually, that's where I'm going," I replied. The driver flashed a look at me in his rearview mirror, and my co-passengers were a little astonished.

We arrived at the address and pulled up in front of a set of huge cast-iron gates. The driver buzzed an intercom, and I told him to announce me. "We have Thomas Dolby for Michael Jackson," he said. After a few moments, the gates swung open. I told the driver he could let me out right there, I'd just walk up the drive. I was too embarrassed to show up with the whole group. The Capitol execs looked dubious, but I stepped out of the limo in the glare of its headlights and stumbled up the driveway, dodging puddles. I walked past a big glass guardhouse; inside I could see a pair of uniformed security guards, their faces lit up by CCTV screens. They motioned me on up the driveway. I waved and caught a glint of semiautomatic weapons on a rack behind them. It was much farther to the house than I had imagined.

Michael's home was an imposing mansion with a fountain and a gravel turnaround. The hefty front door was set in a glass surround, and I could see the grand hallway lit up inside. There was a crystal chandelier, marble floors, and twin Busby Berkeley–style curling staircases. I rang the bell pull and stood there dripping in my sodden T-shirt and jeans. I guess I was expecting some sort of butler or domestic servant. But after a few moments, a small figure in a pink silk leisure suit regally descended one side of the staircase and crossed the marble floor. It was him.

The door swung open, and I stood there, leaving little puddles in the doorway. Michael greeted me with a smile and pointed me to a small bathroom off the hallway. There was a stack of paper towels on the basin, so I used them to dry my hair as best I could and sop up a little of the rain from my drenched clothes.

When I returned, my host was waiting by a gracious seating area at the center of the hallway. "Let's sit," he said, indicating a stuffed leather ottoman. I parked my backside on the ottoman, while he mounted a gigantic, jewel-encrusted medieval throne. It was so massive that he had to clamber up to get into it. His arms barely reached the armrests, as it was clearly designed for someone much larger (Henry VIII, perhaps?). Perched on his throne, Michael looked like an action figure of himself.

I cast my eyes around the room at a curious array of art treasures. There was a solid gold mantelpiece with a Venetian clock in a glass bell jar; a stuffed raccoon; a Chinese ivory chess set on a Biedermeier games table; next to that, a Darth Vader helmet on a plinth. Michael settled into the throne in his leisure suit and we began to talk.

"You're a Libra, aren't you?" he said. "You were born on October 14th. I saw that article in *Creem*. I'm only six weeks older than you."

"You're into that stuff?" I replied. "I don't really follow horoscopes. I don't see how one in every twelve people in the world is going to have the same sort of day as I am."

"What I love is the *symbolism*. It's just so *symbolic*. See, I'm a Virgo. The

Virgo symbol looks exactly like my initials—M.J." He picked up a pad of paper and drew it for me. I noticed that his notepad had isolated words and random lines of lyrics jotted on it, like many of my own.

"Do you have songs and lyrics in your head all the time?" I asked.

"Every day I write a bit, then I go dance a bit," he said. I noticed how brown his eyes were. "Then I go play video games." We both laughed.

He asked about the groove for "She Blinded Me with Science," how I put it together. "Were those Simmons electric drums? I dig those. I have a set upstairs."

"Yes, the SDS5s. But I was triggering them with this weird machine called a PPG Wave Computer. It was built to control Tangerine Dream's light show."

"I love those guys! Did you ever hear the soundtrack to *Sorcerer?* The Roy Scheider film? Brilliant. I've got a copy in my screening room. Oh, and I just got my own Synclav." He was referring to the $120,000 Synclavier computerized sampling keyboard heard on the intro to "Beat It."

And so our conversation meandered. We talked about music production techniques, the fall colors in New England that he missed here in Los Angeles, how we'd each spent much of our childhoods away from home. I was surprised by the breadth of Michael's knowledge and interests. He was remarkably down-to-earth and easy to talk to, and as passionate about his music as I was about mine.

Thriller had been out a few months, but it had already passed the five million sales mark. Michael asked how my album was doing. "It's doing well," I told him—not mentioning any figures—"but now that I'm on the U.S. charts, the music press back in England are saying I've sold out."

"You just have to go on believing," Michael said. "You have to go on believing that you are better than them, that you're better than everybody. You must never let go of your dream."

I was touched by his words, and I felt myself welling up. All evening I'd thought we were alone in the house. But after we'd been chatting for about an hour, what was already a strange evening took an even stranger turn.

Out of the corner of my eye, I noticed tiny faces peeking out from the railing of the upstairs landing. I glanced up—they vanished. Moments later they were back, more of them this time. I heard hysterical giggling. Then a door swung open, and the 12" of "Science" came blasting out at 120 decibels. Now there were at least a dozen little faces staring at me, and fingers pointing through the spindles of the balustrade.

Michael explained that on Thursday evenings he liked to invite the neighbor kids over to play with their radio-controlled toys. I asked, "What's up with the giggling?" He laughed and said, "Oh, they just can't believe you're the guy off the TV." He beckoned to them, and they traipsed down the staircase, each with a toy truck or race car. They were in pajamas and dressing gowns. They laughed and played on the Turkish rug, whizzing model trucks and trains around our feet. Michael directed the proceedings from his perch, like the Thin Controller in *Thomas the Tank Engine*. We carried on chatting, but from time to time he broke off midsentence to issue a directive. "Hey, Jimmy, bring that over here . . . Billy, don't do that! Now what did we say about sharing our toys?"

"I never really had a childhood," Michael told me. "I spent too much of it on the road." It sounded to me as if his dad and his brothers bullied and teased him because they knew he was by far the most talented. When he asked about my family, I told him I was a happy kid and loved my parents very much, although I had to explain to him what a classical archaeologist was.

We discussed our favorite albums and discovered a shared admiration for the Beach Boys album *Surf's Up*. Michael was sad that Brian Wilson had severe psychiatric problems and that his brother Dennis was a drunk and a drug addict. "It's better to die a sudden death than just deteriorate. When I die," said Michael, "I want to die like Elvis."

As the evening drew on, I felt it was time I made my excuses. I asked Michael if I could call a cab to take me to my hotel over in Hollywood. "Wait," he said. "Maybe Randy can give you a ride." He picked up a phone and punched a few buttons. Randy Jackson, his younger brother, must have been hiding out in some other wing of the mansion. "Hi, Funky. Can you drive my friend over to Sunset Strip?"

Ten minutes later, Michael's brother Randy appeared in the hall. He was decked out in a skintight red leather suit, bare chest, gold necklace, and sun-glasses. He said he'd be happy to drop me at my hotel.

"You come right home afterwards, Randy, you hear me?" said Michael em-phatically. "I don't want you going to some club, picking up a fish, smoking those turds you smoke."

As Randy Jackson gunned his Jeep up through the Hollywood Hills, the rain was still lashing down. Laurel Canyon, with its sharp bends and high concrete verges, was like a white-water rapid. KROQ was blaring on the radio. I gripped the armrests and longed for my bed.

Randy had a glint in his eye. "Hey, Dolby, you wanna come check out Club Odyssey with me? They have a great sound system, and the best babes in Hollywood hang out there . . ."

I took a deep breath. "I think I'll pass this time," I said. "I'm English."

Still weak from the mononucleosis, I flew back to England and saw my GP. He said I was suffering from nervous exhaustion, and what I needed was a break. I agreed to take one as soon as I'd completed the recording and mixes for my second album, *The Flat Earth*. Lesley got right on it. She booked us a sailing holiday in the Mediterranean with my parents, my friend and bass player Matthew Seligman, and his girlfriend Miranda. I was running on fumes, but five weeks later I completed the mix of the last song, "Dissidents," at 3 a.m. on the day we were all booked to fly out to Athens for our holiday.

I'd splurged on a skippered fifty-five-foot yacht, and we spent a relaxed fortnight dodging in and out of small Greek harbors. It took me half that time to decompress, but the beauty of the Aegean Sea gradually seeped into me. As it turned out, it was to be the last trip I would make to Greece with my father, Martin. Now in his late seventies, he was completely at home among the islands, with his extraordinary knowledge of ancient Greek cul-ture and pottery. When we sailed past the remains of a temple high on a headland, he told us its story: how the high priest threw a wedding party for his only daughter, but she was kidnapped by Phoenician raiders and carried off to Thrace, where she was raped by the demigod Cychreus and gave birth to a sheep, or some such. This was history that was never written down, but passed on through the centuries in the form of oral poetry and the beautiful paintings on those black and brown pots. The connections he made were unique to Martin, and could only have come from the deep study of classical art. "Those are myths and legends, surely, not hard facts," I said. "Ah," he said, smiling, "but does that matter?"

Anchored in any one of a hundred tiny harbors, where narrow alleyways wound from waterfront cafés up to the white-stoned hilltop villas, my parents would sit in the shade of our boat's cockpit while the young folk explored the island on bikes or on foot. Around the headland from one small fishing village we found a beach where you could take ten-minute waterskiing lessons behind a powerful ski boat. A couple of us had never tried this before, so we all signed up. Matthew went first, and in typical style, he made an immediate and spectacular wipeout, ending up in a pool of foam with his skis and booties and trunks and sunhat scattered about like a yard sale. "You try to stand up too quick!" shouted the Greek speedboat driver. "It must stay down until pick up speed, yes?"

It was my turn on the skis next, and I was determined to stay down until we'd picked up speed. I picked up speed all right, and stayed very low, but the problem was I never managed to get upright at all. When we finally came to an abrupt halt in the shallows, I had the horrible realization that I must have imbibed at least a quart of seawater through my anus. I made a frantic dash for the reed beds, and the floodgates opened.

Waddling back to the yacht harbor in considerable discomfort, I found my father on deck with a novel in the evening sun, dressed in a white linen suit and Panama hat, with an ouzo and a bowl of olives. I told him of the waterskiing incident and my ill-gotten enema. When he'd finished laughing his head off, he picked up a pencil and started to scribble in the back of his notebook. Minutes later as I emerged from the shower he tore off a sheet of paper and handed me the result of his scribbling. It was written in the classical style:

Thomas auf Naxos
Squatting on water skis, a golden boy
Plows, his rump a furrow in the blue.

80

The Sea-God, ardour kindled by the view
The beauteous youth doth cruelly enjoy.

When my mother read the poem, she kissed Martin on the forehead. I believe that was the only time I ever saw my parents kiss. They had that kind of old-fashioned English marriage where you have lots of children, read lots of books, and generally make do.

In that kind of a world, Lesley and I would probably have been married. But I told Les after that holiday that much as I valued her loyalty and friendship, I would never make her my wife. We had never actually talked about it, but of course it was bubbling under. "I do love you," I said, "but I want more from life: I want mystery, urgency, adventure."

"But that's not reality," she said sadly, "it's just a romantic pipe dream. You could search for years and grow old and never find it."

"Ah," I said, "but does that matter?"

Not to me, perhaps, but maybe to her.

On my return to the UK, I set about making a long-form music video, *Live Wireless*. It was based around a one-hour live concert shot at Riverside Studios in London, interspersed with a fictional film noir tableau in which I starred as a projectionist in an old cinema. This was an innovative move, as few artists were venturing at the time beyond the four-minute MTV format. I wrote and directed it myself, and again I could hardly believe how lucky I was that EMI allowed me this kind of freedom. During the last months of 1983 I worked on the mastering and sleeve design for my second album, *The Flat Earth*, as Andy Ferguson prepared a massive U.S. and world tour to promote it.

After the Top 5 success of my single, with over a million sales of *The Golden Age of Wireless* and a platinum-selling remix EP called *Blinded by Science*, the pump was truly primed for my breakthrough as a commercial artist. But I had yet to build a reputation as a live artist, and it was a gamble whether I could sell out large theaters. We decided to go for broke and risk most of the money I'd earned from the first album to pay for the tour. I was hopeful that

The Flat Earth could do even better than its predecessor, and it had a killer first single on it, "Hyperactive!," which lent itself perfectly to a great video that would build on my MTV popularity. The quirky, up-tempo "Hyperactive!" seemed destined to repeat the Top 5 success of its predecessor; yet the new album had some mellow, deeper cuts to follow up with, including the beautiful ballad "Screen Kiss" that I had written after my breakup with Siobhan. I had visions of this coming out as the second single from the album and going all the way to #1.

The grand plan was to use the world tour to consolidate the success of two MTV-powered pop singles and establish my credentials as a serious long-term artist by pushing the more personal and introspective side of my music. We opted to do a full video projection as part of the stage set, which in those days was technically very challenging. It was an ambitious scheme: a trio of suspended video screens, stretched across giant frames that looked exactly like my National Health spectacles. Three-quarter-inch videotapes were loaded into three synchronized U-matic decks, and from there a click track was played into the drummer's wedge monitor so that he could keep tempo with the video projections. The show opened with a pseudo-lecture contrived by my brilliant older brother Matthew Robertson. The lecture was delivered on-screen by a crusty old physicist, who explained with the aid of animated diagrams that, despite the myths and lies perpetrated by NASA and the Kremlin, the Earth is actually *flat*.

I assembled a band from the backing musicians from Lene Lovich's band as well as from my own albums. Lene's drummer, Justin Hildreth, was paired with Matthew Seligman on electric bass. I recruited a cross-dressing keyboard player, Lyndon Connor, who had much better technique than me and could therefore cover the trickier parts from the album while I concentrated on the singing. Lesley would join us on the tour as my personal assistant, also acting as U-matic videotape loader, Fairlight administrator, and occasional backing vocalist. Sadly, Kevin Armstrong was now busy with his own band Bush Telegraph, so the guitar slot was handed to Chucho Merchán, a funky Colombian who dressed like a Guevarista guerrilla. Finally I needed someone to play piano and sing the featured female vocal parts, and my search led me to an outrageous New Yorker called Debra Barsha, who wore a sequined evening dress and performed with a stuffed poodle sewn under her armpit.

We rehearsed for a month in a studio under a South London railway arch, and watched "Hyperactive!" climb into the UK Top 20, aided by a state-of-the-art music video. This one was directed by Danny Kleinman, creator of the excellent James Bond opening title sequences, leaving me free to concentrate on my performance. Everything seemed poised for a renewed assault on the U.S. marketplace. The concert dates were set, kicking off with Radio City Music Hall in New York, then flying across to the West Coast, and back across the country by tour bus.

I couldn't complain about the state of my career. My name was showing up in the gossip columns, my face was frequently in the celebrity press, and I started to get invites to movie premieres or restaurant openings, to add glitz to the occasion. They would offer to send a car for me and tell me to come back any time, free of charge, and bring my friends. The flashbulbs would pop as I walked up the red carpet. "Who is that?" I would hear the paparazzi whisper to each other. "It's the guy that sings 'Science!' . . . you know, with the wacky video."

The view from the inside of my little round glasses was like the view from a fishbowl. I was the center of attention, but it felt alien and uncomfortable. I'd been a naturally shy person all my life, and people took little notice of me. I was never very at ease in social situations, always worried about fitting in or saying the right thing. Now, suddenly, everybody wanted to know me; in a way, they thought they already knew me. When someone called out my name in the street, it was as if they thought they owned a piece of me; but that "me" was just the image I was projecting in my videos. I couldn't help feeling I was acting out a part, a character from a script I'd dreamed up as a sort of joke.

In a hotel suite at the Parker Meridien hotel on Fifty-seventh Street, I began a relentless round of press and radio interviews to promote the release of *The Flat Earth* and the new tour. As the Radio City date approached, I became more and more nervous. It was the biggest venue I'd played by far, and what a history it had! I knew the critics would be there in force. I picked up a copy of *The New York Times* and read a review of a recent gig by Hall and Oates. The *Times* correspondent had ripped them to pieces. The same writer was on the guest list for my gig at Radio City, along with the heads of my record company and numerous showbiz celebrities. The plan was for me to open the show by emerging from the stage on a hydraulic riser copied from pre–World War II aircraft carriers, seated at a white grand piano.

On the morning of the show I had a full-on anxiety attack in my hotel room. I was huddled in a corner behind the couch, shaking profusely. I told my tour manager I couldn't go through with it. The concierge found the number for a private doctor, who showed up within a half hour. His name was something like Dr. Libbitz and he was European and quite elderly. I can't picture his face, but I faintly remember he had bushy white eyebrows. He flipped open an old-fashioned wooden medical box and tapped on a syringe as he held it up to the light. I recall clearly what he said: "This is just a mild sedative to take the edge off. You'll feel calmer in a few minutes. You know, you're not the first singer I've treated for nerves before a Radio City concert. I had to do the same thing for Marvin Gaye. So I suggest you try to pull yourself together. You're twenty-three years old and you're starring in your own show at Radio City Music Hall. I'd say you're a very, very lucky young man!"

It could have backfired. But if even the sublime Marvin Gaye had stage fright, what right had I to feel sorry for myself? He was right, I should just snap out of it and enjoy the moment. He'd talked me down off the ledge.

The show was not perfect, but it was good enough. The band was tight, and whenever I caught a glimpse of the projections on the spectacle-shaped video screens they looked fabulous. We had the audience on their feet for the last few numbers. I felt we could have kept going all night, but the set ran overtime, and because of the union situation I wasn't able to do an encore. After the show a gaggle of VIP guests filed into the backstage bar and I came out to greet them. In a corner, sipping a cocktail, was the *Times*'s rock music critic. He sidled over and congratulated me on my New York debut. His column in the next morning's paper called my lyrics "precious" and my voice "thin and reedy," but he had to concede that the lush synth sounds and video imagery were ahead of their time. Also among the guests was legendary Funkadelic bass maestro Bootsy Collins, who gave me a different kind of review. "Y'all needed that *encore*, baby!" he said. "When you get an audience's *dick* hard, you gots to make 'em *come!*"

The show moved to the West Coast, where we smoothed off some of the rough edges of the set before playing successful gigs in Seattle, Portland, and San Diego, leading up to our big night at the Greek Theatre in Los Angeles. A week or two into the tour my nerves had subsided, and the box office was doing well. But my second album was in big trouble.

In the 1980s, when a record was initially released in the USA, you gauged its impact by how many radio stations added it to their weekly playlist. A top single could expect two or three hundred "adds" in the first few weeks. If you didn't get at least fifty, you were probably going to miss out on the *Billboard* chart regardless of the physical sales. Record companies' marketing and promotion departments needed to be fully focused on your record to maximize those radio adds in the first month, or else the window would close and they would shift their efforts to the next artist.

My single "Hyperactive!" was timed to coincide with the beginning of the Flat Earth Tour, and the album release was to follow on close behind. As we moved from city to city, I watched the single's progress with anticipation. Andy would send faxes ahead to my hotels, and local Capitol reps would turn up at the concerts with copies of the trade journal *Friday Morning Quarterback*. In the first week of release it got forty-three adds—a decent start. Second week—another fifty-six adds. The single entered the Billboard Top 100 at #88. So far so good! MTV added the video into rotation and the single rose to #62. Everything was perfectly poised for another big hit right as the album went on sale.

People hate to be the bearers of bad news. We rolled into Los Angeles on a Monday morning and I met up with the local Capitol rep at the studios of KROQ in Pasadena. I asked him if he'd seen the new chart. He looked like a deer in the headlights. He smiled feebly: "You'd better call your manager. I'm sure it's only a temporary hiccup."

I called Andy Ferguson, who was in New York. In the third week of "Hyperactive!"'s release, we had lost eighty-five of our ninety-nine radio stations. The single stalled out at #62 in the *Billboard* chart, and sales were weak. "I'm trying to find out what's going on," he said. "Just stay focused on your concerts, we'll get this thing back on track."

The following week, the single had bombed out of the chart altogether. I was angry, disoriented, and worried sick. I had too much invested in this tour to allow the record to slip away. I was so proud of this album, the way I'd matured and moved on as a songwriter and producer. The thought of *The Flat Earth* being a failure was unimaginable. What the heck was going on at Capitol Records?

It took Andy a few days to get to the bottom of it. He flew into L.A. for our Greek Theatre gig and sat me down in the back of my tour bus, and over the course of several hours he explained what had happened. Two catastrophic events had taken place within a few days. The first involved the head of rock radio promotion at Capitol Records, Bruce Wendell. He was very well connected, and hung out with a group of independent radio programmers known as the Network. These were highly paid consultants who worked the primary radio stations around the United States, bringing them the latest major label releases. Bruce Wendell's fellow Capitol Records department heads could not figure out why Bruce drove to work every day in a red Ferrari while they themselves were barely earning six-figure salaries. This was starting to cause a lot of friction and seemed to point to irregularities in the way he was doing business. The week after my record came out, the company's president, Jim Mazza, fired Bruce Wendell and severed ties between Capitol and the Network.

The immediate response was a show of power by Bruce's influential friends. They had the ability to dictate to radio stations what went onto their playlists. How? Well, the official line was that these guys "had their ear to the ground" and were totally plugged in to the listening public's wants and needs. They were the "hit men," in the pop chart sense of the term, and if they were enthusiastic about a record, it was because it had the potential to come across well on the radio and delight the listening public.

At least, that was the way it was represented to the Department of Justice, which had had its eye on the music industry for many years and had pressed charges in several high-profile cases of suspected payola—i.e., chart rigging. The record companies had ongoing contracts with the members of the Network and paid them large fees in order to assure that the most important releases would become hits. On the surface, there was nothing illegal about that. In truth, some unspecified portion of this money would go right to the back pockets of the radio station program directors. Once the music industry came under the DOJ's scrutiny in the mid to late 1970s, getting a song played on the radio was no longer as simple as slipping a brown envelope full of unmarked bills into the cellophane cover of the record sleeve. The procedure had to be more subtle. So, speedboats were berthed; golf club subscriptions were paid; college fees were taken care of. And of course, lavish parties were thrown to celebrate new releases. When Capitol fired Bruce Wendell, all of these perks suddenly went away. In retaliation, Capitol's acts were unceremoniously dropped from the playlists of dozens of stations across the country. Hence the downgrading of my single from ninety-nine stations to fourteen in the space of a week. My labelmates Duran Duran had a single out at the same time and encountered the same exact problem. They were considered a higher-priority act, so the entire effort of the Capitol promotion department was refocused on bringing the Duran single back from the brink, while mine was dropped like a hot potato.

The second catastrophe related to MTV. The cable music channel had enjoyed enormous success since its launch at the start of the decade. Its viewing figures were through the roof, and they were plugged in to a new audience demographic that advertisers were able to target directly for the first time. By the third year of its existence, MTV's advertising revenues were in the tens of millions, and its parent company Viacom was already talking about launching a second music channel, VH1. However, the videos they screened were 100 percent produced and paid for by the record companies— and, ultimately, by the music artists, to whose royalty accounts the production costs were billed. So in early 1984, four of the top six record companies approached MTV demanding a piece of the profits. If MTV didn't play ball, the record companies planned to set up their own cable music station in direct competition. MTV was pretty content with its situation, and called the four labels' bluff, removing all their videos from weekly rotation. This included "Hyperactive!" Desperate not to lose out on the vital exposure MTV gave their artists, three of the four labels immediately rescinded their threat. The one record company to stick to its guns was, of course, my label, Capitol Records.

"Hyperactive!" was every bit as catchy and commercial as "She Blinded Me with Science." People couldn't stop themselves from whistling the melody when they saw me in the street. Its video was state-of-the-art for its time and won several awards. As a bonus, it was following on the heels of a certified gold record. I'd have bet the farm on its being an even bigger smash than "Science."

When a record is a hit, you pop the champagne and never stop to analyze what went right. When it flops, you pick over the bones for weeks or months. You start to question the quality of the song, the production, the vocal performance. You wonder about your public image and how you came over in the endless interviews you did. You'd never admit there were brown paper envelopes involved. It's especially hard on the managers, who tend to take all the blame.

When Andy spelled it out to me, I felt ill. I was overcome with the realization that the industry I was part of was so corrupt. I'd seen traces of it before now, in the cozy old-boy collusion of the British music business, but never anything as blatant as this. My record had been flushed out of the charts out of sheer bloody-mindedness. It felt to me as if a handful of coked-up music execs in satin tour jackets had the power to decide that the public would never hear it.

I knew it was not my fault that "Hyperactive!" flopped. There were invisible forces at work. By the same token, I came to realize that my prior chart success with "Science" had also been outside my control. I couldn't take the credit any more than the blame. The fact is, no surefire formula exists for pop music success. Sometimes the stars are just not aligned. As an artist, you just shrug your shoulders and sit down to try again. A great man once told me that you just have to go on believing in yourself. The moment you walk onstage and the spotlight hits you, your self-belief becomes a force field around you.

The last glimmer of a golden sunset faded behind the Hollywood Hills as I took to the stage at the open-air Greek Theatre. It was a warm summer evening and the scent of night-blooming jasmine filled the auditorium. I sat down at the grand piano and played the opening notes of "Screen Kiss." A warm ripple of recognition rose from the stalls. I looked out at the sea of smiling faces. Some of the fans must have already bought the new album and picked out this song to fall in love with. The chord changes fell comfortably beneath my fingers, and I closed my eyes and climbed back into my head the way it was when I wrote them a year earlier. These chords and lyrics were laden with the pain and remorse I'd felt at that dark moment. Could it possibly be that thousands of people, perfect strangers to me, now felt as I felt when I played them? They did. I could feel it. It was a pure connection, a communion of the singer and the crowd. As the last notes died out, the applause swept around the bowl of the Greek, and it didn't stop.

And waiting backstage was Michael Jackson.

CHAPTER 6
LIKE DOLPHINS CAN SWIM

We completed the Flat Earth Tour, and though it was a critical success and well attended, it still lost a ton of money. If the album and single had sold as well as expected, we would have viewed the loss as a worthwhile investment. But *The Flat Earth* had fallen rapidly out of the charts, and its sales were dismal. At Heathrow the band dispersed and we went our separate ways. It was an inevitable letdown. After a long tour you arrive home, jet-lagged, with a suitcase full of dirty clothes, and it feels as if you've forgotten how to do laundry, wash the dishes, or shop for groceries. You check your answering machine and find to your dismay that the mailbox has been full for the last three months. Your friends have adjusted to life without you, and you're no longer on their social radar. And then your manager and record company ask you politely if you've got any new material to play them.

The only new songs I'd worked on were the ones I'd done for Michael Jackson. I had managed to get the tapes over to him the day before I flew back to England, and I waited to hear whether he liked them. Weeks went by and there was no response. Finally I called his number; it had been switched to an answering service. I left a message and one of his assistants contacted me to schedule a call, at 3 a.m. London time.

"How did you like my songs?" I asked. There was a pause.

"I guess I kinda liked the drum parts."

I was disappointed. "Only the drum parts? Well, can I send you any-thing else?"

Another pause. "Are you near Wales?"

"The giant fish, or the country?"

"The country. Could you get me some ragwort for my llamas? Welsh rag-wort is Louie's favorite."

I laughed, but he wasn't joking. That was the last time I ever talked to Michael on the phone.

It was early June and England was in full bloom. I was invited to a sum-mer picnic and celebrity cricket match at Virgin's country studios, set in the grounds of a lovely seventeenth-century manor house outside Oxford, where XTC were finishing an album. I headed for a line of deck chairs and found myself alongside Richard Branson. A shameless promoter of his own enter-prises, Richard was "on" 100 percent of the time. Despite the serenity of the setting, he wanted to talk business. When I mentioned my bad experience with the U.S. record company, he beamed a big smile. "If you ever get off EMI, Tom," he said, "you should really come over to Virgin. We'd sign you up in a heartbeat."

The conversation was cut short by a message from the studio reception desk that there was a phone call for me. It was Lesley. My mother was in the hospital. She had fallen off a ladder in the back garden and fractured her skull. I hurried home to Cambridge along with my brothers and sisters, but she died two days later.

She was a wonderful woman, a mother of six who managed to pursue a busy career as a teacher. The whole family was devastated, not least my father. I hadn't seen much of my parents during the explosive years of my music career, and I felt terrible about it. Being the only one of their kids without a regular job and a family, I cleared my calendar and promised to stay with Martin in Cambridge for as long as he needed me. He was helpless without her—a man who lived in the third century B.C. and could barely boil an egg for himself. We shared our grief during long walks in the meadows.

I set up my Fairlight in my old bedroom. I wanted to write songs, but none seemed to come. While poking around the Fairlight's file system I discovered an old application it contained—a simple word processor, with a blinking cursor on a green screen. I began to transcribe my diaries and journals, dating back to my teenage years. They were written in small notebooks or on leftover school notepads. It was strange to see how rapidly my life had changed and never given me a chance to take stock. I was twenty-five, and I had a great career doing exactly what I loved. I was proud of my albums and live performances. I'd had moderate commercial success, and it had made me comfortable enough not to have to worry for a few years to come. But I was not rich, because I'd poured my royalties back into my career. I'd rolled the dice, and the dice didn't fall for me a second time. Now I had a choice to make: I could try to recapture the magic pop formula that had given me a couple of hits, or I could follow my heart and write songs "from the inside out." The alternative was to turn my back on the rotten music industry altogether and try my hand at something else.

On a certain level, what bothered me most about my life was that I was uncomfortable being the one in the spotlight. I thought of Mutt Lange, a man who crafted immaculate hit records but was virtually unknown to the fans. A way around my discomfort might be to shift my focus to producing other artists. Maybe I could work the controls in the studio while someone else did the press junkets and foreign TV interviews. There were young bands out there that could benefit from my experience—but how to find them? I was in no mood to go out to gigs, where I would get recognized and sometimes bothered by fans and the paparazzi.

Andy Ferguson reminded me that the BBC had a weekly show on Radio 1 called *Round Table*, where a panel of judges reviewed new single releases. He got me invited on as a guest reviewer, along with an up-and-coming DJ called Steve Wright and a woman known as the Queen of the Beehive, singer Mari Wilson.

Andy knew what a snob I was about the state of British pop music. "Remember to be positive, now," he cautioned. "You won't make any new friends at the Beeb if you just slag everything off."

The reviewers were seated around a radio console speaking into furry mics, with headphones around our necks. One by one the new 7" singles went on the turntable, and one by one Steve and Mari gave them an enthusiastic thumbs-up while I groaned and wrung my fingers. Try as I might, I could not find anything positive to say about the Toy Dolls' "Nellie the Elephant" or Alvin Stardust's "So Near to Christmas." But just as I was beginning to feel like a complete curmudgeon, out of the speakers came something miraculous! It started with a lone piano chord and a frantically suspended, strummed acoustic guitar. Next came a desolate harmonica. Then the voice:

> An outlaw stands in a peasant land
> And in every face sees Judas
> The burden of love is so strange . . .

> —From *Don't Sing* © Paddy McAloon, 1984

The song had weird time signatures and key changes and no discernible hook. After three minutes it just faded as though someone was winding down a knob. In short, it was utterly fantastic. By the time the singer started on about "the whiskey priest," my co-reviewers were shifting uncomfortably in their seats. "Not a hit!" Steve said. "Definitely not my cup of tea," added Mari. When it came to my turn, I grinned and heaped all the praise I could on the record. Not only was it a relief to find one I liked, but I was genuinely excited by what I heard.

The band in question was called Prefab Sprout, and somewhere in the far northeast of England they were listening to the show. Later that day their manager, Keith Armstrong, got in touch with Andy to pass on their thanks for the plug; and he asked if I ever did record production for other acts? The band had recently signed a contract with CBS Records and was in the process of choosing songs for their first major-label album. Of course I was delighted, and a meeting was arranged. I traveled by train up to their native County Durham the following week.

Paddy and Martin McAloon had grown up in the former rectory of a Catholic church nestled on the edge of the Pennine hills, about fifteen miles southwest of Newcastle. Their mum, Mary, ran the household. Their father had suffered a stroke many years before and was bedridden. Paddy, the eldest of three brothers, attended a seminary and was clearly destined for the cloth; but his deep interest in literature and music had led him astray, and as teenagers, he and Martin had decided that one day they would have a pop group called Prefab Sprout and that their poster would be up in the window of W. H. Smith in every high street in the country.

The brothers greeted me warmly and Mary made me tea. Paddy led me up a narrow staircase, past icons and crucifixes, to his bedroom, which was barely big enough to swing a cat. His single mattress appeared to be stacked on top of piles of song lyrics. Like me, he was untrained as a musician; but he was a fanatical student of all types of music, from jazz and classical to Stephen Sondheim and Marvin Gaye. He sat on the bed with his acoustic guitar, thumbing through his song sheets. Each set of lyrics had penciled notes denoting chords and harmonies. He would keep strumming for as long as it took him to sing the line, then change chords. This resulted in asymmetrical phrases of five or seven bars, and bars with odd numbers of beats. He would often find himself in the wrong key for his voice, so he'd jump up or down an octave right in the middle of a phrase. I began to understand why many found the music on his debut indie album *Swoon* so challenging. Paddy's band had done their best to accommodate his unusual phrasing, but often their elaborations only added to the complexity. In order to cope with the extra fifth beat at the end of a bar, the drummer would add a paradiddle on his hi-hat; a tricky chord change was covered up with an elaborate slide on the bass guitar. My first job as a producer would be to encourage the band to simplify the arrangements, create space for all the parts, and restructure their songs, without losing the focus of the vocal and lyrics.

Paddy's younger brother, Martin, played the bass. His bass lines contained unexpected inversions, because for most of their teens Martin had picked his notes by sitting face-to-face with Paddy and matching the lowest note on his guitar, which was not always the true root note of the chord. The backing vocals were handled by Wendy Smith, a sweet, shy young woman with a breathy and innocent voice. Paddy would give her a sheet of lyrics with harmonies written over each line as letters—D, F#, A, etc. Wendy had a battery-operated Casio mini-keyboard, and she would go off into a corner and check her notes on the Casio before joining in with a harmony to Paddy's vocal. His voice was extremely intimate and sensual, while Wendy's was sterile and detached; the contrast was unlike anything I'd heard, and with the wide harmonies he wrote for her, it all added up to something beautiful and precious. It seemed to speak to the sadness in my heart.

Their unorthodox approach was exactly what made the Spouts' music so fascinating to me. There are many musicians who devote a lifetime to study, practicing their craft but never achieving the level of emotion and expression that Paddy and his band were able to convey when they played. I was so glad that this originality had never been filtered out of them by conventional music training.

Paddy spent the afternoon taking me through several years' worth of his unrecorded songs, and I was spellbound. "Appetite," "Bonnie," "Hallelujah," "Desire As" . . . the songs came thick and fast, with soaring melodies, finely nuanced chord sequences, and poetry that alternately cut like a knife and tugged at my heartstrings. How could this gentle, unassuming man write like that? I was in awe of Paddy's songwriting prowess, and I wondered if I had the missing link that could bring their next album to life. I ran a Walkman while Paddy played, and jotted down comments to myself in a notebook. On the train back to London I gradually narrowed maybe forty songs down to a dozen that I felt were potentially his strongest.

In the autumn of 1984 we began rehearsing for Prefab Sprout's second album in Olympia, West London. The excellent Neil Conti played the drums, and I added piano, synth, and Fairlight. I brought in Kevin Armstrong to add some grittier chunks on his Les Paul. We carefully practiced the arrangements in advance, measuring out the intros and solo sections, editing each song's structure to propel it along while making space for Paddy and Wendy's vocals to slip into. The secret to great production begins with the arrangement. By the time we began setting up at Marcus Recording Studios in Queensway, the sound engineer Tim Hunt's job was relatively easy. He placed his microphones in the huge wood-paneled recording room, separating us with thick baffles, and pushed up the faders; he found he had very little to do to make it all sound coherent. The result was an open, natural sound, with the punchy and organic rhythm section and piano driving the grooves. Adding several layers of overdubs, I doubled Wendy's crystalline vocals with my keyboards to create a glossy sheen as a backdrop for Paddy's warm voice, rich steel-string acoustic guitar, and direct-injected Stratocaster.

The album cover featured the band posed on a vintage Triumph motorcycle. It was called *Steve McQueen* in the UK—an homage to the actor's iconic final ride in the movie *The Great Escape*—though McQueen's estate prevented CBS from using that title in the USA, where it came out under the name *Two Wheels Good*. To this day, it is listed among many music journalists' greatest rock albums of all time.

I was delighted with the way my first major production project had turned out, and when I watched the Sprouts performing on TV or being interviewed, I was frankly relieved not to be the one in the spotlight. This new role as a sort of caretaker for someone else's music felt like a comfortable fit for me. Still, it created a dilemma for Andy Ferguson: Should we carry on building my reputation as a sideman and producer, or concentrate on my career as a featured solo artist? As fate would have it, we didn't need to make that decision for another twelve months. Nineteen eighty-five turned out to be a banner year, because my music had caught the attention of several of my all-time musical heroes, and they were the ones who sought me out.

In February 1985 I was contacted by the producers of the Grammy Awards ceremony in L.A., inviting me to perform on live TV as part of a "synth supergroup" with Stevie Wonder, Herbie Hancock, and Howard Jones. Apparently it was Stevie himself who had asked for me to be involved. I was flattered and intimidated in equal measures. It was an extremely high-profile appearance, and it seemed like the perfect way to come out of myself after the months of grieving for the death of my mother. The plan was to record a medley combining one hit from each of us, then segue into an electronic rendition of "The Star-Spangled Banner." The recording took place at Wonderland, Stevie's cavernous studio on Western Avenue, a converted 1940s movie house. Each of us put together a short backing track of our chosen song, and the multitracks were assembled at Wonderland to be edited. However, the earliest the four of us were able to meet up there was the evening before the Grammy show dress rehearsal.

I was fascinated to watch Stevie Wonder up close. In his studio, he seemed to be constantly surrounded by his team of assistants, staff, and friends. His extraordinary radar told him exactly where each member of his entourage was at any given moment. He would turn his head and call out to a roadie fifty feet across the room, and ask for his Prophet-5 or his Yamaha DX-7 to be set up and plugged in to a Fender Twin amp. He would feel his way over to a keyboard and start to goof around, making up satirical lyrics about the people in the room, drawing out the syllables gospel-style with the most amazing ribbons of notes. Herbie jammed along on piano, and his playing, of course, was immaculate. Howard and I couldn't do much more than watch and learn, though Howard's keyboard chops were pretty impressive as well.

Stevie had decided to play a prank on his old friend Herbie. We were told that Sony were keen for Stevie to test out their latest, state-of-the-art forty-eight-track digital tape recorder, and two of Sony's top executives had flown over with it from Tokyo. They had brought a film crew with them. A fair chunk of time had been spent painstakingly editing together the four different backing tracks so we could add solos over the top. A few hours into the recording session, while Herbie was laying down a keytar solo, the speakers suddenly went silent for five seconds. We all looked at each other. The tape was stopped and rewound to the same spot—same problem, no sound, just a blank silence. The control room engineer started freaking out, saying the Sony machine had accidentally erased several seconds of everything we'd spent the whole evening recording. It was wiped clean across all the tracks. Herbie Hancock was mortified, and the two Japanese executives looked baffled. They said it must be a software bug and they could send for a new machine tomorrow from Sony HQ. Trying to keep his cool, Herbie pointed out that we had to have this piece finished tonight so we could play it at nine the next morning at the Grammys dress rehearsal.

At that point, Stevie decided his ruse had gone far enough, and he cracked up laughing. The film crew, he said, was actually from a show called *TV Bloop-*

ers and Practical Jokes. Once Herbie realized the joke was on him he started laughing, too, and the two of them hugged and high-fived and slapped each other on the back for several minutes, with the Sony execs grinning and bowing. Stevie's staff helped the camera crew pack up, and everybody agreed it was going to make some great TV. It was all very droll. The problem for me was that it was now approaching midnight, and we still hadn't worked out how to do "The Star-Spangled Banner."

Some takeout food arrived, Herbie got waylaid with a telephone call, and Stevie wandered off somewhere into the depths of the building. The session was deteriorating. I felt I needed to step up and assume leadership or we'd never make it to rehearsals on time. So I quickly programmed a drum groove into a nearby Linn drum machine and left Howard to add a bass line while I went off to look for Stevie.

Being an old cinema, Wonderland had all sorts of nooks and crannies. I searched the foyer and corridors, and behind the stage, and climbed the stairs all the way to the upper balcony; and there among the fading velvet panels I faintly heard the sound of a piano coming from a back room. I stuck my head around the door. As my eyes adjusted to the light I could make out a sort of storage room full of old file boxes and cleaning equipment, not much bigger than a closet. Against one wall was an upright Bechstein piano, and Stevie Wonder was kneeling in front of it, playing some mellow blues. He had somehow escaped his ever-present entourage, and was enjoying a quiet moment to himself.

"Steve, it's Thomas," I said and stepped into the cramped room. "Hey, we need to finish up this medley and get out of here. I had an idea for a way to do it."

"Yeah?" he replied. "Tell me."

"Okay, so how about we get a really cool slow groove going, about like this." I started to click my fingers in tempo. "We add some nice synth horn parts, maybe some sampled congas, a shaker . . ."

Suddenly Stevie's head, which habitually moves from side to side as his radar scans the room, stopped moving altogether. "Nah, man, we can't do that," he said. "You know why? 'Cause Marvin tried that one time, at an NBA basketball final. He went out on the court at halftime with a Roland TR-808 and a bass player, and did this really smooth version, got the whole crowd clapping along. And you know, Marvin never got on TV again until the day he died. The networks just couldn't handle the idea of a black man singing a sexy soul version of the National Anthem."

"Really?" I said. I was appalled, but the notion of Marvin Gaye grooving on "The Star-Spangled Banner" fascinated me. "What did it sound like?"

Stevie took a few moments to think. Then he started to play the piano and sing. Like an *angel*. He was there on his knees, instantaneously translating the chords with luscious jazz-soul voicing, and channeling his memory of Marvin's unique style and inflections. In gaps between lyric phrases he beatboxed the 808's drum sounds. He got through about eight lines of the song like that, and I swear, my heart stopped beating. Any one of those lines, or asides, I would give my right arm for that sound to come out of my mouth in front of a microphone. I could strive my whole life in a studio and never come close. Yet Stevie sang this for me, all alone in a broom closet.

Then he stood up and said, "It was kinda like that," and fumbled his way out of the room.

Twenty years later, thanks to the magic of YouTube, I finally saw a clip of Marvin's performance at the 1983 NBA finals for the first time, and I cried my heart out. He is the only one of my great childhood heroes that I will never get to meet.

In the end we did a rather overblown combination of "God Save the Queen" and "America the Beautiful," accompanied by the Grammys orchestra. I was dressed like Beethoven, and conducted with a baton in manic style. People seemed to like it well enough, and for Howard and me it was very flattering to be sharing the stage with two living legends in front of millions of people. But my abiding memory of the whole episode was that private moment in Stevie Wonder's broom closet.

When you appear on television, you never know who's watching. A few weeks after the Grammys appearance I got a call from my manager saying that Quincy Jones had seen me on the Grammys and wanted to talk to me about a new movie project he was working on. It was a film called *Fever Pitch*, directed by the venerable Richard Brooks and starring Ryan O'Neal, and they were already in postproduction. Apparently Quincy had heard good things from Michael Jackson, and when I told him I had always wanted to take a shot at movie scoring, he took a chance and hired me on the spot. I spent several weeks in Hollywood, driving my rental car onto the MGM lot in Culver City and eating at the commissary alongside faces I recognized from the movies. Though the film turned out a little disappointing, it had been a perfect opportunity to get my feet wet in film scoring, which I had always fantasized about. Plus it led me to signing with a top Hollywood scoring agency, Gorfaine and Schwartz, who felt I had a shot at breaking into the competitive world of movie scoring.

When I was a teenager, and in my most impressionable phase, I had a total adulation for Joni Mitchell. My older siblings each owned a copy of *Blue*, and the first album I ever bought with my own pocket money was *For the Roses*. I still consider *Hejira* one of the greatest albums ever recorded. I taught myself all her piano parts and would often lose myself in her dreamy meandering melodies, her unusual chord sequences, and her evocative lyrics. Artistically she was head and shoulders above her contemporaries; and the way she interacted with jazz-oriented side musicians like Tom Scott and Jaco Pastorius gave me hope that one day I too would get the call.

The approach came in the spring of 1985, as Joni embarked on a new album called *Dog Eat Dog*. She and her husband, Larry Klein, had recently acquired a Fairlight CMI. Their sound engineer Mike Shipley was an old friend, and suggested they call me to come in and program the songs. Joni had heard a cover version I'd done years earlier of her song "The Jungle Line," and she'd fallen in love with the B-side, a ballad of my own called "Urban Tribal." We met for dinner in Los Angeles and had a long talk. I described my working methods and my ideas for her new album. To my great happiness she signed me up as a coproducer, along with Larry and Mike.

She'd booked a top studio in Hollywood, and as the project was likely to take several months I decided to look for a place to live that wasn't a hotel. A real estate agent found me the ideal rental: a Spanish-style cottage just above Sunset Strip, with its own pool, belonging to another childhood heroine of mine, the actress Jenny Agutter. My new landlady had been an icon for a whole generation of adolescent English youths ever since she'd starred in *The Railway Children* and later the cult classics *Logan's Run* and *An American Werewolf in London*. She was an expert horseback rider, having been specially trained for her role in *Equus*. Jenny offered to take me riding by moonlight from the Beachwood Canyon Ranch. We rode over the crest of the Hollywood Hills and down into the San Fernando Valley, where we tied up the horses outside a Mexican family restaurant with velvet murals of cute kittens and Elvis Presley. While cantering up the steep trail home, I dropped my wool sweater. Barely missing a stride, Jenny spun her horse around and galloped back for the sweater; at full stretch, in the light of the full moon, she stooped down from her saddle and snatched it up, catching me in a flash and handing me back my sweater with a sexy smile.

The next morning I met up with Joni at a massive downtown piano warehouse. The studio manager had asked us to pick him out a new Steinway. She and I tried out numerous instruments, dueting together from opposite ends of the cavernous corrugated iron space. I played intros to songs from her old albums that she had long forgotten, albums like *Clouds* and *Ladies of the Canyon*.

Joni made music as if she were splashing paint on a canvas. As we built up the tracks she would ask me for a shard of light here, a deep swamp of cellos and basses there, a jagged grid of synth lines under a fluorescent choral sunset. She loved to eat, and when dinnertime came she would order huge quantities of takeout food from the best L.A. restaurants, then eat only a forkful of each dish. As we sat around she would tell stories—hilarious, twisted stories about her hippie days living in a cave in the Greek islands, or heart-wrenching memories of the poverty she endured as an underage single mother in her homeland of Canada before choosing to put her career first and give up her child—a decision I that believe never stopped haunting her.

Wayne Shorter came in to record some sax parts, and the two of them traded insane tales of Miles Davis's drug-addled excesses. Wayne cracked me up with a story about Miles and his brand-new Ferrari Testarossa. Apparently Miles had gotten pulled over recently by the cops on the Pacific Coast

Highway. He always felt he was unfairly victimized for being a black man driving a nice car, and he went to court to fight the ticket. "Mr. Davis," said the judge, "do you have *any* idea how fast you were going?" In his raspy voice Miles replied: "Hey, man, I just drive it till it *sounds* good."

Joni trumped this with a story of her own. One time she was in Paris and found out Miles was staying in the same hotel. He invited her up to his luxury suite, and Joni was eager to talk music. But the aging jazz legend had other things on his mind. He spent an hour trying to persuade Joni to go with him to the bedroom, and during that time he snorted his way through a couple of grams of cocaine. Finally he lurched across the floor and made a grab for her, but he fell to his knees and passed out, just managing to wrap his bony fingers around one of her ankles before losing consciousness. So now he was lying there with a strychnine grin on his face and Joni's ankle in a death grip. Joni had to drag his insensible body halfway across the carpet to reach the phone so she could call for housekeeping to come and prise his brittle fingers off her ankle.

I could have listened to Joni's stories all night. But we didn't get on well in the studio. Whereas her previous key collaborators had played other instruments—Tom Scott on sax, Jaco on fretless bass—the keyboard was her own instrument. My style of arranging uses small abstract building blocks that add up to the whole. The moment I'd programmed a sound designed for a simple five-note melody, she would come over to my keyboard and start playing a full two-handed piano part. "Ooh, this sound is *gorgeous*," she would say. "Let's put it down." I tried to explain that if she played her ten-fingered part using this rich synth texture, it would destroy the effect of the previous five layers I'd so carefully woven together. "Fuck it," she retorted. "Let's burn our bridges! Mike, wipe them all, give me a pair of fresh tracks, I'm ready to lay this down."

Matters got worse when she started on her vocals. It's pretty hard for a singer to judge his or her own performance in front of the microphone under headphones, which is why you hire a producer. Joni sang a chorus, and I'd make a note that lines 2 and 3 needed to be redone, along with the last few words of line 8. Joni would listen back, and say she wanted to redo the whole chorus except for lines 2 and 3; she wanted to sing it more like the way she'd done the last line. It was plain we were on different wavelengths. I was torn: Did I let her do it her own way when I believed she was wrong? Or put my foot down and say, you hired me to do a job, you have to trust me to do it?

As the tension rose, Larry Klein, a sweet, warmhearted man and a consummate bass player, would try to mediate between us. Mike Shipley was a brilliant sound engineer, but essentially an enthusiastic yes man, and he went along with whatever Joni said. I was plainly the odd man out. After a few weeks I bowed out of the studio, by mutual consent, and set up my rig in the back room at Jenny Agutter's house, creating grooves that I sent to Joni in the studio on floppy disks. Joni, meanwhile, went into a bad decline. A string of events seemed to be conspiring against her. She and Larry got in a nasty car crash on the way home to Malibu; in the hospital she discovered that someone in her organization had been cooking the books and had embezzled tens of thousands of dollars in royalties. She was mad at these United States of America of the Ronald Reagan era, at the money-grabbing TV evangelists and the 1980s culture of greed. She rewrote her lyrics to reflect her growing anger at the world. I became the unwitting victim of her fury when we got in a row about songwriting credits. She accused me of being a chiseler and proceeded to say in an interview with *Rolling Stone* that I had been forced on her by her record company, and she had only accepted because I was "hot at the time." Her hard-core fans were divided in their opinions about the album. Many felt it was too much of a departure from the Joni they knew and loved, and I was the natural scapegoat.

But despite all that, I cannot fault Joni. She was not a diva, by any stretch. She just wanted to sing her songs and paint her canvases. When you have a gift like hers, it's understandable that you want the world to respect and honor you. If you only measure respect in terms of chart positions, radio playlists, and royalty statements, you are bound to feel undervalued. It meant little to her that the legion of female singer-songwriters who followed in her footsteps over the decades all paid homage to her, revered her as a fearless pioneer. She couldn't fathom why she wasn't at the top of the charts, when someone like

Bob Dylan—whom she told magazines she considered "a plagiarist" and "not very musically gifted"—seemed to have so many hit albums. Considering the uncompromising depth of her artistry, it's wonderful that she has achieved the legendary status and worldwide fame she's had.

I am sorry now that I was not more compliant with her wishes. I was probably too much of a brat, with my own blinkered way of working. I'd been impressed with the great despotic producers I'd worked with, like Mutt Lange and Trevor Horn. I was never that pushy with Joni, but I should have taken a leaf out of the evergreen record producer Don Was's book and realized that it's all about the artist, it's not about you.

As the summer approached, word started to circulate about a huge charity concert to be staged at Wembley Stadium in support of relief for the famine in Ethiopia. All the top British rock acts were going to be there—Paul McCartney, the Who, Queen, Wham!, U2. Bob Geldof approached David Bowie to star alongside them. Bowie was already in the UK, but working flat-out on the filming of a George Lucas–produced movie called *Labyrinth*, and not really in live performing mode. His regular backing musicians were off doing other projects. He needed to get a four-song set together in a little less than two weeks, and had decided to go for young English musicians. He'd recently worked with Kevin Armstrong and Matthew Seligman on "Absolute Beginners" and "Dancing in the Street," and now he approached them about putting together a band for his performance. They suggested I should play keyboards.

Bowie had been a huge part of my early life. I had pored over his lyrics and album covers, and paid to see him in concert probably five times. When I took his phone call at Olympic Studios I could barely talk. It was like that familiar dream when you're watching a movie on the big screen and suddenly the leading man turns and starts to speak to you. He was disarmingly civil and gracious. "Oh, Thomas, *would* you play with me at this Live Aid thing?" he said. He sounded the perfect gentleman. You could have cast Edward Fox to play him in a biopic. Having seen *The Man Who Fell to Earth* and the BBC documentary *Cracked Actor*, I was somehow expecting the ethereal, strung-out

Bowie from the Thin White Duke era, looking terrifyingly emaciated in the back of his thirty-foot limo, staring at the drowning fly in his carton of milk.

The band was quickly assembled. Neil Conti from Prefab Sprout was added on drums, along with Pedro Ortiz on percussion, sax player Clare Hirst, and backing singers Tessa Niles and Helena Springs—all part of the generation that had grown up idolizing Bowie. We set up at a rehearsal studio in West Kensington, with a list of songs he wanted us to prepare. We had a total of three evenings' rehearsal. He showed up after his long shooting day at Elstree had wrapped and only stuck around for a couple of hours. When he strode into the room, with slick suit and newly blond hair, he shone like a beacon of light. At first he seemed to view the concert as a promotional opportunity. He wanted to play his current single, "Loving the Alien." Yet as the day approached and he zeroed in on what Live Aid was really all about, he realized this was no time to be plugging your current single: he decided to play his classic rock anthems, songs that would rouse the Wembley crowd and get them singing along. He kept changing his mind about the song selection. It was only on the final rehearsal day that he settled on the set list: "TVC15," "Modern Love," "Rebel Rebel," and finally "Heroes." We rehearsed each of the songs and played them a couple of times through, but never back to back without a break. Still, Bowie filled his young band with confidence, conducting the proceedings from the center of the room and positively radiating sunshine and love.

Morning broke on the day of the Live Aid concert. It was a beautiful day. I walked along the river near my home in Fulham, and everybody had their patio doors open. You could hear the TV commentary preamble coming out from every upstairs window. The whole city was gearing up for the event. Wembley is a distance outside central London, and because of the gridlocked traffic I was required to make my way to Battersea Heliport by the Thames, where I was to share a helicopter to the stadium with Bowie himself.

If the Cracked Actor was conspicuously absent during rehearsals, he reared his ugly head the moment we strapped ourselves into the helicopter. Bowie had always been terrified of flying, and until the early eighties he'd eschewed the airlines completely, preferring to take the weeklong *Queen Mary* transatlantic crossing every time he needed to get to or from America. His friend Brian Eno finally talked him into suppressing his phobia and getting on an airliner to Africa; but this fifteen-minute helicopter ride to Wembley was like confronting a new horror. He pulled his wide-brimmed fedora down over his eyes and sank low in his seat, fidgeting with his cigarette lighter and lighting one Camel after another, despite the pilot's repeated plea that the smoke would mess with the avionics. He kept leaning forward and questioning over and over how long the flight would take, what altitude we'd be at, whether we had to fly through any clouds or close to electrical wires and tall buildings. As we approached Wembley we could see its famous twin gold towers gleaming in the distance, and I caught a glimpse of the massive crowd assembled inside the stadium. Above the stage was a giant video screen, and as we banked over the stadium, the chain-smoking Bowie was silhouetted against a massive close-up of Freddie Mercury, crooning to the heavens, reaching the climax of "We Are the Champions."

We were set down in a park half a mile from the stadium, where a motorcade was waiting. Now the Thin White Duke persona evaporated, and Bowie was back to his cheerful, smiley self. Bundled into a police car with its sirens blaring, and flanked by motorbikes, we were whisked through the narrow back streets of Wembley until we screeched to a halt inside the stadium gates, where about a hundred photographers were awaiting his arrival. They swarmed around the vehicle, cameras pressed up against the windows, shouting "Mr. Bowie! Look this way, Mr. Bowie!" David turned to me and said, "Mmm, I love this bit!" and he flung open his door, stepping into the blaze of dozens of popping flashguns. Policemen ushered us through the crowd. Mere moments later we were standing at the side of the stage, where the roadies were making the final adjustments to our mic stands and line-testing the gear. Bob Geldof was onstage wrapping up a rant about money for Ethiopia and getting ready to introduce the next act. I followed Bowie onstage to a huge roar from the crowd and seated myself at the keyboards, blinking in the sunlight. It was my job to kick off the set with the solo honky-tonk piano opening to "TVC15."

We raced on through "Modern Love" and straight into "Rebel Rebel." Kevin was so excited as he kicked off with the iconic guitar riff that he started pogo dancing, springing two feet in the air like a jack-in-the-box. He claims he's never pogo danced before or since. The girls looked and sounded gorgeous, and Pedro and Matthew were rocking out, working their sides of the large stage. I watched Bowie from behind my keyboards, framed against the seething hordes as he caressed the mic stand in his rather close-cut light blue suit, manipulating the crowd, seducing them. Even though we'd never played the songs back to back, the set had a great flow to it, and the intensity was building.

But I was secretly dreading our finale, "Heroes." Although it's a deceptively simple song with only one or two chord changes, those are sometimes the easiest to mess up, and my synth line was very prominent. The tempo was a clear change down in gears, and as we blasted through the intro the crowd began to raise their bare arms, waving banners and singing along with the words. I barely looked down at my fingers. I didn't have to worry about forgetting the parts, because my teenage fanboy self took over and the keys seemed to play themselves. I joined in and sang the answer phrases to his lead vocal: "I remember . . . by the Wall . . . over our heads . . . nothing could fall." I was at one with the Wembley crowd, loving being a part of this timeless Bowie classic, as if I were still fourteen years old.

CHAPTER 7
LIVING IN A SUITCASE

After Live Aid I went on a fishing trip with George Clinton to relax. The dreadlocked funkmeister was living in Miami and spending odd days in the Bee Gees' studio there, recording an album called *Some of My Best Jokes Are Friends*. He'd asked me to fly down there and put some keyboard and vocal parts on his new album, but today he was in no particular hurry. He'd chartered a large skippered fishing boat, and we flopped about in the Atlantic swell, in close company to several other charter vessels all following a school of albacore tuna. We were ten miles out to sea, yet I could still see the tall buildings of downtown Miami on the horizon like a mirage in the hazy morning sun. Distance can be deceptive.

George sat in a swiveling captain's chair at the stern of the boat, rolling joints in the sunshine, replaying rough mixes of his studio tracks from the night before on a large boom box. Just as he was dozing off, the skipper would yell "Fish on!" and George would spring into action, hit a button on his electric rod, and reel in yet another fifty-pound albacore; then, with the skipper's help, he would net the struggling creature, club it with a baseball bat, and throw it into a giant ice chest before settling back into his captain's chair for a snooze.

I asked George if he felt this was fair to the fish. "I know it's called 'sportfishing,' but I don't get where the sport comes in," I said. "Perhaps if you fished from a canoe, the tuna would stand a fairer chance? And hey, think how cool you'd look paddling back into the marina with a four-foot tuna strapped alongside your kayak, like a hero from a Hemingway novel."

George said fishing mellowed him out. In his younger days, he told me, he liked to go out for several days at a time with Bootsy Collins and a few tabs of LSD. One time they were close to the Bermuda Triangle and had a UFO encounter. He was dead serious. They were running away from a storm when a dense whirling silver and gray cloud enveloped their boat, and blobs of mercury started spattering all over the deck. George thought they were being abducted. Bootsy was yelling that the Space Limousine was here to take them up to the Mothership. They both stripped off their shirts and were dancing around the cockpit like maniacs, giggling incessantly as the blobs of mercury enveloped them. The Haitian charter skipper panicked and locked himself in his cabin getting drunk, and they had to steer the boat back to port themselves.

I laughed and told him he'd experienced the phenomenon of bioluminescence.

"Bio *what?*" he said.

"Bioluminescence. There are small plankton in the ocean that don't instantly re-emit the radiation they absorb. Microscopic organisms that suck up the sun's rays during the day but only release the light at night when they collide with something, in this case the deck of your boat. It's called a 'forbidden' energy state."

"What about the swirling cloud?" he said.

"Probably a fog bank lit up by the full moon above it, or the last rays of the setting sun."

George paused to reflect. "Dolby, you ain't no fun," he said, and rolled himself another joint.

The next day in the studio I came up with a new persona. I was the Space Limousine Driver, and I laid down a rap on George's record. He loved it. "*Now we having fun!*" he sang, and cranked the volume way up on the studio monitors. When the groove is "in the pocket," George's face lights up; he bares his teeth and wiggles his ass. He shouted something inaudible about me coming onstage with him for a James Brown thing two weeks later.

The James Brown thing turned out to be a testimonial concert in Washington, D.C., during the annual Black Urban Music Conference. Backstage at the auditorium, the P-Funk tribe was gathering for the sound check. Musicians, side players, and their families piled into the dressing room, hugging and reminiscing. Before long it was plain that George owed most of them money from previous gigs. "That's how I make sure they show up for the next show," George confided in me. "Trouble is, now even *James* wants to get paid." George decided that in my guise as the Space Limousine Driver I was going to do guest vocals on the song "Get On Up (I Feel Like Being a) Sex Machine." George's band had never performed this live, even though Bootsy had toured as James Brown's bass player and his older brother Catfish Collins had played rhythm guitar on the original track. Bizarrely, George asked me if I could walk Bootsy and Catfish through the changes, as I knew the structure pretty well; so a small Fender Twin amp was set up in a corner of the green room and they both plugged in. I said if there was an available keyboard onstage I would play the piano solo midway through the song. George scribbled *Sex Machine* in the middle of his set list.

The P-Funk All-Stars stepped out on the stage and went into the first song. There were twelve thousand people in the audience, and about three of us were Caucasian. It was an early show and this was a business convention crowd, and the reaction was a little muted. Only a couple of isolated people in the audience were on their feet clapping and dancing. I was wearing a long linen coat, leather gauntlets, peaked chauffeur's cap, and goggles. Standing at the side of the stage, listening to an atrociously bad mix at a thousand decibels, it was very hard to make out where one song ended and the next began. I wasn't all that familiar with the Parliament-Funkadelic repertoire; but each song was, basically, "Funk in the Key of E."

About half an hour into the set I vaguely made out the words as the MC announced: "Ladies and gentlemen, put your hands together for the Space Limousine Driver, a.k.a. Thomas Dolby!" The band launched into the famous "Sex Machine" groove and I took center stage. The audience looked bewildered. As I waited for my vocal cue to come around I glanced down in the front row: James Brown himself was sitting right there, glaring up at me suspiciously. I had no choice but to break into my very best Queen's English: "Get up—get on up! / Get up—get on up, yah? / Stay on the scene, chaps / Like a sex machine, Cordelia."

By the second verse I was thrashing around like Sir Alec Guinness having a seizure. Astonishingly, by the time it got to the solo most of the audience was on its feet, and a party atmosphere ensued. I streaked over to where a Fender Rhodes electric piano was set up at the side of the stage, and launched into my solo. Shit, no sound! I thumped on the keyboard, fiddled with the volume knob; still nothing. I felt down the back panel for an audio cord—it was not even plugged in. I went berserk. Without thinking, I kneed the Rhodes over on its back and started kicking and stamping on it. For an instant the thought flashed across my mind that this was what all those punk rock bands had wanted me to do in 1977. Even James Brown cracked a smile.

By the time the set was over and the band filed back into the green room, which was now thick with marijuana smoke, I had regained my composure. Bootsy and Maceo Parker high-fived me, and "Skeet" Curtis gave me a chest bump. I walked out through the lobby at the convention center, and the throng parted for me reverentially. "*Damn*, TD," someone called out, "you're pretty funky, boy!"

Back in California, Gorfaine and Schwartz had submitted me as composer for a film adaptation of a classic Marvel comic book called *Howard the Duck*, produced by none other than George Lucas. The script called for several original songs, and Lucasfilm needed someone to coach a group of four young actresses to be a band. My new agents got with Andy Ferguson and cut a mouthwatering deal. They would need me on the set to work with the actors while I wrote the songs; and as yet, they had not selected a composer for the instrumental score. So I went straight up to Skywalker Ranch to meet Lucas and review the storyboards, and set up my own room at the Sprockets facility in San Rafael. I was a fan of the comic books, and with George Lucas's track record, how could *Howard the Duck* possibly fail?

The stars of the movie were Lea Thompson—best known as Marty

McFly's mom from *Back to the Future*—and a talented but hitherto unknown actor called Tim Robbins. The budget was reputed to be huge, and a lot of it seemed to be going into the development of computerized, animatronic duck suits for the central character, Howard. The three-foot-tall Howard was a potty-mouthed, cigar-smoking waterfowl from another planet, mistakenly brought to Earth via a teleportation accident. Howard was variously played by several little people and child actors dressed in the duck suits. A team of puppeteers worked his facial muscles with wireless handsets, but take after take was cut short because Howard's bill wouldn't open properly, or his eyeballs rotated in opposite directions. Every time Howard was on the set there seemed to be some serious issue with his remote-controlled prosthetic head. Once, the shooting had to be wrapped midafternoon because one of the eyebrows went into a spasm and jerked skyward, ripping a six-inch tear in his latex scalp.

The more money that was sunk into its production, the more homogenized *Howard* seemed to become. Over two hundred actors were auditioned to provide the on-screen voice of the duck. A committee of studio execs simply couldn't make up their minds. Even Robin Williams was asked to come in a second time for a callback. And Lucas himself was conspicuously absent from the proceedings.

Still, I enjoyed hanging out with the cast and crew, and I loved cruising around Marin County as I got to know the San Francisco Bay Area. The movie was clearly losing its way, and way behind schedule. My contract was extended by ten weeks, so I decided I needed a nicer ride than my silver Hertz rental car. I saw an ad for a 1972 Morris Minor woody convertible that a six-foot-four surfer dude was selling. It was covered in surf decals, and he would drive it up and down Highway 1 with his head and his boards sticking up over the Morris's windshield.

As the weeks went by, it became a common sight to see groups of suited, worried-looking Universal execs milling around the set. I tried in my small way to restore some coolness to the project by contributing quirky left-field music cues with names like "Duck Pâté" and "Mutant Disney." But the producers didn't go for my eclectic approach to the score, and eventually I left

Lucasfilm in a hurry, having been fired as composer for being "too subversive." I was replaced by the great film composer John Barry, though they kept my songs in the movie, along with a brief on-screen cameo as a beatnik bartender.

I planned to ship the Morris Minor convertible back to England and keep it as a summer car to complement my Jag. Somehow I never got around to organizing the export paperwork. Three months later there was a message on my answering machine in London to call the transportation manager at Lucas. I knew he would be wanting to know what to do with my Morris, now presumably sitting abandoned in the parking lot at Lucas, so I erased his message. Many years later a business associate told me how she and her kids had been on a walking tour of Skywalker Ranch during the postproduction of *Star Wars Episode I: The Phantom Menace.* The tour guide had taken the visitors past the Foley stage. He pointed out a twisted mass of metal and rubber lurking in one corner, surrounded by microphone stands: ". . . And over there you will see the remains of a Morris Minor once owned by Thomas Dolby. It is regularly attacked with crowbars and baseball bats when we need to create the sound of road wrecks or space battles."

That was probably about the best thing to come out of the *Howard* experience. It was a lesson in collective self-delusion. The film studio and the entire cast and crew, myself included, managed to maintain our belief that we had made a decent film right up until the weekend of the Hollywood premiere, when real people and film critics started to attend screenings of the movie. It was universally panned in the press as a $50 million waste of time. And that was back in the days when $50 million was a lot of money.

Perhaps as a consolation for being fired from the movie score, they told me I could write and direct the MTV video for the title song. The video had an elaborate premise, involving a rock concert by the movie's all-female rock band, Cherry Bomb, and the centerpiece of their stage show, a twenty-foot-high pyrotechnic egg. I was looking forward to the chance of directing Lea Thompson and Tim Robbins, and I selected Limelight Films' L.A. branch as the production company. The budget was surprisingly large—$250,000, approximately ten times what I'd had available when I made the clip for "She

Blinded Me with Science." But during the run-up to the shoot, I got an interesting insight into exactly how the U.S. music industry moved money around.

I was in Limelight's offices on Melrose Avenue, working with the line producer, who was interviewing key members of the production team. Listed on the proposed crew sheet was a set decorator whom I'll call Joey Gonzales. When the producer asked him what his rate would be, he said calmly that it was $6,500 per day, which would add up to $26,000 for the whole four-day shoot.

"You must mean $650 per day, right?" the producer said.

"No, $6,500. Just check with _____ at the record label. Here's his number."

The producer duly called the number, and was put straight through. "Yup," said _____, "that's the correct figure."

I'd accidentally stumbled on one of the many ways record companies laundered the money they needed to bribe radio programmers and buy radio play. This was how they got large lumps of petty cash off their books without alerting the attention of the DOJ. Gonzales the set decorator would presumably be given a small bonus for laundering the money through his account, and the rest would end up in a brown envelope. The Limelight line producer did not bat an eyelid, and wrote the daily figure of $6,500 into his accounts ledger without a word. This record company was one of Limelight's larger clients; far be it from him to rock the boat.

I was sickened to find myself a part of their ugly crime ring, but we were only days away from the shoot. To blow the whistle at this stage would have meant canning the whole production, and the loss of work for more than thirty people. I struggled with my conscience. What would it really accomplish? It was not as if one individual, exposing a single instance of corruption, would bring down the whole rotten house of cards. And I would probably just get myself ostracized, blacklisted across the whole music industry. It served as a powerful reminder: this was not an industry I really wanted to belong to.

George Clinton cheered me up, once again, when I bumped into him at a

Capitol Records listening party. He said how pleased he was with the way the James Brown concert and his album had turned out, and suggested he'd like to do something for me to return the favor. I had an idea for a song and video called "May the Cube Be with You." We enlisted the help of my old friend Lene Lovich, the Funkadelic rhythm section, and the Brecker brothers on horns, and our makeshift supergroup recorded the track at Battery Studios under the name Dolby's Cube.

The MTV video for the song included a series of short tableaux involving celebrity look-alikes. I helped pick out the actors from a casting catalog, based on their looks. In one scene we reenacted the famous love scene from *Some Like It Hot*, set on a millionaire's yacht. I was in the Tony Curtis role, and I got to make out with a Marilyn Monroe look-alike on a couch, with my glasses all steamed up. While we shot our scene they were busy setting up the next one, in which a leather-capped Marlon Brando impersonator sat astride a vintage Triumph and unwrapped a pack of butter. In a break between takes, the Brando look-alike turned to me and said, "Tom, do you remember me?" I couldn't place him. It turned out to be a guy called Marcus whom I'd been friends with at a boarding school in the English countryside when we were both aged ten. I was amazed that anyone else from that stuffy establishment had ended up in show business. We renewed our friendship. Marcus had an interesting story. In his twenties he headed to Los Angeles to work as an actor, but he couldn't make a living on his looks and talent alone and had to fill in as a personal trainer to the stars. He'd gotten close to one of the biggest divas in showbiz—very close. For several years he lived in her guesthouse in Malibu, ostensibly as her trainer and assistant. She was extremely generous, and when she grew tired of him he was able to afford to buy himself a ranch way out in the mountains, where he lived a hermitlike existence, teaching local kids about Native American history, occasionally renting the property out as a movie location. He adopted—or rather, he was adopted by—a lone white wolf, to whom he became very attached. The wolf was, Marcus said, the love of his life.

When you reconnect with someone from your distant past and listen to their account of the parallel existence they've led during the intervening years, it's like holding up a mirror to your own life. As I drove back to L.A. after an afternoon in the mountains with Marcus, I thought about my career and where I was heading with my life. I'd become isolated from myself as a result of my revulsion with the inner workings of the record industry. It was flattering to get call-ups from my childhood heroes, but they were distracting me from my proper path. It was really in my own music that my passion lay. Even the rigidity of my contract could not prevent me from writing and recording great songs, or performing them in front of my fans. I knew it would soon be time to get back to the source, to the music I loved the most.

I still had yet to write a great instrumental score for a great movie. The opportunity arose when the controversial but highly respected British director Ken Russell approached me with a project he was working on entitled *Gothic*, the true story of the night that *Frankenstein* and *Dracula* were born. Lord Byron, Percy and Mary Shelley, and the sinister Dr. Polidori were sequestered in Byron's villa on Lake Geneva, where they explored their darkest fantasies and nightmares under the influence of laudanum or other hallucinogens. It was a splendid opportunity for me to hone my chops as an orchestral composer, and it was one of the first feature film scores to feature a mixture of real and sampled orchestral instruments, which is nowadays very commonplace.

I visited the *Gothic* film set to get a feel for the movie. The production company was Virgin Films, a brand-new Richard Branson venture. The budget was tight, and to save money, Ken Russell was using his own country estate in Cumbria to double for Byron's Villa Diocanti. Many of the crew were "upgraded" from their usual roles—so for example, a dolly grip was working as the focus puller, a focus puller as the camera operator, and so on—while others had accepted reduced fees, trying to make the move into features from music videos or commercials. In his younger days Ken Russell was considered the enfant terrible of British cinema, with a fearsome reputation as a tyrant on the set. His tantrums were legendary. The *Gothic* crew was on tenterhooks for the first few weeks of the production. Every time a lighting stand got knocked over or there was a hair in the gate, people would glance Ken's way, expecting a violent outburst. But Ken just closed his eyes and counted to ten. There were whispers that perhaps he was mellowing in his old age.

I spent two days watching the director, cast, and crew at work. One scene in the script called for a parrot on a perch. In the whole north of England there was a single movie parrot handler, and he was duly employed for half a day. He showed up in his parrot handler van with a lovely scarlet macaw that was much admired by all. Gabriel Byrne and Natasha Richardson were psyching themselves up for the scene. The cameraman framed the shot, which required the parrot to sit at the left hand end of her perch. Just as Ken yelled "action!" and the actors began their dialogue, the parrot started to waddle sideways and out of frame. "*Cut!*" yelled Ken. "Do it again." The parrot was reset and the camera rolled again, with the same exact result. "*Cut!* Do it again!" Midway through the third take, the unruly parrot sidestepped once more out of frame.

At that moment, all of Ken's pent-up rage from the previous few weeks boiled over. He walked over to the parrot handler and grabbed him by the shoulders, physically shaking him and spitting every known expletive. The poor parrot was sacked on the spot, and its perch was removed from the close-ups. For the remaining weeks of the production, the crew was constantly on the alert. Some mornings, word would go around to look out because Ken had "PHS"—parrot handler syndrome.

Ken Russell was a man with an immense knowledge of the classics. As a young director he'd made many films about the lives of the great composers. He liked the Fairlight CMI–driven score I submitted, but said he wanted "the real thing" for some of the main cues. Virgin Films was reluctant to spend the money, but I was keen to work with a real orchestra and excited to give it a try, so I offered to pay for the additional recording out of my own fee. I worked with an orchestrator and conductor John Fiddy to convert my cues, and the London Symphony Orchestra was booked for a full day's session at Angel Studios.

We started on the dot of 9 a.m. An aspiring French horn player himself, Ken Russell looked forward to this part of the filmmaking process. He and the editor Mike Bradsell were already slumped in a deep couch at the back of the control room, getting stuck into a crate of Burgundy and quietly comparing notes on the latest classical record releases. They looked like a pair of garden gnomes. "This new Deutsche Gramophon recording of Mahler's Second," Ken whispered, "is clearly superior to the 1978 Bernstein production." "In everything other than the *andante* section, I'm inclined to agree," mumbled Mike.

I looked at the clock—two minutes to nine. British orchestral musicians are highly unionized. Many of them were chatting, sipping their tea, or reading the *Daily Mirror*. Their instruments were out of their cases, but the music on their stands was unopened. As the minute hand reached the hour, the conductor tapped his baton, and beginning with the first violin, the whole orchestra tuned up. "Open your scores to cue 1M2, if you please," he said, and he counted them in.

The orchestra began to play, and I marveled as the sounds of my composition rose up all around me. It was wonderful to hear my music come to life, played by musicians who had devoted a lifetime to their craft. I wandered between their chairs, admiring the fine acoustics of the Angel Studios' vaulted ceilings. But every few bars, something was not quite right. I had given the orchestrator my Fairlight sequences to transcribe, and not being a trained musician I'd had no way of checking his work. I took mental notes as they played, and at the end of the first cue there were a few issues I needed to point out. I walked over to the cellos. "Okay, you know the bit that goes 'da-DAAA-da-da'? Just after the tympani roll?" "Bar thirty-five, lads," said one of the cellists, checking his score. "That high top note, you're playing an A sharp, right? That should be . . . a B natural. Yes. B natural." The cellists looked dubious but penciled in the change. Then I went over to the woodwinds and made another set of changes, struggling again for the right terminology. By now it was obvious to these guys that I was completely untrained. I thought I heard a slight snigger somewhere in the back row. I asked the conductor for another take of the cue; this time it was a lot closer to what I wanted. We began to work through each of the cues, with many faltering stops and starts.

As lunchtime approached, we were terribly behind schedule. We had over thirty cues to get through in a single day, and we'd barely completed eight. But we were making progress, and aside from the minor corrections, I thought it all sounded lovely. I gave a couple of pointers to the percussionist in the ninth cue and asked the conductor to count in another take. "I'm afraid not, Mr. Dolby, sir," said the first violin. "Why not?" "Well, it's a minute to one, sir. We go to lunch at one, and this is a two-minute cue." "Really? We can't just add on a few minutes to the end of the lunch break?" "I'm sorry, Mr. Dolby, that's the rules." I was dumbfounded. The orchestra members were already starting to set their instruments back in their cases.

Suddenly the doors of the studio burst open, and in strode Ken Russell, red in the face, fuming. He marched into the middle of the orchestra, the veins visibly bulging out of his neck. "You fucking *bastards!*" he screamed. "You have this wonderful gift, from *God*, to play your instruments, and all you can think about is your fucking *tea break*! Now, cut this young man some slack and *finish your fucking cue!*"

And finish it they did.

After this brief outburst of PHS, Ken and I sat down for a sandwich in the cafeteria. "I'm sorry you got a bit hot and bothered in there, Ken," I said.

"Well, it did the bloody trick, Dolby, didn't it?"

Back at my flat in Fulham, I was interviewed about the upcoming movie by a reporter claiming to be from an important Australian music magazine. The interview had been set up through EMI Records. This was not unusual, so perhaps I was too trusting when I let her visit me in my home. I got a bit suspicious when I left the room to fetch the coffee and came back to find her fingering papers on my desk. Two weeks later I received a letter from a law firm representing Dolby Laboratories, the audio noise reduction company. They had found out about the upcoming *Gothic* score and were threatening to sue me for passing off my music as a Dolby Labs product.

I was born with the family name Robertson. I acquired the nickname Dolby while at boarding school, where I was always the geeky kid who messed around with gadgets. I built my own crystal radio set to listen to Radio Caroline in bed at night. I was the projectionist for the school film club. When portable cassette machines first came out, I used to have my Philips cassette recorder constantly slung over my shoulder and a pair of bulky headphones on my head. The high-end cassette recorders of the era had to have Dolby noise reduction. My friends started to call me Dolby. It was just one of those childhood nicknames that stuck.

In the early days of punk rock I had gone to see the Tom Robinson Band at the Red Cow in Hammersmith. I saw Tom afterwards and introduced myself. "I'm Tom Robertson and I'm a musician, too. Sooner or later one of us is going to have a problem!" We agreed that whoever made it first, the other would change his name, and we shook hands on it. Three months later Tom Robinson made the charts with his smash hit "2-4-6-8 Motorway," and I changed my name to Thomas Dolby.

I had a lot of respect for Dr. Ray Dolby, who had achieved so much in the area of audio technology and marketing. Since the late sixties, consumers had been willing to pay ten or twenty dollars more for a cassette machine with the Dolby logo on the front. Cassette quality in the early days suffered from high levels of unwanted high-frequency noise, and popping in the Dolby button certainly improved the experience. But as recordings got "brighter" in the seventies and eighties, using that button tended to remove *good* musical content, like the sibilance in the vocals, the crispness of the strings, or the clarity of the cymbals. Nobody really knew why the button was still there. Dolby's marketing department had clearly done an admirable job of preserving its perceived value.

Some of Dolby Labs' original patents were beginning to expire around the world, and cassette tape was on the way out. The company wanted to refocus on the world of film and home theater sound, and they weren't too pleased when they saw my name on a cinema marquee advertising *Gothic*. Now they were offering me a choice: I could either accept a lump-sum payment of half a million dollars to change my name, or they would immediately file suit against me.

I was proud of what I had accomplished—proud and obstinate. Half a million dollars was not going to persuade me to drop my name. It was hard to imagine a dollar figure that would have made me change my mind. I replied to their letter that I had no intention of complying with their demands.

During the following few weeks, wherever I was in the world they would manage to find me. One time I was in Los Angeles staying in a friend's guesthouse in the Hollywood Hills. The phone by the bed rang, and it was two of Dolby Labs' lawyers, calling on speakerphone. I have no idea how they obtained the number. They said they were willing to up the offer to $1 million, but they were simultaneously preparing to file suit in the California courts, and this was my ultimate deadline. I didn't appreciate the carrot and stick routine, even less the invasion of my privacy, so I told them to get stuffed and hung up.

In the fall of 1986 Dolby Labs filed for an injunction to prevent me using the name Thomas Dolby, claiming I was deliberately creating confusion with their brand. In the initial court hearing, it was clear that Dolby Labs had been collecting information to try and discredit me. One of their witnesses was the so-called Australian music journalist whom I'd let into my home in London—actually a private investigator on their payroll. She provided evidence about my living conditions, describing how my clothes were strewn about the house. And they had somehow obtained a copy of my bank statement.

I was not present at the hearing, but the transcript of the dialogue between their attorney and Judge Samuel Conti was quite amusing (I'm paraphrasing here): "Are you seriously telling me, Mr. _____, that a consumer has walked into a record store and purchased a Thomas Dolby album in the belief that it was a Dolby noise reduction unit?"

"Well, no, Your Honor . . ."

"What, then?"

[Attorney shuffles papers.] "We have a record here of a phone call received by Dolby Labs' switchboard, from a music fan, asking to speak to Thomas . . ."

"Oh, come, come," said the judge. "Is that the best you can do?"

Judge Conti denied the injunction and said he found no evidence of damage caused to the Dolby Labs brand. I received an initial bill from my lawyers for $104,000. So far, the legal profession were the only ones doing well out of the situation.

Dolby Labs wrote again to say that they were "very pleased" with the outcome of the initial hearing. However, they were willing to sit down and discuss an out-of-court agreement and put an end to the proceedings.

I met Dr. Ray Dolby for the first time in a basement conference room in Lincoln's Inn Fields. We sat face-to-face at a long table. There were at least seven lawyers in the room, and I dreaded to think what the combined hourly fees would add up to. Thankfully it didn't take long for them to formulate a letter agreement, stating that Dolby Labs would drop the suit provided I undertook not to use the name Dolby on its own, or in larger letters than the name Thomas. This seemed reasonable to me, and we were on the point of wrapping up the meeting when Dr. Ray, who had been silent up to that point, locked eyes with me and launched into this bizarre monologue:

"You pop stars think you're so special. You jet-set around the world, lying by swimming pools with your groupies and your drugs and booze. I have *worked* to get myself where I am today! I have built up my little company from nothing to the global brand it has become. How *dare* you try to cash in on my good name?"

I stood up without a word and left the room.

Though the Dolby Labs court case ended in a stalemate, it temporarily cleaned me out. When I sat down with my accountant at the end of 1986, he told me my finances were in bad shape. He also pointed out that I'd spent nearly eight months of the previous twelve living in hotels in America. "If 1987 is going to go the same way," he said, "you'd be better off declaring that you're spending a year outside the UK, then you won't have to pay any tax in either country. It's all perfectly legal, but you can only do it once."

The expatriate scheme didn't sound like a bad idea at all. I could use the time to record and mix some tracks for the new Prefab Sprout album, *From Langley Park to Memphis*, in some of the great L.A. studios. What's more, I felt a year abroad in a new setting might spark some new songs of my own. A great friend of mine named Grant Morris was living up above Beachwood Canyon, near the Hollywood sign, while he made his name as a screenwriter.

He told me there was a house for rent just around the corner from him, on the crest of a hill, with its very own pool and a panoramic view over the city. I took a year's lease on it, sight unseen, with the intention of setting up a small studio and writing material for my third album.

Grant was a craggy New Zealander who seemed to know everybody. For the first half of my year in L.A., he and I were a pair of crazy bachelors, living the L.A. life to the full. We drove around in a pink 1966 Mustang convertible that I'd hired from Rent-A-Wreck. I helped him pitch ideas for feature films, and he helped me with my lyrics. He was extremely gregarious and possessed a wicked sense of humor. In cafés and bars or at the supermarket, he would get talking to random people and invite them up to his house for a party. He would spin impossible yarns about who we were and what we did. On a given day, I was a rally car driver and he was a top plastic surgeon from Cedars Sinai; on another, he was from the Israeli consulate and I was the heir to the twist-tie fortune. I would just sit there cringing, expecting Grant to end up with a black eye or for us both to get arrested, but somehow we would always just end up at a rowdy party back at his house in the hills, trailing an unknown French film director, the elderly checkout clerk from the Mayfair Market, a Guatemalan pool guy, and a couple of waitresses from the Beachwood Café.

The one thing I never understood was Grant's choice of girlfriends. With one or two exceptions he seemed to make disastrous choices and get hitched up to the worst possible women. So I was very pleased when he introduced me one afternoon to his latest date. I'd popped round the corner to his house in the middle of the day expecting to find him working on a script. Sitting there in his living room was a gorgeous brunette. They'd been set up on a blind lunch date by a mutual friend. We chatted a bit, and it was clear she was not like the others. She was warm, witty, and totally unselfconscious. Her name was Kathleen Beller. She was an actress, and unlike many of Grant's friends in Hollywood, she actually had a successful career in show business. I was delighted that he had finally met someone special.

Later that evening I phoned Grant, excited to hear how his date went with Kathleen. "Oh, she's perfectly nice," he said, "but there's no real spark there."

Moron! I thought to myself. Well, Grant might be willing to let this one get away, but I was not about to. A few weeks later, when the same mutual friend, Joan Aguado, invited us to dinner, I asked if Kathleen could come along. As Kathleen tells it, she was in the midst of a bout of bronchitis and had just gone to bed with a fever when she got the call from her friend Joanie, saying that the guy she'd met at Grant's house wanted to ask her out. But Kathleen had met two guys at that day—me, and Grant's roommate Dave— and she was only willing to get dressed and come out for "the one with the pointy shoes." Happily, the one with the pointy shoes was me. At dinner in Los Feliz, we eyed each other shyly. Back at my place later that evening I brought her hot tea on my grandmother's china tea set, and we sat up and talked for hours. Within a week we were in love and inseparable.

Although her name and face were not familiar to me, Kathleen had been acting since she was a teenager, when she got her first break on a daytime TV soap. She'd had small parts in many feature films, including *The Godfather Part II*, in which she played an Italian vaudeville theater owner's daughter, sharing a scene with Robert De Niro. She'd received a Golden Globe nomination for best supporting actress in *Promises in the Dark*, but was probably most famous for her role on *Dynasty*, at that time the number-one TV show in the world. She deeply regretted that role, because although it made her rich for a couple of seasons, her life became very difficult. She suddenly found herself famous for a type of show that seemed to care only about how she wore her clothes, not how she delivered her lines. And hard-core *Dynasty* fans were fanatical, showing little respect for an actor's privacy. There was a period when the only time she could go to the supermarket was while the show was actually airing, so she would be left alone to do her shopping. Often we'd be out sharing a quiet candlelit dinner and she'd have the fork halfway to her mouth when a stranger's hand would wrap around her wrist. "Oh my God—girls, get over here! It's *Kirby*! Kirby *Colby*, from *Dynasty*!"

My own fans, by comparison, were harmless. You could spot one a mile off when he made a beeline for us in a public place. He would probably have an anorak and skin problems. "Excuse me, Mr. Dolby," he would mumble.

"I was wondering—I've got an Oberheim OB-Xa and I want to work out how to sync it to the master clock of my Emulator 3. Have you any advice?"

Kathleen was never less than civil and friendly towards even her pushiest fans. She always arrived on the set ten minutes ahead of her call time, with her lines memorized, and made sure she said hello to each of the electricians and carpenters and props people, using their first names. Even when her script was crap or the director was an idiot, she would find a way to make her lines real and nail them, take after take.

I told her I was amazed by her patience and professionalism. "The way I see it," she said, "it's a collaboration, the whole thing, between the actor and the fan. You wouldn't be where you are without your audience. They often imagine you to be the way you are on-screen. But then they find you're only flesh and blood."

Kathleen's generosity and compassion were a breath of fresh air. In the music industry, I'd always been encouraged to keep fans at arm's length, to maintain the invisible wall that separates stars from mere mortals. While many celebrities do buy into that and behave in a way that perpetuates the illusion, Kathleen saw right through it. She was friendly and civil even to the lowliest busboy or valet parking attendant. She was never starstruck, even in the presence of massive celebrities and the superrich. She had acquired a group of friends over the years who did not judge each other by the box-office receipts of their latest movie.

When she was only seventeen she had landed a small part in Francis Ford Coppola's *Godfather* sequel, the movie that made Robert De Niro a household name. Kathleen was a young and impressionable actress and was blown away by De Niro's dashing looks and utter commitment to his craft. In the weeks she spent on the film set in Little Italy she developed a major crush on him. Her heart was all aflutter when Mr. De Niro invited her out for lunch one day. A chauffeured limousine showed up and she climbed in the back with De Niro, still in costume, and Frank Sivero, who played the part of the hoodlum Genco. She'd never been in a limo before. "Wouldn't one of you like to sit in the front with your friend?" she said, indicating the chauffeur. They drove to an Italian family restaurant that was empty other than a central table set for three. De Niro had it booked out. Each place setting came with its own waiter.

Prior to his move into the acting world, Frank Sivero was reportedly a bona fide New York "wise guy." Born in Sicily and brought up in Brooklyn, it was rumored that he was permanently armed and carried his entire net worth on his person in cash at all times, even when the camera was rolling. Filmmakers like Coppola and Scorsese loved to have Frank around just to make sure everything was "authentic."

De Niro ordered for her from the menu, before turning to Sivero and conversing quietly in Italian. Though her film character was Italian, she didn't understand the language herself and had had to learn her lines phonetically. Every now and then during the meal De Niro would turn to Kathleen to check if the food was to her liking or if her glass needed refilling. But he barely said a word to her. The meal ended, and the limo took her back to the hotel.

Next morning, Francis Coppola noticed her looking distraught. He took her aside. She broke into tears and confessed that she had a big crush on De Niro, but that their lunch date had turned out to be a disaster.

Coppola put a fatherly hand on her shoulder and said, "Kathy, it's not Bobby you've got a crush on, it's the young Vito Corleone. There *is* no Robert De Niro."

I was amazed when Kathleen told me this story, but I caught something she'd missed. I knew that De Niro would totally inhabit his movie roles, living the character twenty-four hours a day, even to the point of spending his off days playing out story lines that were not fully explored in the script. I'd read that when he was filming *Taxi Driver* he used to drive around the New York streets at night picking up real fares. (One night he reportedly picked up a wannabe actor. The actor said, "Jeez, only last year you won an Oscar and already you're back driving a cab?") During Kathleen's scene in *The Godfather Part II*, Vito Corleone and his sidekick Genco go to a theater matinee with the intention of inviting her out to lunch. They get into an altercation with Don Fanucci, whom Corleone later assassinates. It was clear to me that De Niro was merely playing out the lunch date that might have been.

I was deeply in love with this woman. She was witty, good-natured, and fond of books and travel; she had a natural beauty that did not rely on cosmetics or fine clothes. We were both hardworking professionals surrounded by Hollywood bullshit but in search of some balance in our lives. Her tolerance and common sense rubbed off on me right away. Here was someone who understood the pressures on an artist in the public eye, yet shared my pragmatism about showbiz. We were like peas in a pod. When we announced our engagement at a party in late 1986, none of our friends were remotely surprised.

So my "year out" in the USA became a permanent move. Kathleen split her time between her place in Laurel Canyon and my rental above Beachwood, and I started to look for an L.A.-based band for my third album and national tour.

I advertised for musicians in the *Recycler*, narrowing the hundreds of replies down to a few dozen. The tryouts took place in a warehouse in Reseda. Most of the applicants had no track record to speak of, though I was very taken with an excellent drummer called Dave Owens, who had a day job at the Knott's Berry Farm amusement park, where he was sometimes required to perform in a chicken suit. I paired him with an amazing bassist, Terry Jackson, who had once played all day at a Jerry Lewis fundraising telethon. Larry Treadwell's claim to fame was that he'd been the guitarist in a Christian duo supporting Pope John Paul II during his famous "Popemobile" tour of American stadiums. The band was rounded out by curvaceous percussionist and backup singer Laura Creamer, and a frenetic keyboard player named Mike Kapitan.

While driving down Beachwood Canyon one day on my way to rehearsals I caught a glimpse of a flyer pinned to a lamppost advertising a band called Lost Toy People. I thought, what a cool name! The next day I realized it actually said "Lost Toy Poodle, reward $25." So my new band was christened Thomas Dolby and the Lost Toy People.

Kathleen's housemate and childhood friend was Mary Coller. She was looking for a job. Her previous position, by complete coincidence, was as personal assistant to Michael Jackson. For three years she went every day to his Hayvenhurst estate and organized his life—picking out birthday presents for Elizabeth Taylor, inviting the Astaires over for dinner, or rounding up Bubbles the chimp when he escaped into the Encino undergrowth. Mary had a pager and was on call twenty-four hours a day. Michael would beep her at 2 a.m. just to ask where the popcorn was kept. She devoted her life to him. Then, suddenly, for no apparent reason, she was given a fortnight's wages and shown the door. She hadn't messed up or offended anyone. Try as she might, she could not get Michael on the phone. By this stage of his career he was insulated by layers of security staff, aides, and family retainers. Mary was devastated. Kathleen comforted her, but of course there was nothing I could do to intervene. What I was able to do was offer her a job, and she started working for my management team under Andy Ferguson.

Now that I was living full-time in America, I no longer needed Lesley to be my UK-based personal assistant. I hoped we could stay in touch, but it was clearly the end of an era. She had been loyal and supportive for many years, and if things had worked out a little differently, we might have been a couple. I never thanked her enough at the time, but the fact was, towards the end we bickered a lot.

Kathleen and I were married in July 1988, on a Thames sailing barge in my native Suffolk, England. We sold our respective properties—mine in Fulham, hers in Laurel Canyon—and bought a lovely 1923 Spanish-style mansion above Franklin Avenue. Our house had originally belonged to Wallace Beery, an Academy Award–winning actor who was once married to Gloria Swanson, and on whom John Goodman based his wrestler character in the Coen brothers' *Barton Fink*. Although huge, the house was affordably priced because of where it was situated. Whitley Heights was the first hilltop neighborhood in Hollywood. It was developed back in the 1920s and '30s, only to be sliced in two when the 101 freeway was put through the hills in the 1950s. The developer, H. J. Whitley, had modeled his enclave on hilltop villages in Sicily and Spain; but he failed to recognize that unlike those places, Los Angeles is subject to torrential downpours and the occasional 8.3-rated earthquake. The Whitley Heights hillside estate had never been provided with adequate drainage, and all day and night the eighteen-wheeler trucks on the freeway rattled our foundations. Ours was therefore a true house of cards, but we loved it. It had a stately living room with cast-iron gates, velvet curtains, and plaster reliefs. Next to that was a pub with high wicker stools and a full bar. We bought a splendid grand piano, and we used to arrange twisted cocktail evenings and invite over our Hollywood Hills neighbors— who included Julian Lennon, Gary Kemp, the as yet unknown George Clooney, and a very young J. J. Abrams. Across the street was a rambling house rented out to the Red Hot Chili Peppers, still relatively unheard of outside of L.A.

My new band was really starting to cook. We developed some of the grooves that had originated during the auditions. Some were very funky, while others were a kind of high-energy acid swing. I added chord sequences and melodies, Grant chimed in with some lyrics, and we took the songs into a small studio to lay some demos directly to half-inch analog tape. The album was shaping up to be a kind of crazy postcard home from a British expat on a debauched visit to Hollywood. I decided to title it *Aliens Ate My Buick*, a sort of homage to the tabloid newspapers you pick off the racks at American supermarket checkout counters. Before recording started in earnest I needed to fine-tune the new set in front of a live audience; this would also give me a source of revenue to pay the band's wages until the album was complete. So a West Coast club tour for the Lost Toy People was booked, kicking off with a "secret" gig at a dive called Club Lingerie in a seedy part of Hollywood.

To ease the pressure of a first gig, I wanted it to be kept quiet so that the crowd would be minimal and reviewers would stay away. It was a condition of the booking that the club did not advertise my show. On the afternoon of the gig, someone leaked the news to local radio station KROQ that "a bespectacled Englishman" was playing "at a frilly club with a saucy name" that same evening. To my utter dismay, when I arrived at the club for sound check there was already a line outside, stretching clear around the block.

I felt the familiar pangs of a Radio City–style panic attack coming on. Was the band ready? How would the crowd react to my new-style songs? Could I still cut it onstage after a three-year hiatus? Stuck in a traffic jam on Sunset Boulevard, I started chewing my lip and my hands were shaking. Kathleen had never seen me like this, but she had a suggestion: Why not do the gig in drag? It was an insane idea, but it might just work. So after sound check she drove me over to the home of her friend Victoria, who was one of the makeup artists on *Dynasty*. Victoria proceeded to invent a new persona for me: Erica Brady, a deranged Beverly Hills housewife. Erica had OD'd on diet pills and quaaludes and was moonlighting in a punk band, resplendent in leather corset and stiletto heels, with back-combed blond hair and an inflatable synthesizer. She chewed gum and swore like a sailor. Meanwhile Kathleen went the other way and showed up as Erica's bearded boyfriend, with her chest bound and a thick pair of socks stuffed down her Levi's. The crowd at Club Lingerie was not sure what to make of Erica and her diminutive toy boy. The band played each of the new songs twice through. When someone blurted out "Play 'Science'!" it was met with nothing but a stony stare. I certainly didn't make any new fans that day, but it did the trick as far as my stage nerves were concerned. The Lost Toy People officially popped their cherry, the rest of our West Coast gigs were a smash hit, and my agency began setting up a coast-to-coast North American tour covering over thirty cities.

I was delighted with the way the band sounded. I had a special rapport with my bass player, Terry Jackson (no relation to the other Jacksons). He was a young black guy from St. Louis, Missouri, new to L.A. and very green. He was a fabulous, flawless funk bass player, totally intuitive, who never played the same part twice. He had a huge teddy bear smile. We practiced acrobatics at the gym together, and at the climax of our set he would cup his hands together and flip me into a back somersault. Kathleen and I offered him our spare room for a few months to get him settled, and he became like a kid brother. Most evenings our house lit up with Terry's "Happy Hour." This entailed improvised monologues at the piano by characters ranging from pimps and drug dealers to TV evangelists and Bible-thumping politicians, keeping Kathleen, Mary, and my sister-in-law Jane in fits of giggles.

Terry's finest recorded moments are on *Aliens Ate My Buick*. He had this ability to create solid, minimalist note patterns and space them out with outrageous melodic passing licks, never detracting too much from the main vocals or keyboard parts. His playing was the perfect complement for some of my toughest and most hard-hitting songs: on the midtempo groove "Pulp

Culture," where I poked fun at the hedonistic Los Angeles lifestyle, and on the epic "Budapest by Blimp," which was a British expatriate looking back at European imperial splendor through an American lens.

> *See the priceless antiquity, frozen in time*
> *Built on the ashes of the Jews*
> *And for your curiosity, beauty sublime*
> *Signed in the blood of Zulus.*

—From *Budapest by Blimp* © Thomas Dolby, 1988

The *Aliens Ate My Buick* album was a critical success, earning me four Grammy nominations, but the radio play and sales were disappointing. It never gathered momentum. The general feedback from the record label (now EMI Manhattan Records) was that I had gone too far overboard with my tongue-in-cheek funk grooves and risqué lyrics, and alienated radio programmers and retailers. They were not pleased with this new direction and felt I'd been more on the right track with the previous album, the organic and introspective *The Flat Earth*. (*Now* they tell me, I thought! Where were they when I was in my "organic" phase?) The problem, they said, was that their promotion people didn't know whose jurisdiction I fell under—the rock division, which mostly promoted white musicians with guitars and drum kits, or the urban division, which handled black artists whose records featured danceable grooves and soulful vocals. For this and other reasons, they decided (at 8 p.m. on the evening before I was due to depart on a thirty-date tour promoting the new album) to withdraw their tour support, leaving me with two choices: cancel the dates and disappoint my fans, or cover the $60,000 shortfall myself. I chose the latter; but it worried me that my own record company was unwilling to back my efforts to promote the album.

The more I saw of EMI, the more I felt they were a dinosaur corporation from an extinct age. They needed to pigeonhole everything in order to understand it. Artists were supposed to follow tried and trusted formulas, and conform their music to what the corrupt radio networks thought would sell more advertising. I wouldn't play the game, so they pulled the rug out from under me.

There are two kinds of musician in the world. The first wants nothing more in life than to sign a contract with a major record label. The second wants nothing more in life than to tear the contract up. By the end of the 1980s I had a burning desire to extricate myself from EMI, no matter the price—even if it meant getting out of the music business altogether.

Prefab Sprout's manager called. He said Paddy McAloon had demos for a new album he was desperate to play me. "This is not a good time, Keith," I snapped at him. "I'm too wrapped up in my own career!" "Just give them a listen, Thomas," he urged me. I reluctantly agreed, knowing full well there would be new Sprouts songs I would fall in love with and be powerless to turn down. It was always the same story. The tape showed up and sure enough, I got as far as the second track, "Wild Horses," and I was mesmerized. By the time "Jesse James Bolero" faded out I was irretrievably hooked. I called Paddy to tell him how much I loved the new songs.

I flew to London and met up with Paddy and Wendy in a café in Camden Town. "You've got to produce this, Thomas," he said. "It's a nineteen-song double album. It's called *Jordan: The Comeback*. It's about Elvis and death."

As Kathleen is quick to point out, I spent seven months out of our first year of marriage living with the Sprouts in leafy English country recording studios.

CHAPTER 8

STARS EXPLODE, FIREWORKS DON'T

In January 1990, Michael Jackson concluded a yearlong world tour with a series of five concerts at the Los Angeles Sports Arena. Now at the peak of his fame, Michael had smashed all the record books. He had also become a global curiosity, yet his quirky habits and strange lifestyle choices, intriguing to some and revolting to others, did nothing to take away from his commercial appeal. With his *Bad* album topping the charts, the L.A. dates were sold out within hours of going on sale.

On the last night of the tour, all of Hollywood turned out to see him. He had sent personal messages to every A-list celebrity, inviting them backstage for a reception before the show. His office sent Mary Coller four complimentary tickets, and she brought Kathleen and me, along with my bass player and lodger Terry Jackson. Under the bleachers in the huge concrete backstage area of the arena, the scene was chaotic. Michael's people had set up a large Bedouin tent surrounded by exotic Persian rugs. Wolfgang Puck was doing the catering, but there were dozens more VIPs than he'd anticipated. By the time we arrived, glasses were dry and the hors d'oeuvres were long gone. No paparazzi were allowed backstage, but there was a professional camera set up inside the tent, as Michael's desire was to create the photo album to end all photo albums, featuring himself posing with the top names in show business.

With less than an hour until Michael was due onstage, time was running short. The staff began to herd the celebs towards the tent in a long unruly line that was moving very slowly. This did not go over too well. Lou "the Hulk" Ferrigno stepped on Danny DeVito's toe. Paula Abdul was getting antsy, and Arnold Schwarzenegger started complaining loudly to one of Michael's staff, who was talking helplessly into his headset microphone. Michael's trusted family retainer Bill usually ran things in this situation, but he seemed to be absent. Ahead of us in the line, I heard Joan Rivers's whiny voice call out, "This *sucks*, Michael!"

Without missing a beat, Mary Coller stepped up to the front of the line and started directing traffic. Most of Michael's staff knew her as his assistant and must have assumed she was still on his payroll. Mary waved her arms and issued orders this way and that, reassuring the listless celebs that their turn with Michael would arrive very soon. You could see the flashes popping inside the tent. Once Mary took charge the line began to thin out, and our foursome were the last to step inside to Michael's inner sanctum.

The tent interior was brightly lit and lavishly decorated, like a Rudolph Valentino movie set. Michael greeted me warmly, and I introduced Kathleen and Terry. He briefly clutched Mary's hand, then turned directly to the photographer and struck a rigid camera pose, smiling from ear to ear. The photographer motioned for the guests to huddle close to Michael and compose the shot. Much to my surprise, out of the corner of my eye I saw Kathleen lean in to whisper something in his ear. As he took in Kathleen's words, his face slowly crumbled. By the time she had finished, he looked utterly miserable. Then he turned to her and said, "Well, maybe Bill could do that?" And with that his smile returned, the photographer snapped a couple of shots, and our audience with the King of Pop was over.

Outside, I asked Kathleen what on earth she had said. "I told him, 'You should be ashamed of yourself. Mary was devoted to you. You really need to apologize to her, because you broke her heart.'"

I instantly wrapped my arms around my wife and told her I loved her. This was certainly the only real thing anyone had said to him all evening. But he never did apologize, and it's only because of Mary's complete loyalty to Michael and the Jackson legacy that she has never to this day spilled the beans about her three years working as his personal assistant.

Mary was a brilliant fixer. Still, I dropped her right in the deep end when we accepted an invitation to take part in a historic event in Moscow, USSR.

It was a quarter past midnight at Moscow's OPJS Central Telegraph office—the allocated time for my call to the USA from a dilapidated row of phone booths. All the phones at our hotel—the mammoth Cosmos Hotel, a monument to the achievement of the Socialist Worker—were out of order. I'd had a hard time flagging down a taxi in the street, not knowing that in Moscow at that time there were two ways to do it: (1) hold up a number of fingers indicating the multiple of the meter price you were willing to pay, or (2) hold up a packet of Marlboro cigarettes, which was enough to get you a ride anywhere in the city.

This was to be the first ever transglobal simulcast of a rock concert. Produced by MuchMusic, Canada's answer to MTV, the show was being filmed live in Toronto, New York, London, Paris, Moscow, and Sydney. Earlier in the evening I'd shared the stage with Canadian rock superstar Bryan Adams, performing in front of a Russian audience who totally failed to see the significance of the event. The ten-minute satellite window during which Moscow broadcast to the world was part of their regular Saturday-evening TV variety show, and the producers couldn't wait to hustle us off the stage so they could set up a Gypsy juggling troupe, who were much more to the audience's taste.

We'd gone right to the TV studio from a grueling, three-leg, twenty-two-hour flight to Russia, and after the show I was desperate to call Kathleen back in L.A. to let her know I was alive. With the Cosmos Hotel phones out of order, my only option was the grim Central Telegraph office. I made it down there at about 11 p.m., and though the booths appeared to be empty, the clerk told me the first slot she had available was at 12:15 a.m. I sat on the hard wooden bench grinning at her and watching the clock above her head.

Finally, at the appointed time, she pointed me in the direction of booth number seven.

My call was put through to the USA. The operator connected me and after a few rings Kathleen answered the phone. She was relieved to hear my voice. Then she said, "Sweetie, I hope you're sitting down—I'm PREGNANT!" "You're *what?*" I blurted out. Then suddenly the line went very quiet. I could just about hear her voice, but I could barely make out the words.

It was fantastic news. "Yes—you—heard—me—I'm—pregnant!—when—are—you—coming—home?"

"I'll—change—my—flight—and—try—to—be—there—the—day—after—tomorrow!" I yelled.

The next day our guide and interpreter told me why the phone line had gone so quiet. "It's the KGB," she said. "If they can't understand what you're saying they turn down the volume, so you have to speak extra loud and slow."

I managed to find a taxi back to the Cosmos Hotel, feeling on top of the world. It was nearly 1 a.m. and the place was hopping. A huge throng filled the massive atrium bar area, composed mainly of Russian prostitutes and foreign businessmen. I found Mary Coller in the middle of a group of Hungarian salesmen and their dates, playing drinking games. Their umpire and ringleader was Bryan Adams, and it appeared he had decided Mary was the main prize. Tray upon tray of vodka shots were lined up on the bar, charged to Bryan's tab. He urged me to join in. Any other night I'd have declined; but I'd just found out I was going to be a father, and tonight I was celebrating, too. I watched the other players to get the hang of it. Before each vodka shot, you had to smack yourself on the cheek with the back of your hand. The harder the slap, the louder the cheer from your fellow drinkers. As time went on, the preamble got more elaborate. You rolled down your shirt collar, undoing your tie if need be, then . . . *smack!* and down in one. The ladies were not to be left out. For one Russian prostitute this meant removing her gaudy earrings and undoing her top buttons, revealing a lacy bra strap. The poor girl must have had a dozen shots, and her makeup was starting to run from the tears of laughter rolling down her rosy cheeks.

Two on-duty Soviet soldiers with semiautomatic weapons eyed the proceedings disapprovingly from across the hall. When they felt matters had gone far enough, they decided to break up the game. They pushed their way into the scrum and tried to eject the prostitute. Their progress was impeded by several drunken Hungarians, who clapped them on the back and urged them to lighten up, thrusting vodka shots under their noses. Mary was loving all this, and Bryan Adams was on the top of his game, conducting a singalong in pig-Russian from atop the bar. A cross-eyed businessman started fingering one soldier's Kalashnikov. That was when I decided it was time to call it a night. I dragged Mary to the elevator and sent her to her room. The next day, heavily hungover, Mary and the interpreter arranged for us to take an early flight out of the USSR; and twenty-four hours later, after a brief stopover in Ireland, we finally made it home, exhausted, to L.A.

Kathleen and I were delighted with our news. We cleared our calendars for a few months. Our home needed a rethink to make it a suitable place to bring up a baby. We soundproofed the bedrooms to block out the ever-present drone of the 101 freeway, and I set about converting an extension to the basement to make room for a small studio for me and an office for Mary.

I was determined to use this time to see if I could get myself out of my record contract. Andy Ferguson, ever the pragmatist, advised me to try to stick it out, but my mind was made up. On the surface my contract was watertight, and even if I stopped recording I would continue to be tied to the contract in perpetuity. But by asking around, I found out that several of the other artists on my label were as unhappy as I was. One of them, the platinum-selling pop balladeer Richard Marx, was in a dispute over his royalties. Richard told me EMI had tried to withhold hundreds of thousands of dollars owed to him in order to boost their quarterly earnings and make the parent company, Thorn EMI, look good to its shareholders. Richard's aggressive manager, Allen Kovac, was having none of it. He threatened to sue EMI unless they released Richard and two other artists he represented. I briefly had the idea of hiring Allen myself, to add some leverage and get me out of my contract. Fortunately, EMI made that unnecessary, because halfway through the recording of my fourth album, *Astronauts and Heretics*, they declined to pick up their option to release it. This was all very well, but the timing was far from ideal: I had already been in the studio for several months, and now those bills would come directly to me. I put this out of my mind and tried to block out any business concerns while I got the record finished. I left Andy and my lawyers to sort out the formalities.

After eight years and three albums I was no longer an EMI artist, although of course the company would continue to own my recordings and videos, and still do. It left me high and dry, and desperately short of funds, but it felt great to be a free agent. Great, and little scary.

Hindsight is 20/20, but in 1989 none of us could see the big picture. All I knew was that EMI and most of the major labels were so bogged down with their conventional way of doing things, they would resist change in any form. I was finally rid of EMI, but I still needed to get my half-finished album released. There were other labels to approach, including several up-and-coming indies; I wondered if it was going to be a case of out of the frying pan, into the fire.

The one company that seemed to be forward thinking was Virgin. They were expanding their brand into many different areas, from films and TV to airlines, insurance, even health and fitness. They had the reputation for sticking to their belief in their artists, allowing them the freedom to experiment and grow. And Andy had a great relationship with Virgin Records' bosses, Paul Conroy and Simon Draper. So when my EMI termination letter finally arrived, I headed straight back to London and showed up, metaphorically speaking, on Richard Branson's doorstep, hoping he'd be as good as his word at that cricket match many years before. I doubt Branson knew much about it—or even remembered I existed—but in November 1989 Virgin Records offered me a lucrative new record contract. It included a huge advance, and was for the UK only, leaving us free to negotiate a separate deal for the USA. This was a major coup on Andy's part considering how poorly my previous two albums had performed. With a new label eager to hear it, I hurried to complete the recording of *Astronauts and Heretics*. In the press I thumbed my nose at my former label, and I called several of the top guys at EMI to tell them exactly what I thought of them!

Six months later, Richard Branson sold Virgin Records to EMI.

There was a great sixties cult TV show called *The Prisoner*. Each episode had Patrick McGoohan, as Number 6, trying to outwit an invisible, repressive governing force, in order to escape the surreal island where he was held captive. The final shot of every episode was a close-up of McGoohan's face as a heavy cast-iron grate clanged down in front of it.

When I heard the Virgin news, I felt just like Number 6. So when I got a call from Roger Waters offering me a part in a giant production of *The Wall* in Berlin, it seemed just the ticket. It's a miserable piece, and it matched my mood entirely.

Pink Floyd had last performed *The Wall* in concert in 1981. Waters said the only way he would ever revive it was amid the ruins of the Berlin Wall. In November 1989 the Wall came triumphantly crashing down, and Waters agreed to perform his piece again. A spectacular live production was planned, to be broadcast live to thirty-five countries via satellite and staged in front of 350,000 people at what had formerly been no-man's-land near the Brandenburg Gate. A 591-by-82-foot fully collapsible wall was constructed, stretching from West to East Berlin. The land had hardly been used since the end of World War II, and in preparation for the show, West German military personnel were brought in to scan for unexploded ordnances. During this process they uncovered a maze of tunnels that had made up part of Hitler's bunker, complete with faded Nazi banners still hanging on the walls.

It was the largest one-day rock concert ever staged, and the most multilayered: what with the live TV production crew, video and laser projectionists, pyrotechnics, giant puppets, and a cast of thousands all tripping over each other in a construction site, rehearsals were a catastrophe. High winds were playing havoc with the puppets; polystyrene bricks were flying out of the wall; camera crews were stepping on pyrotechnic devices. The 150 Red Army Chorus singers had nowhere to pee. Roger Waters, who had a hand in every last detail of the show, was walking around with a black cloud over his head.

Among the all-star cast were Marianne Faithfull, Jerry Hall, Sinéad O'Connor, Bryan Adams, Albert Finney, and Tim Curry, along with several of my all-time heroes such as Van Morrison, Joni Mitchell, and Garth

Hudson. My role was as the ghoulish Scottish schoolteacher. I came on-stage during "Another Brick in the Wall" to play a synth solo on a keytar, jousting with Cyndi Lauper the vocalist, who was dressed up as a schoolgirl. In the final trial scene, I was to be suspended from the top of the eighty-foot wall, like Gerald Scarfe's grotesque puppet, screaming at the top of my voice in Glaswegian. My head was shaved, aside from three nasty little tufts. I wore a special suit with fifteen-foot-long arms and legs, and under it a mountaineering harness. As my cue approached, I was shown down into a deep well behind the stage but in front of the wall. Wires were attached to the shoulders of my harness, which led up over pulleys at the top of the Wall and down to a sandbag that was roughly my weight. As I lay there in the darkness, two dozen U.S. Seventh Airborne commandos in jackboots abseiled down the wall and landed all around me. Then, as my musical intro started, stagehands yanked on the sandbag and I was catapulted halfway up the wall and into the beam of a powerful searchlight. I thrashed around on my wire doing my best puppet imitation and glared out across the Potsdamer Platz at the delirious crowd of nearly half a million people.

Kathleen was with me in Berlin, and suffering from extreme morning sickness. She spent most of the trip on the couch in our hotel suite with the blinds drawn. When room service wheeled in a trolley to set up our dinner, she withdrew to the bedroom and told me to bring her only a small side plate of food at a time. She'd never drunk alcohol in her life, but now she suddenly announced that she needed to sniff my red wine before she could stomach a mouthful of food. On top of everything, her breasts were huge. They're on the large side anyway, but even at this early stage of pregnancy they were fair bursting out of her top. She urgently needed me to go out and buy her a bigger brassiere. I speak a few words of German, but this called for vocabulary that was way beyond me. I bought an English-German phrasebook and hailed a cab to take me to the nearest department store.

In the taxi I found the phrase I needed: "*Meine Frau ist Schwanger. Sie braucht einen neuen Büstenhalter.*" A *Büstenhalter*? Are you serious? I checked inside the front cover to make sure the publisher was not Monty Python, Inc.

Imminent parenthood does strange things to your mind: you take a long hard look at the world you're about to bring a child into. I returned from Berlin determined not to let record industry politics stop me from making a great album. I wanted to get as much music as I could in the can before the baby's arrival. As Kathleen's belly swelled, I spent long hours in the studio, writing and recording a set of songs that were more introspective and more metaphysical than any I'd attempted. The new direction called out for a curious collection of maverick musicians. It also took me on some wild road trips.

While I was in Europe my great friend Grant Morris made a snap decision to move to New Orleans. He loved the music and the food there, and found it conducive to his screenwriting. After offloading his crumbling one-story bungalow in the Hollywood Hills, he was able to buy a precious gem of a house in the Garden District, with change to spare. I'd never been to Louisiana, but when I realized Grant was seriously quitting L.A. for good, I decided to go and see him in his new locale. The four-day trip was a musical whirlwind. He took me to a venue called the Maple Leaf deep in the housing projects, where my jaw dropped on hearing the dizzying funk of Rebirth for the first time. There were at least nine brass players crammed onto the small stage, ranging in age from fourteen to eighty-five, and a single marching drum. How could their sound be so tight and so loose at the same time? It unraveled in my mind a musicological thread dating from Louis Armstrong all the way through to James Brown, George Clinton, and Prince. Pouring out of there at nine in the morning we went to the Zydeco bowling alley, where the bourbon tasted pretty good in plastic cups. Later we hung out with the rickety Ernie K-Doe at his own moth-eaten lounge bar, and watched him mime to his 1960s hit "Mother-in-Law" in a sequined suit, like a scene right out of *Blue Velvet*.

I had tapes with me of some of the grooves from my album. Grant rustled up a car and we trekked out to the bayou in search of a couple of local Cajun musicians he knew, Wayne Toups and Michael Doucet. We met them in a ramshackle recording studio in the back of a record shop. I set up some mics and began to run the grooves. Within minutes the word got out around town that there was a session on. Every time I turned around somebody's second cousin had shown up unannounced with a different instrument, and soon it was a nonstop party. The whole experience was eventually distilled into a couple of fine songs, "Silk Pyjamas" and the epic "I Love You Goodbye." It was the last mad road trip with my friend before the responsibilities of fatherhood took over.

Our daughter Lilian Harper Robertson was born on February 3, 1991. She was a delightful, bouncy baby girl, and a very light sleeper. Our sleep patterns were severely disrupted, and my album ground to a temporary halt. But we were very, very happy. On a rare occasion that I was able to sneak downstairs and do some writing, I played the piano until the sun came up and wrote a love song for Kathleen. Around 7 a.m. she wandered sleepily into the living room in her pajamas and told me the baby was fast asleep. I sat her down next to me on the piano stool. She rested her head on my shoulder and I sang the ballad I'd written for her, "The Beauty of a Dream."

The song had a coda that was crying out for some great guitar playing. I had a crazy idea that perhaps Jerry Garcia and Bob Weir of the Grateful Dead would do it. I'd been a bit of a Deadhead in my early teens, having seen a couple of their rare British appearances, at Knebworth and Alexandra Palace, in front of their famous wall of loudspeakers. I'd always liked the way the two of them interacted, Weir's choppy rhythm chords intuitively voicing Garcia's melodic phrases. But I had no idea if my album's recording budget would stretch that far. To my delight, not only did they return my phone call, but they said if I was willing to visit them in Northern California they would have a crack at my song. They refused to be paid a penny for their work.

I was unsure what to expect. Garcia had been in and out of rehab, and I'd heard his health was fading. I flew up to San Francisco with my multitrack tapes under my arm, and drove a rental car over the Golden Gate Bridge to Marin County, which I still knew my way around. The Dead had a combined storage warehouse and rehearsal space in a shabby industrial estate on the outskirts of San Rafael. It was packed to the rafters with their mountainous PA rig. In the midst of it a rehearsal space had been cleared, and they were busy preparing for a new tour with Bruce Hornsby on piano. There was a giant mixing desk and a pair of Studer twenty-four-tracks to record their rehearsals. I suppose I naïvely expected the Dead to turn up on Harleys in Hells Angels denim and leather, or in a psychedelic-painted VW bus. So I was quite surprised when a brand-new BMW 7-series sedan pulled up in front of the warehouse, and out stepped Jerry Garcia in an impeccable Giorgio Armani suit. While the engineer set up the tapes, we pulled up a pair of stools and chatted.

I was surprised to hear Jerry say that he owned a copy of my first album and really liked "One of Our Submarines." He'd heard some of my newer stuff on KFOG. These days, Jerry said, the Grateful Dead didn't sell many records. "Maybe not," I pointed out, "but aren't you still the biggest-grossing rock-and-roll band in the world?"

Garcia shrugged and flashed me a big grin. "I can't really explain it, man," he said. "These dirty hippie chicks just keep following us around."

Bobby Weir showed up and was very keen to get on with the track. We sat in a circle and began to run through the last twenty-four bars of my song. Weir was very on the ball and quickly worked out the chords, easily finding his way to the correct inversions. Jerry, on the other hand, was lost. He seemed to be having a hard time getting to grips with the changes, or finding gaps between the vocal lines. He didn't sound like himself at all. At one point I realized he was actually trying to make the synth melody from "One of Our Submarines" fit into this very different song. Weir tried to follow him, but it just wasn't working. In my imagination they would sound just like the Dead always did, but overlaid on top of my music. In Jerry's mind, I was asking him to make his guitar sound like my synths.

Between takes, as the tape was rewinding, Jerry doodled absentmindedly on the lovely custom guitar he called Rosebud. I'd learned years earlier from the masterful Mutt Lange that for the duration of a tracking session you should always run a two-track recorder alongside the multitrack, just to capture the little asides that happen even when the twenty-four-track isn't rolling. So I'd brought my portable DAT recorder with me, and as Jerry doodled, I glanced over to make sure the meters on the DAT were lighting up. His licks were a little incoherent, but it sounded like Jerry—or at least, it sounded as if someone had dug up Jerry's cadaver and attached electrodes to his tendons, and the muscle memory had triggered a few random riffs in B major left over from the Summer of Love.

The session was over in about three hours. I tipped the engineers and expressed my gratitude to Bob and Jerry. Bob took me aside and apologized profusely. He felt terrible that I had come all this way and he and his bandmate hadn't delivered. "Far from it," I told him. "I've got plenty I can use!"

Back at my basement studio in L.A., I set to work on the tracks. Although multitrack analog tape was still the norm in 1991, computers were just starting to come into the frame. I had new software on my Mac Plus called Opcode Studio Vision, and it could do a limited amount of sixteen-bit digital recording. The consensus among sound engineers was that computers were not yet a replacement for analog tape, but to me, the most exciting aspect was the ability to chop up recordings into small chunks and use them as building blocks, cutting and pasting phrases and bars of music the way an author would manipulate prose in a word processor. I transferred Jerry's off-the-cuff improvisations from my DAT tapes into the Mac and began to piece together a solo that, I hoped, would be worthy of his name. A week later I sent the results up to San Rafael, and Bob Weir called me, plainly relieved. He said I'd done wonders considering what Jerry had played, and asked if I would return the favor one day and do some work on one of their albums. I said I'd be honored to. Sadly, it was never to be, as Jerry died only a few years later.

Whereas the lyrics I wrote in my early twenties tended to be at arm's length—about submarines, dissidents, and wind turbines—the songs on my new album were increasingly personal, growing out of the episodes and relationships that mattered in my life. On one song, I did a duet with the wonderful Scottish female vocalist Eddi Reader. Being a songwriter occasionally gives you back the opportunity to say things you wish you'd said in person, and to put words into other people's mouths. In this case, Lesley's:

> "And I know that it was just the fear of flying
> And I know it's hard to keep myself from crying

But when my tears are washed away you'll still be blind
Skin diving for jewels."
You were a shining pearl under moonlight.
And I was cruel.

—From *Cruel* © Thomas Dolby, 1992

The album was full of joy, as well. I was amazed by the way Kathleen's body and mind were transforming before my eyes as she grew into her role as a mother. And of course, I was in love with our delightful daughter.

My album was taking shape, but a couple of songs still needed a few guitar touches. Kathleen used to hang out with the actress Valerie Bertinelli, who was married to Eddie Van Halen. Eddie and I had met before at awards shows. He was possibly the best rock-and-roll guitarist on the planet, and I wondered if I could nab him to play a few notes on my album. Like me, he was an odd mixture of very shy and very arrogant. Kathleen called Val and she connected us. Eddie was interested, but he and his band were midway through their own album *For Unlawful Carnal Knowledge*, and he warned me that his bandmates—especially his older brother Alex—were not keen on him guesting for other people. But he said he could do a few hours' recording over a weekend at his home studio in the hills above Coldwater Canyon.

I followed a winding drive to Eddie's fifty-six-room Tudor mansion with my multitrack tapes. The studio was a little farther up the hill. Eddie's engineer was the legendary Andy Johns, a towering Cockney, and he was apparently on a weekend bender of booze and drugs. Eddie himself was stone-cold sober. We sat in the control room surrounded by about a dozen electric guitars on stands, including his famous red-and-white-striped "Frankenstrat," and chatted nervously.

Usually when you meet a fellow musician from any corner of the world you can break the ice by quoting a random line from *This Is Spinal Tap*. It is the universal currency. So when Eddie wanted to illustrate an idea for my song and reached for his as-yet-unplugged Frankenstrat, I said: "Shh! Listen to that sustain. You could go out for a bite to eat while that's going on."

147

I waited, but Eddie looked at me completely blankly. "Um, did you ever see that movie?" I asked. *"This Is Spinal Tap?* The mock-rockumentary?"

"Yeah, dude," said Eddie. "We saw that piece of shit."

"You weren't so into it?"

"We didn't think it was funny. It was like, someone followed us around with a camera, put it up on a screen, and everybody fell over laughing."

Over the course of that weekend I understood. Eddie's playing on my songs was out of this world, but every hour of his day was a scene from *Spinal Tap.* The studio was like a padded den for adolescent schoolboys. In the back room there was an automated hot dog vending machine, an electronic dartboard, and a row of four Grand Prix Racer arcade game machines, so the band could have races.

A little way into our session, it became apparent that Andy Johns was the worse for wear. Eddie could operate the twenty-four-track himself, so he told Johns to go home. "All right, you little Dutch git," said Johns affectionately. "I'll see you Monday. Come here and gimme a hug." He smothered Eddie in a bear hug and exited the studio.

Moments later we heard a deafening crash. Eddie ran outside and I followed behind. Johns had reversed his large mauve Cadillac convertible into a stone statue. "Wanker!" shouted Eddie. He turned to me. "He's knocked an arm off one of the statues. Val's gonna kill me."

It was a warm Saturday evening and we'd been working with the studio door open, Eddie laying down a righteous chunky rhythm guitar on one song and an array of dizzying solo licks on another. When it was time for a break, he suggested we head down the hill to the main house.

"Shall we walk or drive?" Eddie said.

"We might as well walk, no?" I said.

He grinned slyly. "I never walk," he said, and disappeared around the back. Seconds later he emerged at the wheel of an electric golf cart, its roof painted in his personalized red-and-white-striped Frankenstrat color scheme. We pootled a hundred yards around the hillside, eventually arriving at the front door of the mansion, not fifty feet below the studio.

As we stepped out, I suddenly heard the honking of horns and shrill distant cries of "EDDIE! EDDIE! YEAH!!" High up above his property a group of fans had parked their trucks and hot rods on a scenic overlook off of Mulholland, and they were screaming and flashing their headlights, amazed to get an actual sighting of their favorite guitar god.

Down at the Tudor mansion, Eddie sank into an oversized armchair and grabbed a remote to flick on the massive gas fireplace with a loud *whooomf!*

"Eddie!" complained Val. "It's ninety degrees out!"

"Crank up the AC then, would you, babe? I'm beat."

He told me to help myself to a soda from the fridge. In the kitchen I ran into his brother Alex. He looked at me suspiciously.

"I hear you're not nuts about Eddie playing on my album?" I inquired.

"You got that right, bro," Alex said. "Last time we let him do that, he did a solo on that little fucker Michael Jackson's record. That was the only reason *1984* got stuck at #2."

On the Sunday evening, after a marathon recording session lasting most of the weekend, Eddie and I completed his overdubs on two of my songs, "Easter Bloc" and "Close but No Cigar." I felt that familiar mixture of satisfaction and fatigue, when you know you've got something great down on tape but you're too tired to edit it.

At home, Kathleen and baby Lily, now six weeks old, were waiting for me. We were sitting on a couch in the smallest room in the house when we got the news that Terry Jackson had been in an accident. He was on a small charter jet with other members of country singer Reba McEntire's band and crew. It took off in bad visibility from Brown Field near San Diego, and six minutes later it flew into the side of a mountain. There were no survivors.

Terry was dead. I stumbled out of the house in a daze, unable to process the news. I reached the top of the trail up above the Griffith Observatory and sat down on a rock still warm from the afternoon sun. Over the distant Pacific Ocean the sky was starting to turn pink. Way below I could make out the taillights of the commuter traffic on Sunset Boulevard. A melody took root in my head and kept repeating over and over: "I live in a suitcase . . . I live in a suitcase . . ." I stared out over the darkening city as the mathematical grid of lights began to throb and glow. Somewhere away in the undergrowth a pack of howling coyotes had ambushed their prey, probably a domestic pet. Above downtown a police helicopter was rotating around the beam of its own searchlight. Los Angeles was a glittering lake of lights.

Beyond the city I could now see the silhouette of the high mountains to the south, and above them the deep blue of the night sky, with a faint flicker of the early stars and planets. Then my trance was suddenly broken. Half the city of Los Angeles flickered and went black, leaving a river of red and white light flowing along the network of freeways. There must have been a massive power outage, a brownout of some sort. It was as if one side of L.A.'s bloated torso wore a resplendent cloak; the other, its skin peeled away, was exposing its arterial veins. My breathing slowed, and the lines came to me:

> *When all the lights go down*
> *This dirty desert town*
> *Is theater in the round*
> *With stars instead of a crowd.*

> —From *I Live in a Suitcase* © Thomas Dolby, 1991

It was the spring of 1991. The fallout from the Gulf War and the generally weak economy was hitting Los Angeles hard. Movie theaters weren't filling, concert receipts were down, and even *Billboard*'s top-selling albums were barely going platinum. L.A.'s restaurants and bars were deserted. In the wake of the Rodney King case, in which four police officers were acquitted after being caught on camera beating up a black civilian, there were widespread riots, with looting and arson in the streets. The view from the picture window of our living room a few blocks down the hill to where Hollywood Boulevard shops were on fire looked like a disaster movie—not least because our view was dominated by the Capitol Records Tower, always the first building to get blown away in disaster movies.

The fires were put out, but Capitol Records and their major label cousins had other problems to contend with. The world they ruled over was one of brick and mortar. Their total control of consumer music sales was built on a network of pressing plants, fleets of vans, and historical relationships with retail chains and media channels. They had beefed up their revenues by re-selling fans music they already owned, in the novel CD format. That was a limited market, and it took the focus away from developing new artists. Meanwhile, the mega stadium acts of the 1980s—Bruce Springsteen, Bon Jovi, George Michael, Prince, Madonna, even Michael Jackson—began to lose their selling power.

With that as a backdrop, I found it very hard to find a label that would release my fourth album, *Astronauts and Heretics*, in the USA. I was immensely proud of it, but I had to admit it was a moody and introspective piece, with-out any of the synthpop quirkiness that had been a benchmark of hits like "Science" and "Hyperactive!" The only offer came from the recently launched Giant Records, run by a music industry "giant" by the name of Irving Azoff— all five feet and three inches of him. Irving was known in the business as the Poison Dwarf. His commercial track record was astonishing, as were the rudeness and disdain with which he treated me, along with most of his staff. *Astronauts and Heretics* came out in the USA on Giant in 1992, sank without a trace, and left a deep gash in my heart, still barely healing from the death of my dear friend.

It was time to move on.

PART 2

CHAPTER 9
RIDE THE BULLET TRAIN

My son once slid down our attic steps with an armful of old vinyl jazz albums, shouting, "Daddy, look what I found—giant CDs!"

If you were born later than 1985, you'll scarcely remember the days before music went digital. Perhaps as a child you heard your mum and dad fondly reminiscing about turntables and tuners and transistors. You may remember those dusty crates of eight-track tapes on the top shelf in the garage, with their pictorial labels featuring Cat Stevens and the Bee Gees and Fleetwood Mac.

Today, even compact discs seem like ancient archaeology. When my daughter was a teenager, and already an avid iTunes user, her grandparents gave her a CD for Christmas, *Fallen*, by her favorite band, Evanescence. She took it to a party at a friend's house and left it by the stereo. Later that evening she discovered that both the CD and its jewel case were gone. The poor girl came home distraught and bewildered. She just could not process the idea: one moment you own music, the next moment you don't. She couldn't just restore it from a backup, or reauthorize her music collection?

The current generation of music fans has seen technology evolve so rapidly that they no longer think of it in terms of a particular format or device. They still have their favorite artists and songs, but the music is decoupled from the delivery method. They know they can access a single or an album via whatever means are handy at the time—a mobile phone, an iPod, a computer in a public library, a friend's Spotify account, a rental car stereo, a hotel room TV, and so on. It no longer matters where the bits or atoms reside. The fan just logs in somewhere and knows he can hear the latest release by Coldplay, because he's a Coldplay follower.

To the fan, the concept of following is much fairer and more intuitive than the old model, where you had to go to a store and buy a physical product. Aside from the inconvenience of the store visit, if your record got scratched or lost or stolen, or snatched by an ex-girlfriend, you'd be back to square one. It's also better for Coldplay, because millions of fans who register to follow them are glad to submit their names and details, giving the band permission to gently push future releases, concert tickets, and merchandise their way as well.

I can state this with confidence as I sit here writing in the second decade of the twenty-first century. Music went digital, the major record labels foundered, the new bosses are companies like Apple and Google and Spotify; that's all water under the bridge. But let me transport you back to the uncertainty of 1992, the year I abandoned the music business (or did it abandon me?)—and pursued a career in technology.

A small but growing number of computer users were starting to connect to the Internet via subscription services like CompuServe and America Online. Using these services you could access and download digital files such as photos, applications, and songs. The user interfaces were unappealing, and connection speeds were very slow, but there were new compression formats starting to appear, including Fraunhofer's MP3 format, which improved song downloads and storage by a factor of at least ten to one, with a quality loss that was barely discernible to the average listener.

I'd been sending and receiving Internet song files since the days of my Radio Shack TRS-80, fumbling around with acoustic cups in Nevada desert phone booths. In the 1980s, that method of sending music from A to B was limited to the professional recording world; but when I first saw CompuServe, with its folders of downloadable song files, my worldview was radically altered. It was a beautiful thing. My fans and I were now connected to the same network and using the same equipment; all I had to do was hit "upload" and I could potentially distribute a song to millions of users worldwide, at a negligible cost.

I began to speak in press interviews about the Internet and its exciting possibilities. You didn't have to be a visionary to see this potential or understand its implications. Many of my peers recognized the possibilities around the same time. I would find myself sitting on panels at tech conferences alongside people like Peter Gabriel, Laurie Anderson, and Todd Rundgren—the same fearless and forward-looking artists who were the first to embrace music videos, the first to experiment with games and interactive CD-ROMs. We shared an enthusiasm for these technologies and couldn't wait to get our hands on the new tools that would allow us to explore their creative possibilities.

Alongside us on those tech panels would be representatives of the record labels and copyright societies. Their concerns were very different: they worried about the risk of music distributed illegally via the Internet, which would eat into their profits. Music piracy, they claimed, was already a major issue around the world, especially in third-world countries where physical CDs were much easier to duplicate than vinyl. They saw the Internet as an even greater threat, and appealed to government and the courts to help them prevent services like CompuServe from facilitating song downloads.

I wasn't interested in getting into debates with music industry types. I was there to wander the exhibition booths and make contacts in the tech world. Every booth seemed to offer a new tool or service, with intriguing artistic implications. For several years I'd had a close relationship with a couple of companies that made my favored music software, Opcode and Digidesign. I often sat down with their salesmen to discuss their newest products; sometimes this led to invitations to visit their headquarters and meet the software designers themselves. When I showed them my own projects, they were amazed and surprised that I was using their tools in ways they'd never envisioned. I recall a lunchtime session at Opcode's offices in Menlo Park shortly after the company released its first version of Studio Vision, a MIDI sequencer with a feature that allowed you to add actual digital recordings to the synthesized notes. I showed them the wave forms of a few bars of a drum groove, played in real time by my drummer Dave Owens. I selected a single four-beat bar of the groove, chopped it up, copied it, and pasted it over sixty-four bars to make up a whole song. Then I started jamming over the top of the loop. They were impressed; they'd never seen this method in practice before. But I pointed out that it was a bit laborious. Why not add a command called "Repeat Paste" with a field to enter the number of bars?

On another occasion I showed Digidesign how I was using its Pro Tools workstation, which had a feature that allowed you to change the pitch of a passage of audio. I'd been recording some songs with a vocalist called Dr. Fiorella Terenzi, a noted Italian astrophysicist with blond pinup looks and a geeky cult music following. Her accent was delightful but her singing voice was, by her own admission, not very in-tune, so I had to carefully splice her vocal takes into individual chunks and retune each syllable via a numerical value. Though the end result was musically more palatable, the artifacts made it sound a little unnatural. We chose to make this robotic effect a feature of the song (it later became known as the Cher Effect), but I told Digidesign that if they could automate the retuning process and give me finer control over the tone and inflections to make the vocal sound more natural, they could have a revolutionary product on their hands.

Far be it for me to take the credit for the invention of Auto-Tune (a dubious honor, I think). Conversations like these were going on in the workshops of many software companies at the same time, and with several other professional musicians. I didn't really care who came out with a product first or whose name went on the resulting patent applications. The excitement, for me, was that technological innovation was happening at a rapid speed within my own area of expertise, and that I was in a position to influence the direction it took by creating early musical examples of what might be possible.

So I began saying yes to projects that put my new techniques to the test. In 1992–93 I wrote soundtracks for several computer games, such as *Double Switch* for Sega and *Cyberia* for PC. I worked on an early multimedia CD-ROM product called *The Dark Eye*, based on the works of Edgar Allan

Poe. I recorded an entire soundtrack album for a computer-generated animation compilation called *Gate to the Mind's Eye*. The new buzz in Hollywood was around celebrity-backed theme restaurants and motion platform rides. As my reputation in the interactive sector grew, I was asked to create the soundtrack for a live-action sequence at the Dive, an elaborate submarine-themed burger joint in Beverly Hills that was co-owned by Steven Spielberg, and to compose music for a trio of immersive motion platform rides at the Universal Studios Tour.

Two things became very apparent. First, there was plenty of work available in these emerging areas, enough for me to form a small group of composers and sound designers in order to tackle multiple projects at the same time. Second, the music software tools available to me were woefully inadequate for the task. They were designed to create *linear* music, in other words music that has a set beginning, middle, and end. Yet the projects I was now composing for were *nonlinear* experiences. Their whole appeal was that the user could help determine the outcome, either making choices in branching story lines or by entering a fully immersive real-time world, as in shoot-'em-up games like *Wolfenstein* and *Doom*. How could a composer provide a single musical score when the experience could turn out so many different ways?

This problem was fascinating to me, to the extent that I became obsessed by it. I began to tinker with ideas about how to solve the puzzle using computer software. I was exploring uncharted territory, and I felt again the thrill of being a maverick, a pioneer. I was Booker T. Boffin all over again.

The idea of going back to the conventional music-industry cycle of album, tour, album, seemed dull and uninspiring. I wanted nothing to do with Giant Records or any other label. Nor was I interested in producing other bands. When Keith Armstrong called with a proposal for a new Prefab Sprout project based on Paddy's latest cycle of demos—this time, a rock musical based on the story of Zorro—I refused to even get into a discussion about it. In fact, I was terrified to even listen to the demos, because I knew there would be at least one song on the tape that I'd be powerless to resist.

Back in the UK, Andy Ferguson, quite understandably, was losing patience with my lack of cooperation. Over the years he had worked hard to get me the best possible deals with labels and music publishers; he constantly urged me to stay focused, and I constantly disregarded his advice. He couldn't understand my new obsession with nonlinear entertainment, and his frustrations were becoming evident. We met and talked it through, and decided that Andy would continue to manage my business affairs in the UK, while Mary Coller took over as my manager for the USA and the rest of the world. This was a big career move for her, but she must have wondered what she'd gotten herself into.

One morning I marched into Mary's office and asked her to make me up a thousand business cards with my name and number and the words HEADSPACE INC. When she looked at me blankly, I explained that this was going to be our new company. It didn't really matter that we weren't actually incorporated or that we had no employees yet. That would come later. I was traveling back and forth to Silicon Valley every couple of weeks for meetings, attending many tech conferences, and each time I came home with a pocketful of business cards. Business cards were like a rash in those days before cell phones. I needed to be able to flash my own. Mary duly headed on down to Kinko's, and that very afternoon I boarded a plane for San Francisco as the CEO of my own company, Headspace Inc.

My destination was Francis Coppola's winery in Napa Valley. Coppola had invited a select group of twenty-five or thirty guests to spend a weekend at his ranch discussing the implications of nonlinear entertainment. It was a fascinating premise. So much of the filmmaker's art was based on classical story structure dating back to the Greeks, Shakespeare, and Japanese narrative aesthetics. If structure and story line could now be jumbled—or if the audience itself could determine the outcome of a plot—how would filmmakers be forced to adapt?

In a barn behind the main house, Coppola's eclectic guests discussed their forays into interactive art and debated its meaning. Francis excused himself quite early on to attend to dinner. He loves to cook, and he had a true feast in store for us. We were summoned back to the splendid Victorian farmhouse, where tables had been set out around the veranda. As the September sun went down behind the avenues of vines, vast pots of pasta were brought out and topped with Francis's secret sauce. We ate and laughed, and sampled the winery's finest cabernets and pinot noirs. Francis produced a small vial of balm to fend off mosquitoes. He said he'd discovered and learned to swear by it while filming *Apocalypse Now* in the Philippines. He moved among his guests like some sort of cinematic high priest, anointing each of us with a dab between the eyebrows.

After dinner we retired to the screening room, where Coppola had arranged a screening of one of his favorite films, Antonioni's *Blow-Up*, but with the reels in random order. Truth be told, it didn't make a very good advertisement for nonlinear storytelling.

One of the guests was a venture capitalist called Tom Byers, the first of his breed I had met. As we talked I explained my ideas about digital music and the reasons I'd formed my own company. I handed him my business card, inscribed with the name HEADSPACE INC. He looked at it thoughtfully.

"Do you mind me asking, what's your business model?" he said.

I stared at him. "What's a business model?" I said.

Byers roared with laughter, taking this for a Silicon Valley in-joke. He didn't know I wasn't joking.

Film music composers have to learn many skills and tricks. When you're writing the soundtrack for a film, it's not enough to just compose a great piece of music. Its form and function are more important than its intrinsic quality. You might be required to establish the geographical location via the style and instrumentation, or evoke a particular era in history. Perhaps you'll set the mood—mysterious, triumphant, sexy. Even after you've submitted the piece, the director may change his mind and ask you to rewrite it to create more empathy for a given character or to provide subtext, such as the presence of a lurking danger. The editor might send you a new cut with the sequence of shots unexpectedly changed around; or the studio might decide a certain musical style appeals to the wrong audience demographic. You need to be ready to cope with some or all of these requests, and often you'll have half an hour to make the changes while the orchestra is on its lunch break.

In a computer game, the musical changes have to happen *instantaneously*—in real time, without unpleasant glitches or overlaps or gaps. So as a game music composer, how do I allow for multiple variations in the user experience, when I won't be there to tweak the score? How do I inject the skills and tricks I've learned from years of trial and error into the brain of the game itself?

The games industry at the time was unaware that this was a problem, and programmers were perfectly happy for games to have low-quality audio with clunky transitions between cues. It gave me an earache to play most computer games, yet I was convinced if they could be made to sound better, it would dramatically improve the user experience.

What I needed was some software of my own. I dreamed of a music engine that could receive messages from the player's interactions with the game and translate them into changes to the music. For example, in a chase sequence I could gradually increase the tempo of the score, using certain milestones in the game play to modulate the key. When the player solved a clue or picked up a trophy, it would trigger a musical flourish and introduce a new instrument into the arrangement. In a branching story line, the tempo and arrangement of the incoming piece would be matched to the outgoing, to create a smooth transition.

The communication language of electronic music is MIDI, and the most powerful programming environment for MIDI was called Max. I looked for a Max programmer that could interpret my ideas and build my dream music engine, and my inquiries led me to a guy called Steve Ellison. Over a period of weeks in 1993, we sat together in his backyard shed in Pasadena and mapped out the software. Once the planning was done, it took Steve only a few days to build me a prototype. I went to work on it, using my MIDI drum pads to simulate random commands coming in from the game, and we swapped iterations back and forth. We decided to name our technology the Audio Virtual Reality Engine, or AVRe for short.

As a way to demo the AVRe software, I came up with a typical adventure game scenario. The visuals would be simple, consisting of a sort of pictorial storyboard with different branches. Once loaded up on my state-of-the-art

Macintosh Color Classic, you could click your way around it with the mouse. You enter a mystical cave, where you sound a gong, summoning a wise old hermit. He speaks to you in riddles, and you have to decide which tunnel to take. One tunnel leads to a pile of glistening treasure guarded by a serpent, while the other leads to a deadly trapdoor and an agonizing death. As you move through the cave, the musical score precisely matches your choices. AVRe takes its tempo from your progress, and each prize or threat you encounter alters the music in a perceptible way.

The demo was fun and compelling, and it was time to get some feedback. I dug out Tom Byers's business card and called him in Menlo Park at the offices of Kleiner Perkins Caufield & Byers, a prominent venture capital company. I described my demo and said I wanted somewhere to show it off. Tom put me in touch with a man named Richard Saul Wurman, who ran the annual TED conference in Monterey, California. If I could persuade Wurman to let me speak at TED, it would be a good way to get a measure of how compelling my invention really was.

TED was in its fourth year, and still a well-kept secret. It was a cliquey four-day retreat that attracted a few hundred Silicon Valley technologists, entrepreneurs, and futurists, who paid several thousand dollars apiece to attend. Wurman ran it like a talk-show host, watching each talk from his armchair on the stage, sometimes bumbling across the stage to shoo away a speaker he didn't like. The event had a velvet-rope approach to admissions: even if you could afford the four-figure registration fee, you had to know somebody to get yourself invited; and Wurman might just as easily uninvite you without warning, editing the printed program without first contacting the speakers. His event had a mystique about it, like an exclusive nightclub. So I was delighted, though a little apprehensive, to be confirmed as a TED speaker and given twelve minutes to show off my demo.

I took a fifty-minute flight from Burbank up to Monterey in a puddle-jumper turbojet. As there was not enough overhead storage space for my Mac Color Classic, I had to purchase a second ticket and strap the computer into the seat beside me. The flight attendant brought me a glass of chardonnay. "How about something for your little friend?" she asked furtively.

The TED conference turned out to be a lot of fun, for those that could afford it. Being one of the speakers, my ticket was a comp. I stuck around for the whole four days of the conference. We got to drive the latest BMW concept cars around a racetrack, and sipped cocktails after hours at the Monterey Aquarium. The range of speakers impressed me, though there were some obvious duds. A few just showed their corporate PowerPoints and trotted out the company jargon, but this was frowned on. The best speakers quoted one another, building on ideas, so that a discernible flow emerged over the course of the four days. Spontaneity was applauded. One speaker got up onstage and tore his notes to shreds, saying they were nothing but corporate claptrap; instead he wanted to use his time to introduce us to his ninety-year-old grandmother, who had survived Auschwitz, and he ran down the steps and pulled her out of the audience. Another speaker, a famous brain surgeon, began telling us about the history of electroconvulsive therapy as a treatment for severe depression; a few minutes in, he broke down in near-tears and confessed that he himself had been an ECT patient, and his colleagues had covered up for him for several years.

When my turn came, Wurman introduced me as the "former MTV star turned CEO of Headspace Inc." I took to the stage and found to my horror that my Macintosh was not even plugged in. I fumbled for the power button. "Get a PC!" shouted a heckler to a chorus of titters, as I scrambled to boot it and load my software. But from there on my demo went like a dream. The AVRe beta software behaved itself, and there were audible "oohs" and "aahs" as I clicked my way through the cave scenario, with the sampled orchestral score sounding massive on the theater's PA system.

Afterwards I stood in the foyer with the Mac under my arm. A circle of men in suits formed around me, eyeing my Mac covetously. Two or three thrust their business cards into my hand and said they wanted to talk about funding my company. I felt, for the first time, the power and influence that come with the possession of new technology.

With several meetings set up in my calendar, I headed back to L.A. There were other TEDsters on the flight. Like me, they were splitting their time between the Hollywood entertainment industry and the software universe of Silicon Valley. We joked that they ought to build a bullet train between the two.

One of my meetings was with Kevin Teixeira at Intel Corporation. It puzzled me that Intel, maker of microchips, might be remotely interested in my application. Teixeira explained that his company was always looking for new ways to push real-time computation to its limits. Intel had a problem: Moore's Law, which states that processor speeds double every eighteen months, was proving to be correct. But this made it harder for computer companies to justify the need for a consumer to buy the latest machine just to make spreadsheets and edit Word documents. So Intel had a fund set up to help start-up companies with interesting applications that required lots of processing power.

Intel had struck a deal with the Guggenheim Museum in New York City to present an exhibition that fall of some exciting new technologies. Kevin Teixeira said Intel was prepared to give me a grant to develop an artistic installation at the Guggenheim featuring my AVRe software; and he asked if I was at all interested in virtual reality. Perhaps there was a way to combine my sonic approach with some real-time 3-D graphics. He introduced me to a mad VR programmer by the name of Eric Gullickson, who lived on a half-sunken coal barge in a Sausalito marina, surrounded by the rusting hulks of mainframe computers. We took Intel's money and spent the next seven weeks getting down to work.

In the 1990s, everybody was very excited by the prospect of virtual reality. It was an easy concept to grasp—you'd just "jack in" and you'd find yourself in an alternative universe that seemed totally real, like *The Matrix*. However, most people's actual experience of VR fell far short of the promise. The hardware was clunky and cumbersome, and the head-mounted graphics at the time (often running on IBM 286 machines at 20 megahertz or less) were jerky and low-res, running at a few frames a second. One user described the experience thus: "It's a quick way to make yourself seasick with someone's old sneaker stuck to your face."

My feeling was that there was no excuse for the audio to be bad, too. (As George Lucas knew well, high-quality audio really helps sell a substandard picture. Try watching a space battle from the original *Star Wars* with the sound muted!) So my concept for the Guggenheim exhibit was *The Virtual String Quartet*, and it was all about the music. It owed quite a lot to my experience on the *Gothic* sound-scoring stage many years before. Donning a head-mounted display, you walked freely in the midst of four computer-generated musicians playing Mozart's String Quartet no. 18 in A Major. As you moved around the nine-by-nine-foot space, the sound was "convolved" around you in quadraphonic sound. You were creating your own mix of the quartet in real time. If you put your ear really close to the cellist, you could hear the rosin on her bow. Or, if you were feeling naughty, you could tickle her, using the trigger on your joystick, and she would start to play variations in another random musical style—Appalachian bluegrass, maybe—while the other three musicians stuck with the Mozart.

For the first few days of October 1993 the Guggenheim exhibit had lines around the block, such was the allure of VR. Unfortunately, the crowds dwindled as word of mouth spread that the graphics were nothing to write home about. But most agreed that my audio at least made the experience tolerable!

I was standing there helping people on and off with the headset when a familiar face stepped forward out of the crowd. It was my old friend Andy Partridge, the genius behind XTC, who was on a rare visit to New York, where he was courting the lovely Erica Wexler. I gave Andy and Erica a quick demo of my VR experience. It was plain Andy was not too impressed.

"Tom, this is all very well, but . . . why don't you just unplug, get with some real musicians, write some great songs, and start making music again? We miss you. Millions of music fans out there miss you."

I laughed his question off with some flippant remark about how VR was the future. But if I had answered sincerely, I would have said this:

"Andy, I can't make music right now because of the pain. The pain of Terry Jackson's death; the pain of the commercial failure of the music I am most proud of; and my revulsion at the state of the record industry, which is rotten to its fucking core."

CHAPTER 10

HOUSEQUAKE

As if it weren't already written in the tea leaves that Kathleen and I had to get the hell out of Los Angeles, the events of January 1994 made up our minds for us.

Hello! magazine, the glossy British celebrity periodical, had published a story about us and our family home, shortly after the birth of our second child, Talia. They sent a professional photographer who was very adept at setting up a shot to maximize the opulence of the subjects. Our Hollywood Hills house was highly photogenic, with its lovely 1920s Spanish-style architectural details, and we'd taken a slightly tongue-in-cheek approach to our decorating, creating the atmosphere of a Hollywood brothel from the Clark Gable era. The photographer's assistant brought in armloads of flowers, and each photo was crammed full of blooms and overstuffed cushions, red velvet drapes and crystal. We were posed with happy babies bouncing on our knees, the ideal nuclear showbiz family.

The article focused on my chart hits and Kathleen's movie and TV credits, and the impressive list of our friends and collaborators. The overall effect was one of runaway success and wealth, and it surprised even us. While it was a pleasant change to have a magazine article build you up instead of kicking you in the ribs, *Hello!* went a little too far in the other direction—it made us look like royalty. When the magazine came out in the UK, we received a couple of over-friendly letters from relatives I hadn't heard from in years, and I got the distinct impression that some of our close friends wondered if we were now out of their social league.

What the photos didn't show, of course, was the close proximity of our house to the 101 freeway, which roared and rumbled all day and all night, shaking the foundations of Whitley Heights and coating the old stucco in soot.

At 4:30 a.m. on January 17, we woke to a deafening crash. At first I thought an eighteen-wheeler had actually smashed off the freeway and into our house, but the shaking and rattling just continued, growing in intensity. "It's an earthquake!" I screamed to Kathleen, and we sprung out of bed to grab the two kids and get them into a doorway. Lily, nearly three, looked bleary and bewildered; she asked me if a giant was outside shaking the house. Talia was barely a year old and her eyes were wide as saucers. The concert grand piano jolted off its coasters, denting the floor, and rolled sideways about a meter. Plates and glasses flew off the shelves. All the car alarms went off in the neighborhood. It was a 6.7 on the Richter scale, with its epicenter just a couple of miles north of us, in Reseda. The aftershocks lasted a month, and you could hear each one come rolling towards you across the city. We were more fortunate than most: the death toll was fifty-seven and more than five thousand people were injured.

It was several months before we realized our house had major structural problems. The office extension had pulled away from the main house, and we could see a thin strip of daylight along the ceiling where it joined my studio. It turned out that the terraced garden at the rear of the house had become unstable and was slipping down the hill. Underneath it was a confluence where the two sewers from our neighbors' houses joined our own, and this had cracked, its contents gradually saturating the soil.

"Bad news," our builder said. "This is a pretty major project. It's going to cost you around $240,000 to fix."

Ramps were built down our steps and bulldozers and excavators moved into the yard. The hot tub was removed and a couple of trees had to be replanted. The work started in earnest, but there were multiple delays. The workmen started coming fewer and fewer days of the week. Finally the work ground to a complete halt, leaving the front wall knocked down, scaffolding supporting one corner of the house, and dust everywhere. The construction equipment had caused further damage to the retaining wall, and our neighbor down the hill threatened a lawsuit because she was worried our terrace would collapse on her property.

Then it transpired that both the construction company and our insurers were under criminal investigation for fraud. The money for the repairs had gone AWOL, and so had our contacts. We sought legal advice but were told that we had no clear recourse against either company, due to the liability limitations in their contracts.

Our property looked like a bomb site. Kathleen, our two small children, and I were sleeping and eating in two upstairs rooms. My dwindling royalty payments and irregular income from new projects were nowhere near enough to cover the repairs ourselves. We were rapidly heading into bankruptcy.

It was then that Kathleen discovered she was pregnant with our third child. "There's no way!" I said. "Not unless we get the hell out of L.A. and find somewhere cheaper and safer to live."

"Well, make it happen!" she replied.

We made the decision to do a quick sale of the house despite its condition, in order to pay off what we owed on the mortgage. There were a couple of offers, but they were for less than what we owed. The next month we defaulted on our loan and the house went into receivership.

We felt like vandals, leaving a lovely house like that in a state of ruin. But every cloud has a silver lining. I managed to get us the hell out of L.A., and later that year, in the bathroom of a small rented condo in Northern California, Kathleen gave birth to our son, Graham, and I caught him on the way out. He grew up to be a fabulous young man and an excellent drummer, and I wouldn't trade him for all the bulldozers in Burbank.

In our final years in L.A. I had become an avid windsurfer. I found it the perfect escape from my career woes and the pressures of parenthood. Kathleen used to encourage me. "Go recharge your batteries!" she would say. "You're too stressed out." I had a car full of boards and sails, and I would head down to the beach at San Pedro or out to the county line north of Malibu and spend whole afternoons hopping waves and bombing back and forth over the deep waters of the Pacific. I got friendly with another windsurfing enthusiast named Paul Sebastien. Like me, he was an electronic music nut, with a keen interest in music software and multimedia authoring. We seemed to have a natural affinity. Sitting on the beach one day we found we shared a dream: to move to the San Francisco Bay Area, close to the hub of Silicon Valley excitement and some of the best windsurfing on the planet.

"What we need," Paul said, "is to find a rich guy to pay us to make software in the morning, then spend our afternoons shredding the bay!" I couldn't agree more.

There's a lot to be said for the power of positive visualization. Within three months I managed to secure a grant from an organization called Interval Research in Palo Alto, owned by Paul Allen, cofounder of Microsoft and one of the richest men in America. The grant enabled my company, Headspace Inc., to put together a team of music and software experts to investigate ways of sending music and sound over the Internet.

At Interval's offices near the Stanford University campus, Paul Allen was assembling an illustrious group of technologists, academics, and business entrepreneurs in an effort to create a variant of Xerox's Palo Alto Research Center (PARC). This was the legendary research organization where many of the key elements of modern computing had been invented, including the laser printer, the mouse, and the desk-based graphical user interface that was adopted by Jobs and Wozniak for the first Macintosh. In every nook and cranny of the building there were strange experiments going on. There seemed to be no formal hierarchy among the hundred or so employees. Everyone reported to the venerable David Liddle—Xerox PARC alumnus, Stanford computer science professor, and one of the inventors of Ethernet.

It was late 1993, and Silicon Valley's reputation and mystique were still in their infancy. It was not yet cool to be a geek, despite the best efforts of cult magazines like *Mondo 2000* and *Wired*. Only a few years previously, the pastures of Palo Alto, Atherton, Woodside, and Mountain View were filled with orange groves. By the early nineties, the orderly rows of fruit trees had been replaced with gleaming industrial parks, home to the giant tech corporations. In spanking-new housing zones, reclaimed from the mud of the San Francisco Bay, entrepreneurial computer geeks planted seeds of their own, working through the night in rented garages or one-story maisonettes.

While Silicon Valley was full of rising tech companies, the rest of the country still viewed technology in terms of IBM and Microsoft. Both companies were located outside California, though their presence was strongly felt from San Francisco to San Jose. Intel's giant chip plants were close by, as were Oracle and Sun and Silicon Graphics; Apple was only a marginal player. Yet among the digerati and creative types like me, the Apple Macintosh was the only computer to be seen with. I loved my Mac, and it was constantly with me as I moved through my day. The notion of using a computer outside the office, let alone for anything artistic, was still very novel. One afternoon I was sitting in a small café with my headphones on, clattering away on the keyboard of my first PowerBook laptop. A little old lady came over to me, smiling, to ask me what I was doing. I was about to say I was calibrating some of the MIDI parameters on the latest rev of my Max patch, when I realized her question was more innocent than that. "It's a *computer*," I said, gently. "A *computer*? Really? How fascinating!" she exclaimed.

Apple geeks were even a curiosity among other breeds of geek. We would sniff around each other like dogs. I remember buying a highly rated novel by Douglas Coupland called *Microserfs*. In his story, a group of nerdy Microsoft employees make a pilgrimage to Palo Alto to glimpse the offices of Xerox PARC. After dark they make a detour through the parking lot at Interval Research and peer in through the windows. As I read this passage I was half expecting to turn a page and read ". . . and there, sitting at a desk programming interactive music software on his Mac, was the lonely figure of Thomas Dolby." It would still be many years before geeks became cool. To most, we were just sad human beings who spent far too long locked away in our cubicles, eating what Coupland referred to as "flat food"—pizza or chocolate or anything flat enough to be slipped under the cubicle door by concerned friends.

Yet there was an excitement that gripped us and bound us together, those early Internet geeks. I myself was caught up in it, hook, line, and sinker. The music business, after all, hadn't really evolved much in decades. The Internet had the potential to create a total sea change in our culture, a turning point in the history of our species. I really felt that way, even in 1994. Despite my success in the music business, and ultimate frustration with it, I knew I was now embarking on an adventure with far grander horizons.

And humble beginnings. With the Interval project in full swing, I moved Headspace's business address up to a small office on Third Avenue in unglamorous San Mateo. It was me, Paul Sebastien, and Mary Coller, who still commuted from L.A. We chose San Mateo because it was midway between San Francisco and the business parks where the top tech companies located their HQs, yet it felt like a real town, with a mixed commercial center to wander around and plenty of shops and restaurants. The space we selected was upstairs from a basement club of some sort. In the middle of the morning on our second day in the building, I saw that the club's door was open and decided to go down and introduce myself to our new neighbors. As I reached the bottom of the staircase I had to squint to adjust my eyes to the dim light. There was a long bar, a dance floor, and a small stage. The room was completely deserted aside from two lone figures on the stage. A large African American man was sitting on a wooden chair, immobile. Dancing around him provocatively was a middle-aged Hispanic stripper covered in tattoos. They didn't seem to notice my presence. After a minute or two I turned to leave. Was this an audition? I wondered. Perhaps he was the first customer of the day? Or the last customer of the night, who just refused to leave?

If I was slightly concerned that having our offices located upstairs from such an establishment would be bad for business, I needn't have worried. Over the next few years Headspace Inc. became known among Silicon Valley venture capitalists and the tech community as "the Internet start-up above the titty bar," which did nothing to harm our ability to attract investors to our offices.

What did more damage was the fact that we all used Macs. One potential angel investor took me aside after he'd brought some of his rich friends by for a meeting. "Thomas," he said, "you've got to get some of these Macintoshes off the desktops. When investors see Macs they think you're a bunch of hippies and dreamers. Get some proper Windows PCs!"

Our research contract stated that Interval would fund our project for a period of six months, with an option to renew. We were paid a fee of $30,000 per month. This was nonreturnable, rather than an investment or stock purchase. Ours was one of many projects Paul Allen was underwriting under the Interval umbrella, mainly in the area of consumer entertainment on computers. "Let a thousand flowers bloom," David Liddle said. "Some may wither and die; a few will thrive and cross-pollinate."

Our brief at Headspace was to find ways to send music and sound over the Internet in real time. Another Interval group was investigating video games targeted at girls and women; yet another was working with haptic feedback, trying to get keyboards and mice to vibrate in response to a user's input. There were strange tests and hush-hush experiments going on all over the peninsula, with the results being brought back to Palo Alto and scrutinized by panels of academics. Paul Allen's venture capital firm, Vulcan Ventures, was waiting in the wings to pounce on anything that showed real commercial promise and spin off commercial start-up companies.

I was now rubbing shoulders with a group of distinguished technologists, academics, engineers, writers, and filmmakers. Exciting though it was to be a part of it, I was a little wary of the work Headspace was doing becoming the property of Paul Allen. I'd seen how EMI Records had ended up owning all my recordings in perpetuity, and I wasn't about to let the same thing happen with my software inventions. So I made extensive notes about AVRe and applications Headspace planned to develop from the technology, and made sure they were attached to the agreement and excluded from my work for Interval. I filed and dated detailed descriptions of our "prior art" and made a set of password-protected floppy disks containing the source code.

As it turned out, this was a smart move. As the six-month period drew to a close, it became apparent to me that Interval was primarily a rich man's playground. Between the enormous amounts of cash it took to set up and the tremendous monthly payroll required for the star-studded research team, it must have added up to a great tax write-off for the Microsoft cofounder. When I met Paul Allen to show him a demo of our work in progress, he seemed uninterested. He preferred to talk about the professional recording studio he was installing in Interval's basement. Allen was a big rock music fan and was stoked to tell us how he'd recently purchased the guitar Jimi Hendrix played at Woodstock. He founded a pop culture museum in a Frank Gehry–designed building in his native Seattle, where he also owned the Seahawks football team and, later, a soccer stadium. Though he was a modest man, he loved to swan around with music and showbiz celebrities, throwing lavish parties for them on his megayacht, which also housed a helicopter, a submarine, and another recording studio.

A tiny proportion of the projects developed at Interval Research were ever actually spun off into commercial enterprises. Of those, most (such as games company ePlanet) went belly-up within the first few years. What Interval seemed more concerned with was accruing U.S. patents. We generated stacks of them. My name was on several, as our group came under increasing pressure to quantify and validate our work. Many years later, in 2010, long after Interval had ceased doing business, Paul Allen's lawyers filed a massive lawsuit claiming infringements of Interval's patents by Apple, Google, Yahoo, AOL, Facebook, Netflix, and eBay—almost every major American technology company, in fact, except Microsoft.

So, in the end, Interval was the polar opposite of its progenitor and inspiration, Xerox PARC. Whereas PARC gave birth to wondrous technical innovations that became the cornerstones of modern computing, yet failed to protect them under the law, Interval Research created nothing of real value but filed 130 U.S. patents with which it now intends to hold the rest of the computer industry for ransom.

I was blissfully unaware of this at the time. All I cared about was that Paul Allen had made my wish come true: he was paying me and my team to fool around with music software in the morning, then go windsurfing in the afternoon. When the wind picked up, Paul Sebastien and I would pack our cars and head to Candlestick Park or Crissy Field to blast back and forth across the choppy whitecaps of the bay. In the mornings and late evenings we succeeded, in a limited way, in making musical "jamming" work over the Internet. The first song we used as a demo was Bob Marley's "Jammin'." We designed simple interfaces that would allow musicians in multiple locations to interact in real time using just a QWERTY keyboard and mouse. While the inherent latency and variance of the network made it hard for the players to respond to each other the way they would have in the same room or a recording studio, it was relatively straightforward to trigger "meta" tasks such as setting the tempo or key and swapping out instruments. It was also possible to send musical "gestures" such as a drum roll, a strum on a guitar, or a predetermined riff or lick.

The unexpected advantage of this gestural interaction was that even nonmusicians could get instant gratification from the app. It was rather like hitting the "auto-accompaniment" button on a home organ, or pressing chord buttons while strumming on an autoharp. While typical computer users might have lacked the dexterity and years of practice required to master a real musical instrument, they did possess highly developed computer skills derived from typing, navigation, and game play. Our goal was to translate these everyday skills into musical enjoyment and socialization via the Web.

Some of our experimental interfaces were very elegant in themselves. One involved a sort of 2-D graphical representation of an imaginary solar system. In a menu bar down the side of the screen was a column of small, multicolored planets. The user could drag these onto the screen and send them into orbit around a central star with a powerful gravitational field. Each planet played a different musical drone; as the planet came into focus at the peak of the orbit, the volume of its note would swell. The harmony between the notes was predetermined, so the result was always pleasing. The effect reminded me a little of the intro to the Foreigner song "Waiting for a Girl Like You" that I had created a decade earlier. But now I was on the verge of sharing the same kind of musical satisfaction with millions of nonmusicians via the Internet. My team was invited to London to the Royal College of Art to demo our application in front of a number of European luminaries, including Peter Gabriel, legendary producer Alan Parsons, and computer graphics guru Kai Krause.

Though the simple apps we created were compelling and beautiful, it was hard to make a business case for a commercial product line. Computer software was viewed as something you bought for productivity at work. Video games were becoming big business, but they were mostly shoot-'em-ups or race-car simulations. Vulcan Ventures didn't see a bright future for music on computers.

At first it came as a bit of a kick in the teeth when David Liddle's lackeys told me Interval would not be renewing its relationship with Headspace Inc. after the six-month grant had expired. However, it didn't take long for me to realize this was a blessing in disguise. The contract had enabled me to relocate my fledgling company and my family to Silicon Valley, and assemble a small team of excellent programmers and musicians in a cool San Mateo office, with a core technology under our belts. We were debt free, we owned our own technology, and our star was rising fast.

By early 1994, the atmosphere in Silicon Valley was changing at an astonishing rate, driven by consumer adoption of the Internet. Hordes of people were logging on for the first time via CompuServe or AOL, which provided basic applications like e-mail, community forums, and file browsing. Their subscriber lists were doubling every quarter, but as consumers became more savvy, they tended to migrate away from these paid "on-ramp" services towards more open-ended Internet use, made possible by a new phenomenon called the World Wide Web. This mass migration set alarm bells ringing in the investment community and among entrepreneurs who, in the grand American tradition, rushed to build homesteads on the new frontier.

Wall Street understands companies and economics, but it has never understood technology. The bankers and analysts assume that technology will "just work." Silicon Valley venture capitalists have a better handle on it; more than anything, VCs are impressed by sheer statistics of consumer adoption. It's less a case of "If we build it, they will come," more a case of "When they come, we need to find something to sell them!" Nobody had a clear idea of how to make money from an activity that was essentially free. Yet this was more than a passing fad. Among the hundreds of struggling start-ups, there would surely be a handful of gems that would grow into the next IBM or Microsoft.

In 1994, investment started to pour into small Internet start-ups from San Francisco to San Jose. If you were an eager young entrepreneur with a germ of an idea, you could take several meetings in a week with angel investors and VCs. Anyone who could sketch out a plan for world domination on the back of a paper napkin was a strong contender for an infusion of cash. A hundred and fifty years after the first hungry speculators poured into the Bay Area, the new Gold Rush had begun.

I'd fled one earthquake in Los Angeles and stumbled into the epicenter of another.

CHAPTER 11
THE UNTOUCHABLES

Headspace's technology and demos excited investors, who clamored to come to San Mateo and check out my little start-up for themselves. It didn't seem to matter to them that I was not a businessman. They would offer their own ideas of how my company could make money, and I would say, "What a great idea—why didn't I think of that?"

I was focused on making our demos as sexy as possible. By now we had some pretty compelling visuals and music. Paul Sebastien was a dab hand at 3-D graphics, and between the two of us we came up with a new environment that would show off the capabilities of AVRe to the full. It was called Offworld, a name we nicked from the sci-fi cult movie *Blade Runner*. A computer user could wander at will around a Cartesian space, turning left and right among lakes and pyramids, climbing to the peaks of hills and strolling along lush streams. Hidden among these fantastical landscapes and vistas were what we called Glyphs, a type of musical instrument that you could approach and play, using your keyboard and mouse. There was a marble birdbath with carvings that triggered exotic percussion loops; a wood flute you could play by hovering your cursor over the blow holes; and a harp you could strum while holding down a key on your QWERTY to create chord sequences. In the distance you could see other Glyphs that were being played by multiple users in different locations. Your music would be layered and blended by the AVRe engine. It was a sort of music with training wheels: a way for millions of nonmusicians to feel the satisfaction of jamming together using skills they already possessed. Nothing like this had been attempted before in a commercial product.

Out of the blue, I got a long e-mail from someone named Chris van Rensburg. Skipping the niceties, he launched into a long rant about the communicator devices on *Star Trek: The Next Generation*. Minutes later he followed it up with a phone call. "Do I know you?" I asked. "No," he said, "but you really should. I'm a programmer. In fact, I'm probably the *only* programmer you'll ever need. Unless of course you're not serious about Cartesian physics and nonlinear storytelling."

We hired him on the spot, and he became known as ChrisVR.

I loved the work we were doing. Every day brought about a new 3-D rendering, a new part of Offworld to explore, a new mythical musical instrument to jam with. It was way ahead of its time, long before multiuser environments like Second Life, let alone the plethora of ninety-nine-cent musical apps that appeared in the iPhone era. Everyone who tried out our demos fell in love with them. But I had absolutely no idea how to write a business plan around what we'd created. The money we'd saved from the Interval project would not last forever. I needed a new source of funds, and it was becoming critical for me to get out and sell myself to the investment community. So I started to use my fame from the rock music world—such as it was—to set up interviews with the media, hype my new company, and get myself invited to speak at the technology conferences that were springing up all over San Francisco, L.A., and the East Coast.

One such conference took place in late 1994 in Washington, D.C. It was the beginning of the most remarkable month of my life, and a pivotal moment for the modern world and the century we now live in. When I reread the journals I kept in that period, I still find it hard to believe that I had a ringside seat at the moment the rules of engagement were laid down. At the time, my observations were laughably naïve. And the irony is, they were mostly jotted on my Apple Newton—a clunky handheld brick of a device that Apple has conveniently written out of its history books. But studying my scrawled Newton notes brings it all back in vivid detail:

It's the early evening of September 17, 1994. Outside an ivy-covered building in the heart of the Georgetown district in Washington, D.C., five black limousines pull to a halt. Al fresco diners in the cobblestone street watch as the drivers open the rear doors in perfect sync, and out step their VIP passengers. Around twenty serious-looking middle-aged guys, dressed for dinner in black suits, white shirts, and ties—and me.

A motorcade is not an unusual sight in this town, but these are not politicians or diplomats. They are a group of the most powerful individuals in international media, technology, and telecommunications. The chairman of Deutsch Telecom is here, as are chief executives from AOL, Adobe, and Vodafone. Cable tycoon Barry Diller. A pair of Kleiner Perkins venture capitalists. A representative of the newly launched CNN.com. Jim Clark, founder of Netscape, and several of Silicon Valley's most promising new software entrepreneurs.

And Bill Gates, probably the fattest cat of them all. Though in real life he is a skinny little guy.

I am the odd one out. I don't own a black suit. I am wearing a lightweight khaki-colored safari outfit, a beat-up Panama hat, and round tortoiseshell specs with clip-on sunglasses. My tattered leather sandals have definitely seen better days. I am feeling mildly out of place as we file in through the double doors of the restaurant and up a staircase. A team of smiling apron-clad waiters lines the hallway leading to the quiet of a private dining room, where the last of the evening sun is filtering in through the shutters onto paneled walls of ancient oak. The rugs are Persian. There are two large round tables, beautifully laid out with silverware, flowers, and place cards. I find my name (Thomas Dolby, Headspace Inc.) and settle in right between the CTO of CompuServe and a super-smart, thirty-something technologist named Marc Porat.

I knew it was a huge deal. This was the eve of the first-ever Digital Media Convergence Conference, and the dinner was for the keynote speakers and panelists. I'm not sure how I got to be there—because I was a token showbiz type, adding color to the speaker roster? Because the organizers viewed me as a rock musician with a brain—someone they might be able to hit up for Rolling Stones tickets? Or was it to do with the fact that I had recently given that talk about my own little software experiment, the Audio Virtual Reality Engine (AVRe), at the influential TED conference?

There'd been a massive buzz leading up to the event. *Wired* called it out in an article entitled "10 Things You Need to Know About Multimedia, the Internet, and the Information Superhighway." *The Wall Street Journal* was reporting a big increase in new subscriptions for online services that offered electronic mail and user forums. People were flocking to Radio Shack to purchase modems for their personal computers. But nobody really knew what it all meant. Would these radical technologies change the way companies did business? Would they revolutionize family entertainment—meaning an end to TV, movies, and compact discs as we knew them? Or was the Internet just an overhyped fad that would evaporate faster than you could say "Sega Genesis"?

One thing was abundantly clear to my fellow diners: when the revolution came, it had to be tightly owned and controlled by corporate America.

Waiters served up the soup course as we sipped our chilled Chablis. The conversation was eager but muted. So this is Washington, I thought to myself, where big-money deals get done in hushed voices and votes are counted behind closed doors. I had to try to blend in. I turned to talk to my neighbor, Marc Porat, and he gave me his business card; the logo on it was a conjurer's top hat. He had been at Apple for many years and left to cofound an innovative software start-up called General Magic, where he'd designed a new operating system for small devices. Marc told me a handheld "personal digital assistant" such as my Newton would never succeed, because it didn't do much beyond storing phone contacts and calendar entries—like a battery-powered Filofax. So he had invented a new technology that would put your PDA to work for you, wirelessly trawling the Internet for the best deals while you went about your day. He'd already attracted over $75 million in venture capital and strategic investments.

Directly across the table from us, the CEOs of two European telecom companies were competing for Bill Gates's attention. On paper, multinational telecoms like these are actually bigger and richer than Microsoft, with stronger political ties. Yet Bill Gates's Windows operating system was running 90 percent of the computers on the planet. He would only have to alter a line of source code and the entire infrastructure behind the world's corporations would grind to a halt. There was another big difference: most of these guys had to answer to their shareholders on a quarterly basis, and to government regulators, while Gates was his own boss—a maverick, a loose cannon.

Marc Porat and I were eyeball-to-eyeball as he continued to fill me in about his company. Marc didn't notice, but across the table, Bill Gates was ignoring the sycophants to his left and right, and straining to eavesdrop on Marc's jargon-laden elevator pitch. Gates seemed to be getting more and more agitated, and was poking at his beef Wellington. As Marc explained his technology in more detail, Gates began rocking nervily back and forth in his chair.

"You'll have these intelligent agents, as I call them," said Marc quietly, "scouting and negotiating on your behalf, pulling in data from all over the Net. Eventually you won't really need a PC, because all your work will be in a sort of cloud."

Suddenly there was an explosion from across the table. "MARC, THAT'S FUCKING BULLSHIT AND YOU KNOW IT!" It was Gates.

His tie was too tight and the veins were bulging on his neck. In the wake of this high-decibel outburst, a deadly silence descended on the room. Startled faces at both tables turned our way. Even the waiters froze, silver ladles in their hands. Amid the hush that had fallen, Marc Porat visibly shriveled in his seat, looking like he wished a hole would swallow him up. Then Gates turned to the Frenchman next to him, as if to casually pick up the conversation where they left off. Gradually, the murmur of talk around the room resumed.

It was a moment of astonishing brutality. I flashed on the scene in *The Untouchables* where Al Capone, icily portrayed by Robert De Niro, struts behind a row of seated Mafia bosses at a dinner before bashing one unsuspecting mobster's brains out with a baseball bat, leaving him to hemorrhage all over the white tablecloth.

Gates's savage assault on Marc Porat came as such a shock that when I picture it now, I can't really separate it in my mind from the Capone movie.

Yet Gates was never some kind of street thug. He was just a man who believed in the utter correctness of his programming code—the inherent truth of his own version of the digital universe. It was the first time I'd seen the Gates persona up close, but it wouldn't be the last.

The next morning, the Digital Convergence show was packed to the brim. My panel went pretty well. Seated at a long table on a makeshift stage in a hotel ballroom were some highly celebrated digerati, including Nicholas Negroponte from MIT's Media Lab, 3DO game console developer Trip Hawkins, and the curiously named editor of *Mondo 2000*, R. U. Sirius. My intelligence quotient was well below the mean for this ensemble, but as a former London punk rocker who was working in a fruit-and-veg shop while the rest of these guys were getting their multiple Ph.D.s, I was able to add a spot of Pythonesque levity to the proceedings.

Bill Gates was due onstage for his lunchtime keynote right after our panel, and he was sitting in the front row. Actually, although the room was full, he was the *only* person in the front row. He was again swaying backward and forward in his seat. I speculated that perhaps this is how he assimilates new information. But he seemed to be staring right at me as he rocked, and it was a little unsettling.

There was the usual twenty-minute scrum at the steps down from the stage that follows each session at these events, where enthusiastic networkers thrust their business cards under your nose and ask for one of yours. You leave with pockets bulging. (I briefly considered keeping them all to input into my Newton on the plane back to California, but instead I chucked them guiltily into the hotel room wastebasket. No wonder the Amazon rain forest was shrinking.) Finally the ushers shooed us out of the ballroom doors so they could get the next session started. After the customary business prattle I returned to a vacant seat and listened to some of Mr. Gates's presentation. He was clicking through a PowerPoint that detailed a new product called Microsoft World Wide Web Server. This Internet on-ramp was to be preinstalled in every new copy of Windows 95, enabling users to surf the Information Superhighway at will, safe in the knowledge that the data gatherers in Redmond would be watching over them every step of the way.

From the aisle at the end of my row, somebody was trying to catch my eye. It was Jim Clark, Netscape's founder. He pointed at me and beckoned. I joined him outside in the foyer, by the coffee service. He was standing with an executive he introduced to me as Karen White from Oracle. I have always been bad at remembering business names, so I was trying to train myself to make associations with something memorable about a person's appearance. Ms. White, for example, was wearing *black* stockings and stilettos.

"I need to show you both the new Web browser we're developing," Jim said. "It's called Mosaic, and it's the future. This is how the world is going to access and share everyday information—not only with hyperlinked text, but pictures and video you can search through. And the beauty of it is, *that guy*"— he motioned to the open door of the ballroom, where Gates was mid-keynote—"can never own it."

We headed up to Jim's hotel suite and he fired up his laptop. I perched on the edge of the bed. Karen White, long bestockinged legs crossed demurely, looked on from an armchair. Jim showed me what looked like a newspaper front page come to life. There was live weather and local traffic, NASDAQ and NYSE stock tickers, sports scores and CNN news headlines. I'd never seen anything like it. I asked if there was any sound.

"Oh, no. No sound," he replied. "One of my partners thinks sound would annoy the guy in the next cubicle while he's trying to do his spreadsheets."

I was disappointed that Clark, like others in Silicon Valley, seemed to have overlooked audio as a key requirement. Yet I was encouraged that this could open up an opportunity for me and my company.

"Look, Jim, the World Wide Web really *needs* sound. Otherwise it's no more than a flashy brochure," I said. "Sound is warmth, connection, humanity."

"But sound files are huge," he retorted. "It'd take too long to load them for every Web page."

"It doesn't have to. You can break music up into tiny compressed chunks controlled by a markup language—just like JPEGs and hypertext. And I'm the *only* one that knows how to do it."

He shrugged. "Come and see us," he said. "We're down in Mountain View."

The following afternoon I was at the Delta ticket counter at Reagan airport, about to get checked in, when I heard a voice somewhere off to my right. It was Karen White. She was standing at the first-class check-in desk. I realized we must be on the same flight back to San Francisco. "Are you flying coach, honey? Hang on a mo . . ." She leaned over the counter and started talking intently at the clerk. She waved me over. I trundled my suitcase across to her counter. Karen White said, "Marylou here has sweetly offered to check you in, and she's working on getting you an upgrade to first."

Roughly thirty-four thousand feet over Indiana, Karen White and I bonded over a glass of Moët. She was smart and ambitious. She was also a single mum. I was curious as to why she was at Oracle, a rapidly expanding database company that had a reputation for burning good people out by the time they were thirty. "Larry Ellison recruited me himself over dinner," she said. "I told him I was concerned about working for Oracle and still having enough time to bring up my daughter. On the way home from dinner we drove past Woodside Middle School, where construction was nearly complete on a brand-new, state-of-the-art library. 'See that library?' he said. 'That's the *Larry Ellison* Library.' I guess that clinched it for me." And the silver-tongued Mr. Ellison, presumably, had sent her to the Washington conference as a kind of . . . talent scout? a high-tech Mata Hari? Intriguing . . .

Karen White was eager to hear what I thought of Jim Clark's Web browser, Mosaic. I told her I thought it was terrific. "He didn't seem bowled over with your idea of adding sound, did he?" she asked, probing my face. She lowered her voice. "If you're serious, I could make some introductions for you to certain of our clients who can . . . make things happen."

How could I pass up an offer like that? I drove home from SFO with an exciting new contact for my Rolodex: the number for the senior director of marketing at Coca-Cola Corporation.

At 1 a.m. on September 28, 1994, the lights were still burning at Headspace's office on Third Avenue in San Mateo. The house music from the strip club downstairs was pumping through the floor. Under headphones, I was trying to replicate a vintage Coca-Cola jingle using a small MIDI synthesizer. In other cubicles, my small team of programmers and musicians, headed by Chris van Rensburg and Paul Sebastien, was frantically working up a demo showing how sound and music might work within a typical Web page. For this purpose, we'd selected the CocaCola.com home page to "sonify." It was one of the most popular bookmarks on the World Wide Web—the kind you would show off to your envious next-door neighbor, along with HotWired.com, WhiteHouse.gov, and coolsiteoftheday.com. Not because there was anything to *do* there—but because the Web was very new and snazzy, and computer users bookmarked sites like CocaCola.com to show the Web off to their friends. It was eye-catching, garish, loaded with nostalgic Coke logos and icons of various sizes—and painfully absent one key ingredient.

Sound and music have been synonymous with Coke's global branding for decades. Coca-Cola is a company that believes sound can stimulate your taste buds. Everybody knows the famous Coke songs, jingles, and other sounds, ranging from "I'd Like to Buy the World a Coke," to the satisfying, trademarked *pshhht!* sound in those ads where a supermodel pops the cap off an ice-cold bottle at a desert gas stop. Coca-Cola once made a TV ad with no moving pictures, only thirty seconds of a still frame showing two Coke bottles, accompanied by the sounds of ice cubes clinking and people having fun. The ad won all sorts of awards. It was clear that Coca-Cola understood the power of music and sound: I imagined those Madison Avenue ad agency guys bursting into applause when they heard the way we'd woven a vital piece of Coke's brand identity into their client's home page.

Earlier in the day I'd had a call from Jim Clark's assistant at Netscape. Mr. Clark would like to take me and my associates out to lunch, she said. This news spurred my team into frantic action. We were desperate to get the sonified Coca-Cola.com site working by morning so I could give Jim a demo on my laptop.

I visualized myself at Jim Clark's power table at Il Fornaio restaurant, casually flipping open my Mac notebook and blowing his mind, while heads all around the restaurant swiveled for a peek. It's the way I always come up with my best stuff: I picture the actual moment of performance as an empty spotlight, a blank canvas; then let my imagination fill it, working backward as I select the brushstrokes, the sights and sounds that will make up my content. That's the way I write songs; that's how I storyboard music videos.

By 5 a.m., the demo was working really well, and I sent everybody home for a few hours' sleep before the big meeting, aside from a guy called Kurt, who was already crashed out on the couch. There remained one problem: we'd be picking Jim Clark up at Netscape HQ in Mountain View. He was going to ride in my car, and my car was a disgrace.

Most workdays at Headspace, I used to knock off early and go windsurfing on the San Francisco Bay. I had a pager on my belt that beeped whenever the wind gusts got above twelve knots at Coyote Point. In the summer months, this happens like clockwork between 2 and 2:30 p.m. On more than one occasion, that beep was the cue for me to excuse myself from a "vital" meeting. And therein lay the problem: four programmers and I had to get down to Mountain View. I was the only one with a reliable car. My ride was a dusty Buick Roadmaster station wagon with mock-woody side panels, a personalized number plate that read HD5P8CE, and a stack of sails and surfboards in the back covered with damp wetsuits. There would certainly not be room for all of us plus Mr. Clark; and I doubted Netscape's millionaire founder would be too impressed when our motley crew spilled out of my dinged-up Roadmaster in front of his shiny offices.

There was only one thing to do: I had to rent a flashier car. I called Hertz at SFO airport. Good news—they had one BMW 740i on the lot, and it was $285 a day plus insurance. Sorted!

At noon, I dropped off the Buick and returned in the BMW, and every-one piled into its cushy leather and wood interior. It was just a fifteen-minute trip down the freeway from San Mateo to Mountain View, and we were in a great mood. The sun was shining and the stereo was blasting Massive At-tack at top volume. I was in the carpool lane and pushing the speed limit, in the shadow of Silicon Valley's towering edifices—Genentech, Oracle, Sun Microsystems, and the new pretenders, Lycos and eXcite. Dodging traffic, I switched to the 280 and we glided past the exit to Sand Hill Road, lined with venture capital firms waiting to write us big checks. We skipped past Xerox PARC, where it all began, thumbed our noses as we passed our former sugar daddies at Interval Research, and cut through the scholarly Stanford Busi-ness School campus, down into Mountain View.

Pulling up outside the front doors of Netscape's HQ, engine at idle, I called Jim Clark's private extension on my cell phone, as per his assistant's instructions. Jim himself answered. "Hi. Actually I thought we'd just order from the café here in the building, if that's okay with you guys. So park up. There are some people I want you to meet."

I was a little miffed that I just blew $285 on the BMW and now we'd be eating chicken Caesar wraps in the Netscape cafeteria. At least we'd trav-eled in style, even if nobody saw us.

Jim greeted us in the lobby and we followed him down a corridor to a win-dowless conference room. A meeting was already in progress, and Jim made the intros. I already knew many in the room by reputation. There was Marc Andreessen, the brilliant young software designer whom Clark recruited from the University of Nebraska; Netscape's soon-to-be-announced CEO, former FedEx supremo James Barksdale; David Hoffman, an independent marketing consultant and documentary filmmaker; and a geeky-looking beanpole in spectacles peeling an orange, whose name I instantly forgot. Prac-ticing my memory technique, I decided to dub him Little Alex, in a nod to *A Clockwork Orange*.

I whipped out my laptop and fired up the demo. In a few minutes I was showing them how the CocaCola.com experience came alive with sound and music. Music played from the moment I loaded the page. A photo of an antique radio lit up with the voice from a classic radio commercial. I hovered my cursor over the Coke logo, which triggered a little jingle in the same key as the background music. Clicking buttons and typing in text fields became a sonic delight—the whole user experience of the Web just jumped up a level.

As I finished my presentation and shut the lid, I could see looks darting between Clark, Barksdale, and Andreessen. Clark was clearly impressed. But to my dismay I realized Andreessen had smoked us out. "It's not really Mosaic, though, is it? It's a mock-up," he said, smiling. My programmers froze, waiting for me to say something. I knew as well as they did that we'd basically *faked* the demo, using a rapid prototyping application called MacroMind Director. We'd taken screen shots of the Mosaic user interface and the Coke Web site, chopped them together, and added our own sound effects and music engine "under the hood." I thought it looked indistinguishable from the original, but we must have made a mistake with one of the URLs.

Andreessen saved my blushes. He knew that in its present form, Mosaic wasn't capable of sounding like this. "What would it take to make this real?" asked Clark. "Theoretically, user interactions in our browser could make calls to the exposed parameters of your synthesizer via JavaScript," Andreessen said. My programmers nodded enthusiastically. "That's exactly what we were thinking!" said ChrisVR. "We're working on a custom extension to Hyper-Text Markup Language that we're calling HMML, specifically for music. It's far more efficient than streaming protocols like RealAudio because it's derived from MIDI. It's essentially a description language just like HTML—so it's super-quick to load, and it triggers instantaneously because you only need to get small chunks of audio over to the client side on a one-time basis. . . ."

Barksdale cut him off. "I think it's marginally useful at best." There was an awkward silence.

Then David Hoffman chimed in. "Wait—let me see if I'm understanding this. You're telling me a company like Coca-Cola, that's invested billions in its brand identity on TV and radio, can have their logos on the Web with the jingles and sounds? And if Coke needs music, what about NBC? Intel Inside? Oscar Mayer? Wrigley's? *McDonald's*, for crissakes?"

Barksdale shuffled his papers and stood up. "I'm saying it's questionable for the enterprise. It might even be a distraction."

Clark said, "Well, we should look into it at least. Let's get some feedback from Madison Avenue. That story *The New York Times* is planning to run—I could see the advertising angle as a neat sidebar. Who's gonna own this?" He looked to Barksdale, who looked to Andreessen. They all turned to Little Alex. "You're in charge of business for third-party developers, right? You take care of these guys." Alex was jotting notes furiously. Barksdale left.

"See if we can ship Headspace in the install package without adding too much to the footprint," added Andreessen, poking Alex's notepad. He was referring to the size (and therefore the download time) of their browser. Little Alex nodded. "And of course, it's got to be 100 percent robust."

I was thinking, of *course* we can make it "robust"—whatever that means—even if my whole programming team has to stay up for nights on end.

"Does Coca-Cola know about this?" Jim Clark asked me on the way back to the cafeteria.

"Well . . . not exactly," I fudged.

"Okay. So get the green light from Coke, make that page over for real, and we'll look at making you part of the feature showcase in our next rev."

My mind was racing. I felt my head was about to explode. Clark's remark could mean anything from a straightforward bundling deal to . . . I gasped to think what else. Our company was still small enough that Netscape could acquire us without even blinking. There'd be no cash involved, but we'd be allocated hefty salaries and a big chunk of stock, which could be worth a fortune if they ever went public.

More important, our technology would become a standard feature in the Internet's standard Web browser, and my dream of a "sonified Web" would become an everyday reality.

The whole meeting was over in less than half an hour, but we walked out of there on cloud nine. It was three thirty in the afternoon, and we decided to drive over to a seedy cocktail bar in East Palo Alto. David Hoffman tagged along and joined us in our booth, and we toasted ourselves with a tray of martinis. David is a feisty East Coaster who's been around the block a few times. This is not a guy that gives or takes any bullshit; James Cagney would play him in a movie. He told us that the meeting we'd just left was the most astonishing he's ever witnessed. He believed Headspace was on its way to overnight tech superstardom. The Web would soon be lit up with music and sound, he exclaimed, and our little start-up would be the keepers of the code.

I just needed the green light from Coca-Cola. Using the Karen White connection, I set up an appointment to give my presentation at Coke's corporate headquarters. By the end of that week I was on a plane to Atlanta, feeling like a rock star once again. Still high from our big meeting at Netscape, I took a cab straight from the airport, and minutes later I was sitting at a long table in a wood-paneled boardroom fifty-six floors above downtown Atlanta. Given the intro from Oracle, I was convinced that the Coke execs would wet themselves when they saw their Web page sonified, and rubber-stamp the project.

I projected the demo from my laptop onto a big screen and swung around, waiting for the applause. In the semidarkness, two fat cats with loud ties stared at it from their leather-clad chairs. There was a long silence. They looked grave. I could hear the ticking of a grandfather clock in a corner of the room.

Finally one of them looked me in the eye and began to speak in a strong southern basso. "That there Internet is pissin' away a *heck of a lot* of our money," he drawled. "We may be in touch. Then again, we may not. Meantime, you just hang tight."

As I closed up my laptop and headed for the door, he threw in a chaser. "And I better not be hearing 'bout how you took this thing right on over to *Pepsi*-frikkin'-Cola."

That gave me an idea: I took it to 7Up instead.

With a few phone calls, I changed my tickets home and flew standby to New York to a meeting at 7Up's Madison Avenue ad agency, Young & Rubicam. They loved my Coke demo and instantly hired Headspace to make a similar demo for 7Up. Over the following weeks, we came up with a great Web page for them. It featured a map of the USA emblazoned with the 7Up logo. The vocals from their TV jingle, "It's the UN-cola . . . Ahhh!" played in the background. As you moved your mouse towards Seattle, the accompaniment morphed seamlessly into a Nirvana-style grunge version; move down to New Orleans and it turned jazzy; hover over Chicago and it became a techno/house mix; over Nashville, it became a fiddle-and-banjo country-and-western jam. The company's marketing people were delighted with my creation and agreed to feature it prominently on their Web site, along with a swanky press release about their partnership with Headspace and Netscape.

It was the first time anything remotely like this had been seen on the Web. Before long, Headspace's switchboard was lighting up like the Fourth of July. There was a little piece about us in the business section of *USA Today*, and I showed it proudly to my family. It was, ironically, the first time that my kids had seen my name in print.

I went and sat alone high up on the bluffs overlooking the Pacific. Gentle waves broke on the rocks below, and sea otters played in the billowing kelp beds. As the sun sank below the horizon I stared out over the vast expanse of the Pacific Ocean and thought about the true implications of interactive music on the Internet.

And at that moment, I realized how insignificant the Pacific Ocean really is.

CHAPTER 12
STEP UP TO THE PLATE

We had no infrastructure per se and no money in the bank. We had five full-time employees, not including Mary Coller, who still had one foot in the music business and was flying back and forth weekly from L.A. We had nobody to take care of accounting, sales, or human resources. We needed new programmers, another graphics person, and another audio designer. In the second week of January, a memorandum of understanding arrived from Netscape, with a deadline for us to deliver a multiplatform-compatible version of our audio engine, using their brand-new plug-in API. I held the MoU in my hands and read it over and over. This was really happening. And it was then that I realized I was in way over my head.

Help came in the form of a guy called Joe Rizzi. He had been successful in the semiconductor world and was now working out of the offices of a firm called Matrix, where he was beginning to invest his own money in young companies. I liked Joe. Now in his early sixties, he was a ham radio enthusiast who played the banjo and rode around on a vintage Harley-Davidson. He was intrigued by our technology and believed he could sell the big VC firms on the idea that Thomas Dolby was a tech visionary.

Our second meeting was at a café-bakery in Woodside, and we worked out a rough capitalization of my company on the back of an envelope. It was the first time I'd seen this done, but it looked fairly straightforward. Joe's arithmetic valued my company at $2 million (very flattering!) and his aim was to quickly put together a seed round of about $500,000 in cash, enabling us to make the new hires and cover payroll for a few months, taking us through to the completion of the Netscape integration. "Just a ballpark number," Joe said. "Enough to get you to first base." I would retain 75 percent ownership of the company. Within six months, he said, we would do a much larger "Series A" round in the millions of dollars. Netscape had just completed a fantastically successful IPO that gave them a market cap of $2.9 billion, launching a new era in tech stock valuations; Joe was convinced that our company would be in a position to raise some serious money once our technology was integrated into Netscape's browser.

I was secretly amazed that Joe trusted me to run this thing myself. I'd never managed a group larger than my backing band; I had no experience in business and could barely look at an Excel sheet without glazing over. Really all I wanted was to ensure that music and sound were a key part of the Internet revolution. Now here I was playing at being a tech start-up entrepreneur. But business intrigued me, like a mysterious new language. This was not the first time I'd dived into beta software without glancing at the user manual.

Over the next couple of weeks, Joe made up a list of potential coinvestors he assured me were heavy hitters. He brought several around to Headspace's small office and had me pitch them my demos. One was Thampy Thomas, an Indian associate of Joe's. Thampy agreed to make up the balance of the seed round, but he had a couple of caveats. First, he wanted me to hire a full-time accountant and paralegal, and said he happened to know just the right person, a man named Alan Thompson. Second, he wanted us to take on his son Ahin as a summer intern. And third, he demanded that I get myself a proper computer, and quit using that "strange thing," waving a disdainful hand at my fur-covered PowerBook 500. Apple products, he said, had no place in a serious software CEO's office. The next day, I duly complied and drove to Fry's to purchase my first Windows PC, a Toshiba laptop. It was truly horrible, but I had to bite the bullet.

With half a million bucks in the bank, we set about meeting Netscape's deadline to deliver a plug-in version of our engine. We would certainly need more programming firepower: development had to take place across multiple operating systems now, because Netscape was determined to be the dominant browser on PCs and Macs, Silicon Graphics and Sun workstations, and a couple of TV set-top boxes. So I recruited a VP of technology, Chris Muir, who had the software engineering experience to pull off this complicated development. Muir was a pragmatist. I needed someone like him to push back on my pie-in-the-sky ideas. A musician himself, he had at one time worked for the Gibson guitar company. Our biggest challenge, he said, was that each computer platform had a different way of handling audio. In order to be truly cross-platform, we needed to have our own integral audio generator—in effect, a synthesizer.

One of the TV set-top boxes we had to integrate with was made by WebTV, a small outfit in Palo Alto set up by three alumni from Apple's QuickTime division. I was impressed with the audio capabilities of their box. They told me they'd licensed a software-based synthesizer from a game design engineer named Steve Hales. The synth was called Igor—a sort of homage to *Young Frankenstein* actor Marty Feldman, because Steve was legally blind and had to program with his right eyeball an inch away from his computer screen. I arranged to meet Steve and we instantly clicked. His visual impairment gave him an amazing capacity to map out problems and solutions in his mind. I made several suggestions of ways to improve his synth and gave him a few library sounds I liked; I was delighted when the very next morning he sent me an updated version of his software with all my features and sounds already integrated. By the end of the week, I'd driven out to his house in the East Bay and managed to persuade him to come on board with us at Headspace, in return for a decent chunk of our newly established stock.

Before long we had a great programming team in place. At one point Headspace Inc. had twelve employees, and seven of them were called either Chris or Steve. They were a motley-looking bunch. One day Kathleen and I went out to lunch with an actor friend. He was visiting from L.A. and wanted to get a taste of what all the "dot-com" excitement was about. As we drove

197

back towards the office on a San Mateo back street, I motioned to a group of unkempt geeks staggering down the sidewalk. I made some crack about how, with all the new software start-ups moving into the area, San Mateo was beginning to look like *Night of the Living Dead.* As we got to the corner of Third Avenue I realized, to my dismay, that those zombies were *my* zombies.

Paul Sebastien and I thought hard about a name and an identity for our new hybrid audio engine. Once we were integrated into the Netscape installation package, we'd be able to display a small logo that would show up on the screen whenever our audio plug-in was used. I imagined this logo as something that would represent the constant flow of music and sound. There was already a Java. This was more like Lava. But that sounded too close; people would get us confused. I thought about volcanoes. Aha! *Krakatoa!* "Krak" for short! We came up with a tiny logo that looked like an active volcano with red lava pouring out of it in a looped animation. "This is your site," boomed Paul in his best movie-trailer-narrator voice, "and this is your site on *Krak!*"

Joe and Thampy soon vetoed that one. "Why would anyone want to buy *crack?*" Thampy asked. We backed down. They reluctantly agreed to our second idea: *Beatnik.* Joe was still skeptical—having grown up in Little Italy in the fifties with a disdain for what was going on over in Greenwich Village— but for me it conjured up all sorts of images: cool poets in smoky basement nightclubs, pretty girls in berets and striped T-shirts riding around on the backs of scooters. Plus, I liked the musical play on words. "Okay," Joe said, "but you're too small to push two screwball brand names and make them both stick. If Beatnik is the product, Beatnik should be the name of your company, too." This made solid sense, so we changed the name to Beatnik Inc.

For the first half of 1996 our engineers worked closely with Netscape's to define a third-party plug-in API. This would allow not only Beatnik but also many other companies to build proprietary extensions to the Netscape browser. There was a lot of talk about "e-commerce" and "intranets" that would enable large organizations to run their own internal applications over Internet protocols. Netscape's CEO, Jim Barksdale, was terrified of Microsoft, which had essentially declared war on him. Barksdale knew Netscape was in a race to establish a new, defensible business in a sector where Microsoft could not crush it. It was clear that multimedia features for the consumer market were not at the top of Netscape's agenda; still, we completed our plug-in and delivered it to them as set out in the MoU—and I waited. And waited.

It didn't take me long to learn the first rule of tech entrepreneurship: VC investment cash is like a ticking time bomb. Unless you succeed early on and start earning some real money, you and that time bomb are going for a long walk on a short pier.

Five months after our MoU arrived from Netscape, I was still waiting for the promised first draft of the contract. I had been calling Little Alex a couple of times a week, and he kept saying that Netscape's lawyers were backed up. But our new in-house accountant–paralegal, Alan Thompson, insisted that the MoU was not binding in itself, and that we had an obligation to disclose this to our potential Series A investors. Following our new hires and the acquisition of Igor, the bank account was already running low.

The same month, I had to ask Kathleen if she minded if I dug into our kids' college fund in order to meet payroll at Beatnik. I was still adamant that Netscape would come through any day with a contract, meaning we could close the Series A round and the company could repay me. Kathleen reluctantly agreed, and we loaned the company $22,500. This stung. At the time we were still living in a rented condo with our three kids, and we were hoping to be able to buy a new house once our credit was clear following the repossession of the L.A. house we had lost.

I made an appointment to meet with Little Alex down at the Netscape HQ. During the months that had passed since my last visit, Netscape had gone from the low hundreds to over two thousand employees. The place was a zoo. Jim Clark, of course, was nowhere to be seen. Little Alex met me in the lobby wearing an immaculate Italian tailored suit and handmade oxford shoes. He took me to a room where he had gathered a group of employees, several of whom looked like they had come straight from New Employee Orientation. I asked him if he had a draft contract for me.

"I've been thinking that Netscape needs a little more out of the deal," he said.

With butterflies in my stomach, I asked what he had in mind. "Well, there is only limited space in the browser for third-party plug-ins," he said, "and there is some overlap between the features of your audio engine and the plug-ins of two of our major strategic partners, Macromedia and RealAudio."

Keeping my game face on, I pointed out to him that until we'd met the previous fall and they had written up the MoU, there *was* no third-party plug-in capability. In fact, what we'd demonstrated to Marc Andreessen was the need for a plug-in API to enable real-time interactions between the browser and external modules. We were pleased to see that we'd helped them define the new framework. As well as opening the door for partnerships with multimedia companies like Macromedia and RealNetworks, we'd helped pave the way for all sorts of enterprise-based functions, including "shopping carts" and e-commerce. Why wasn't he now going to hold up his side of the deal?

After a pause, Little Alex said, "Well, it's nothing that a million dollars wouldn't fix." There was a sharp intake of breath from the junior Netscape employees.

"You want to pay us a million bucks to be in your browser?" I said, dryly.

"That wasn't what I had in mind," chuckled Little Alex. "I thought I read your company had solid VC backing? Maybe I was wrong about you. Look, it's quite simple, really: if Beatnik is not ready to make a $1 million commitment, it's no skin off our nose. There's a company in Arizona that's made an audio plug-in not unlike yours. It's run by a cousin of mine, actually."

While I was still squirming from this, Little Alex introduced a young guy called Tim Hickman, who he said was taking over the Beatnik relationship as of today. Alex himself had been promoted. His new role was executive assistant to the CEO. He was going to be Jim Barksdale's right-hand man. He stood up and walked out of the room.

Two weeks later I read a Netscape press release announcing that the latest revision of their browser would include a selection of third-party plug-ins made by companies including Adobe, Macromedia, and RealNetworks . . . and that for the first time, it would have the capability to do interactive audio.

I downloaded the new installer in vain hope. Of course, the bundled audio plug-in wasn't Beatnik's, it was Cousin Inc.'s. Now I would have to go to Joe and Thampy and explain. The end of the month was coming round again, and there was no way I could personally cover the payroll for a second month running. In desperation, I made a decision to track down Jim Clark and plead with him in person. If need be I would guilt him into reversing Little Alex's decision.

Clark was a serial entrepreneur and never stuck around for long in one place. He was now working from the offices of his latest creation, Healtheon. I met with him in the middle of the afternoon in his new building off the 280 freeway. He had a large corner office with tinted windows. The venetian blinds were down. On his desktop were three computer monitors, attached to a cluster of Silicon Graphics workstations. I made my plea, but his face didn't react. I could hear the whirring of the fans.

"Come and look at this," he said. I moved behind him at his desk, and saw that the three monitors were showing a 3-D model of a huge sailing yacht. "This is my new boat, *Hyperion*. Look, I can control the sheets and halyards with my mouse. See that? I just adjusted the boom vang. The *actual* boom vang."

"Where is it?" I said. "Your yacht?"

"Holland," he replied. "In the dry dock. She's not in the water yet. It'll be another year at least."

So Clark was actually moving parts around on his yacht six thousand miles away. I tried to divert his attention long enough to remind him about my issue with Little Alex. "Who?" he said. "Oh. Barksdale's running all that now, I'm not really involved. I can put in a word, but don't hold your breath. He's shit scared that Gates is just picking his moment to annihilate us."

I left the building fuming. Clark wasn't willing to stick his neck out for me. But there was a secret part of me that envied his ability to detach himself from his company.

When I told Joe and Thampy that Netscape had done a U-turn, and now our money was running low, Thampy's frustrations boiled over. "If you put all your eggs in one basket, Thomas, you're likely to get burned," he shouted, accusingly.

Joe Rizzi was more philosophical. He didn't blame me. "You'll just have to find another way to skin the cat," Joe said. "This is really the time for you to step up to the plate." He was trying to keep me positive, but they could both see I was pretty downcast. The flood of mixed metaphors did little to cushion the blow.

I mentioned that Little Alex had been promoted to a new job as Barksdale's right-hand man.

"Sounds like the ejector seat to me," said Joe. In among Joe's baffling baseball tropes there were a few mysterious pearls of wisdom, which you never dared challenge; you just sort of believed. Sure enough, Little Alex lasted about a fortnight in his new role before he was fired. I only saw him once more, a year or so later, on a plane to L.A. By then he was running his own humble start-up, whereas Beatnik had become big news. Little Alex begged me to take a meeting and read his business plan. I said I was too busy. "It's a tough life in the minors, Alex," I said. Shit, I thought, now they've got me doing it. Years later I heard he was living in Las Vegas, working in real estate.

I sat in a Belmont coffee bar a few days afterwards in the company of a fellow Brit named Chris Anderson, and found I was able to joke feebly about the Silicon Valley vernacular and how hard it was to deal with the nonstop baseball jargon when you grew up playing cricket.

Anderson was a magazine publisher and editor, and we instantly bonded. He had built up a massive magazine portfolio in the UK and sold the whole lot to Pearson. He was reinvesting his wealth to move the publishing world into the digital era, and funding several online magazines; he knew the readers' experience needed to evolve if advertisers were going to migrate from printed media to the Web. He believed me when I told him that sound could make a big difference. We agreed that I would sonify the front page of his Imagine Media Web site for a fee; he also enquired, unprompted, about our investment situation, and asked to be introduced to Joe and Thampy. We all met for lunch. They were targeting a figure of $7 million for Beatnik's "Series A" investment round, and Anderson said he was on board for at least six figures.

His interest got Joe and Thampy thinking that perhaps we should cast a wider net and look for new investment from outside the regular Sand Hill Road VC community.

They suggested another potential investor who owned a meat-processing company in Arkansas. Payroll day was rapidly approaching, so I welcomed all comers. We still needed $5 million. I'd been thinking about going vegetarian, but I quickly dropped that idea. Mr. Arkansas was in.

It occurred to me I could approach Clive Calder, the head of my former publishers Zomba Music. I hadn't seen him for over ten years. With Clive at the helm, Zomba had grown into a huge music empire. His label Jive had moved beyond rap, and its roster boasted many of the top pop groups of the day, including Britney Spears, 'NSync, and the Backstreet Boys. Joe Rizzi and I made a trip to New York to meet with him. We sat in a conference room on the top floor of his offices close to Times Square. It was clear from the outset that Clive had cash coming out of his ears. His conference room was decorated with platinum albums and aerial photos of the CD-pressing plant he had just bought in Central America. Like most of the showbiz world, he was excited by what was happening in Silicon Valley and on the NASDAQ, and had been watching from a distance. I gave him the background on my company, and he scanned a copy of our balance sheet. I explained the Netscape situation—how we thought we'd had the keys to the city, but that it had fallen through and we were looking for other ways to make Beatnik the core audio engine for the Web.

Clive was ever the realist. "What's Netscape's market share?" he asked me.

"Around 87 percent of all browsers, at the last count," I said.

"Who else has that kind of dominance and ubiquity in their sector?"

"Only Microsoft," I said.

"Microsoft and, arguably, Sun Microsystems, who control Java," Joe added, "though the jury's still out on that one."

Clive leaned back in his chair. "As I see it, Tom, you've got two options," he said in his jagged South African twang. "In the next two months, either you bring in a deal with Microsoft, or you bring in a deal with Sun. Then I will happily bankroll your company," he said. "There is a third option: you shut up shop and bugger off back to England to make synthpop."

Clive's words were a little harsh, but he had a point. The only way to survive as a small company on the Web was to wedge yourself in with one of its gatekeepers, make yourself indispensable, and pray for the best. If you were lucky you would get acquired, in return for a pile of stock. In the meantime, the best you could do was try to win "eyeballs." Tens of millions of consumers were swarming online, and they all believed Web content should be free. Portal sites like Yahoo and Lycos were in a race to win enough user registrations to make them look impressive to Wall Street, so they could emulate Netscape and raise a war chest from an IPO; charging a subscription of even a few dollars per month would have scared away 99 percent of their users. Nobody had figured out how to bill consumers directly. Advertising banners annoyed people. It was still early days for sites like Amazon and eBay. Social media was not yet even a glint in Mark Zuckerberg's eye.

We had to complete the "Series A" round before our cash ran out: that meant we needed Clive Calder at the table. Back in California I set about arranging calls with Microsoft and Sun. While I knew quite a lot about the Redmond giant and its billionaire founder, I knew next to nothing about Sun Microsystems or its Java programming language. I recalled having a conversation at TED with a senior Sun scientist by the name of John Gage, who had said nice things about my AVRe technology. I rifled through my drawers and found his business card. He was friendly on the phone and invited me to Sun's offices to give a demo of Beatnik. He and Sun cofounder Bill Joy were amused by the concept, but they didn't really see a clear business case for music on the Web.

My only contact at Microsoft was a guy called Todor Fay in the game audio department, and he put me in touch with one of the business development executives. When I pitched him Beatnik over the phone, he seemed uninterested at first. Then I mentioned that I had a "relationship" with Sun. Suddenly his tone changed altogether, and he said that he and a colleague would fly down to San Francisco the following week.

It was a big moment. Joe and Thampy were very excited and told me we should put all our cards on the table and consider any kind of a deal with Microsoft, from licensing to a full acquisition. But it made me uneasy, and I needed to mentally prepare. I viewed Microsoft as the enemy. Their dominance of the PC world was such that, if Microsoft merely hinted at a new interactive audio feature in a forthcoming version of Windows, their legions of partners would cease doing business with Beatnik. As David Liddle once told me, "Microsoft is like a snoring giant—it can roll over in its sleep and squish you like a bug."

A friend of mine from TED, Kim Polese, had an experience when Microsoft briefly courted her start-up Marimba and got quite far into its due diligence, taking a close look at her technology before deciding not to invest. Kim warned me about Microsoft's "trip reports." Apparently, whenever Microsoft executives returned from a visit to an unknown company's offices, they were required to fill out a form in a database. It included questions such as "How many employees were there? Did they appear engaged with their work? How would you describe the corporate culture? What computers were on the desktops? What operating systems were they running? Exactly what was discussed in the meeting?" The company was gradually compiling a database of all its knowledge about the competitive landscape.

Logical. Machiavellian. The hive mind! Microsoft was like the Borg.

We showed the two Microsoft execs into our conference room, where I had set up a range of Beatnik demos, just the standard ones that were also available on the Web. Mary Coller and Chris Muir were on our side of the table. They asked us some very direct questions about how our engine was coded, its footprint, and its processor requirements; and about our company infrastructure, including the names of our investors and how much capital we had raised to date. Muir danced around the technical questions, while I managed to keep my cool and dodge the corporate ones, simply smiling and saying: "We're a privately held company and that information is confidential."

It was all very civil. After a couple of hours they stood up. "Oh, by the way," said one of them, "we'd like to leave you with this." And he produced a small, beautifully inlaid wooden box with the words MICROSOFT INC. engraved on the lid. We shook hands and Mary showed them to the door. After they had left, I opened the box. It was a platinum fountain pen, but it was perforated with small holes with black fabric backing, so it looked exactly like a microphone.

Could they be that blatant? I slid the open pen box into the middle of the conference table and we sat in silence and stared at it. After a moment we all broke out in a fit of giggles. Mary started to say something, but I held a finger to my lips and shushed her. I felt like someone needed to go and turn on a water tap. Finally I picked up the pen and smashed it to smithereens on the edge of the table. It had nothing inside but an ink cartridge and a small spring. It had been a perfectly good pen! Not anymore.

Later that week we headed down to Sun Microsystems to talk about Java. I realized I had no clue what Java really did. Chris Muir, our VP of technology, was invaluable in a situation like this. He had an extensive knowledge of operating systems and programming languages, and was able to explain things in terms I understood. This ability to bridge the divide was to become a major asset over the years as my company twisted and turned, looking for a business model that would stick. The changes of direction that filtered down from the boardroom must have been incredibly frustrating for our programmers. Muir was always cheerful and mellow, and broke the news to the engineers gently. They respected him enormously. He liked to sit in his cubicle and play his acoustic guitar, making up meandering Philip Glass–esque compositions.

However, Muir was very adept at missing the point. One day I brought in a demo for a beta audio software program called Acid. The engineer who had created it was looking for a buyer. I loved the way it worked: it allowed the user to drag small loops of audio into a timeline, automatically conforming their tempo and key, making it very easy for nonmusicians to quickly create professional-sounding musical pieces. "Why would anyone want to do that?" Muir said. Over the years, I've never had the heart to ask him what he thought of Ableton Live or Apple's GarageBand, the direct successors to Acid that have been enjoyed by hundreds of millions of people.

I think also of the day we went out for coffee with a young guy who said he wanted to make a system of connected links called a "social network"; or the time we visited a small Internet TV company in Sacramento that had a vision for thousands of channels of user-uploaded content—long before You-Tube and its acquisition by Google. Muir was equally dismissive of both. "In Detroit in the 1920s there were over a hundred and sixty automobile companies," he said. "Some were making cars you steered with a tiller. You just can't take most of these start-ups seriously."

When smartphones began to appear around 2003, I questioned whether we needed to make sure Beatnik was also the standard for sound in these high-end devices, even to the extent of making the Beatnik Audio Engine (BAE) free or cheap to license for companies like Palm, RIM, and Apple. Muir said no. "Nokia sells a hundred million cell phones a quarter. Smartphones have an installed base in the low hundreds of thousands. Why bother?" Even Chris Muir, the world's most die-hard Apple believer, couldn't see that the total dominance of the iPhone was just around the corner.

At a Beatnik board meeting a couple of years later we were struggling to decide what business to be in, where to place our bets. "Let's just ask Chris Muir what he thinks," said Joe Rizzi, "and do the *opposite*."

When I called on Muir to explain Java to me and join me on the half-hour drive down to Sun's head offices, he fed me enough information to make me not feel like an idiot. That part, he was utterly great at.

Java was a new cross-platform programming language designed to run independently of hardware. It had its own "virtual machine" that enabled it to work on PCs, Macs, SPARC workstations, even set-top boxes and domestic appliances. As yet, Java had no programmable sound at all. If we played our cards right, Muir said, we had a shot at licensing Sun the BAE as the core audio layer in Java. He warned me that Sun would probably not want to pay for this, but once we were part of the Java Virtual Machine, we would have a ubiquitous platform from which to launch other Beatnik-related products such as sound editing tools and music libraries.

Muir also warned me that the biggest hurdle was likely to be Microsoft. The very idea of an open-source, cross-platform operating system was poisonous to Microsoft, and what we were doing was sure to incur the wrath of Bill Gates. And I'd seen what Bill Gates's wrath looked like up close.

Whereas dealing with Netscape was like trying to talk to a headless

chicken, and Microsoft was downright chilling, the Sun relationship ran disarmingly smoothly. Within days I got a call from the speechwriter for Sun's
CEO, Scott McNealy. He asked if I could do a five-minute Beatnik demo
during McNealy's keynote speech at the massive JavaOne conference. Really?
Twist my arm.

Thousands of programmers and developers flocked to the Moscone Center in San Francisco for the opening of the show. There was a huge stage,
with revolving lights, dry ice, lasers, and a powerful sound system. Now this
was a world I knew and understood!

I took the stage and gazed out over a sea of eager, spotty, white male faces.
It felt just like a rock concert—except this was 8:30 a.m. on a Thursday. I
demoed a Java-based version of the interactive 7Up page on the jumbo video
screen, and thousands of cheering computer programmers jumped to their
feet and erupted in geeky adulation.

Backstage, the morning San Francisco TV news show wanted to interview Scott McNealy and me. With a note of sarcasm, Scott thanked me for
having him on as a guest during my keynote speech. But I could tell he was
impressed.

That Monday morning, Sun called to tell us they wanted to negotiate a
deal for Beatnik Inc. to create the audio layer for Java. They sent over two
representatives: a director from their technical strategy department and a
marketing guy. They said there was no need for this negotiation to drag out,
so why didn't we just make two columns on the whiteboard—one for Sun's
requirements, and one for the price they would pay us? Muir and the Sun
strategist jabbered away about Java code, and in a few minutes they'd filled
in the bullets for the first column. Then the marketing guy stepped up and
grabbed the marker. He pointed to the first bullet, an initial five-year nonexclusive license to Beatnik's intellectual property. Muir scrawled a number
on a pad and pushed it along the table to me. I nodded.

"We were thinking you'd pay $300,000," I said.

"Might as well round it up to $450K," the Sun guy said, grinning, and
wrote that number in the right-hand column.

Muir and I glanced at each other, astonished. He went on to the next item, and the routine was the same—we threw out a number, this time for NRE (nonreturnable engineering) costs, and he added a hefty markup to it and chalked it in the right column. By the time we'd gotten through the half-dozen items in the left-hand list, I could see that the numbers on the right were adding up to what must be a healthy seven-figure total, which . . . now that I came to look at it . . . totaled *exactly* $1.5 million.

The meeting was over in about forty minutes. Muir told me that in all his years in business, it was the weirdest negotiation he'd ever taken part in.

I have a theory, though: In those days, value on Wall Street was all about perception. Sun was late to the Internet game, and it needed to show its analysts and shareholders that it was making solid investments in Web infrastructure. Sun's market cap would soon justify the outlay. Some accountant must have come up with an arbitrary figure of a $1.5 million contract for Beatnik. I wondered how many other small companies would be celebrating as these guys hurried to fill their quota?

Unlike Netscape's legal department, Sun Microsystems' lawyers made good on their promise to get us a draft of the contract within a week. We worked through the night on a round of edits. Sun signed the second revision, and on a Friday afternoon, I banked a check for an initial $375,000 installment on the contract. Our payroll worries were behind us for a month or two.

My dream of a sonified Web was starting to seem within reach. Yet after two years running a tech start-up I was already feeling pretty shell-shocked. I told Kathleen the world of Silicon Valley felt almost as random and unjust as the music business, only the numbers were way higher. She could see how elated and relieved I was to have signed the Java deal, but she also knew me well enough to see that I was exhausted. She urged me to take a step back from Beatnik. Our kids were now six months, three years, and five years old. Home life was happy but hectic. The kids needed a dad who could laugh and clown around with them and enjoy their energy. I would be useless until I could get a few proper nights' sleep and some R&R.

So at six the following morning I boarded a plane at SFO to San José del Cabo, where I rented a four-by-four and a trunkful of windsurfing equipment and headed to the fabled Mexican windsurfing mecca Los Barilles, on the Sea of Cortez. As I drove along the gravel coast road, scanning for whitecaps on the water, the stress started to melt away and a sense of deep satisfaction set in. This Java deal was the first real money I'd made in Silicon Valley. The last few months and the Netscape debacle had taken a lot out of me, but now the Sun contract was signed and there was money in the bank. And as I'd fulfilled Clive Calder's requirement, Joe and Thampy could press Zomba to fill out their new round of equity.

There wasn't much wind that week in Baja, not enough for the windsurfing to thrill me. I sat in a deck chair on the beach and a waiter brought me long drinks with umbrellas in them. I wrote some postcards, and when I got bored with that I pulled out my Toshiba laptop and a pair of headphones. Beatnik had been given access to a beta version of the new Java Virtual Machine that included our audio engine, and I was curious to play around with it. I had no musical keyboard with me, but I remembered I had a folder somewhere on my hard drive containing the separate musical multitrack files from David Bowie's classic hit song "Fame." I decided to see if I could make a program that would allow me to create a real-time remix of "Fame" just using the buttons on my QWERTY. It took me a couple of days of nonstop programming, but I got it grooving, and it felt fantastic. Just by clicking on my laptop keys, I could switch instantly between different drum grooves and fills; turn the bass and guitars on and off; bring in solos, backing vocals, and percussion. I could even alternate between Bowie's lead vocal and some never-heard John Lennon asides that were buried in the multitrack, adding reverb and delay effects.

Here I was on a beach in Mexico, playing at being a record producer in my shorts. At that moment in time, I was the only man in the world with that capability. But I was using a typical consumer PC and Web browser no different to half a billion others on the planet. I couldn't wait for my team back in San Mateo to hear it. I bounced down a mix and took my laptop inside to see if I could connect via the hotel room phone. Of course, I had the usual hassle trying to get a modem connection over an international phone line. It seemed to take hours, but I finally got the thirty-five-megabyte file uploaded. I chuckled as I remembered the farcical phone call to Michael Jackson in the Nevada desert. That was many years earlier. Moore's Law may have sped up microprocessors, but bandwidth was still a major problem!

Next day I got an e-mail back from ChrisVR. "It sounds good, but you know you needn't have sent me that whopping file, right?" he wrote. "Your remix information boils down to about seven kilobytes. That's tiny. Assuming I already have the audio chunks of *Fame* on my end, we could send remixes back and forth in a few seconds. I've written you a little routine that will allow you to save a remix and e-mail it to me directly from a Web page." Below there was a link to the URL.

ChrisVR's Web page was just a row of buttons and sliders on a beige background. It was plain and ugly. But I realized the graphics could be anything we liked—a photo of David Bowie, for example, or 3-D graphics representing the instruments. *Jesus Christ.* This was a marketing gem!

Joe and Thampy called me at my Baja hotel from a speakerphone. "Oh, so ChrisVR told you about my remix?" I asked gleefully. That wasn't the purpose of their call at all. Though they spoke calmly, I could sense they were furious that I'd gone AWOL just when things were heating up at Beatnik. They told me the board members had been talking, and they'd decided it was time I stepped aside as CEO and brought in an experienced business leader to head up the company.

"We need someone at the head of the table who can read an Excel spreadsheet," said Thampy.

"Without gagging!" added Joe. "We need a CEO we can *fire*."

CHAPTER 13
THE APPLE MAFIA

There is a well-known phenomenon that affects Silicon Valley start-ups called Founder's Syndrome. I suppose I'd heard of it early on during my time as a tech entrepreneur in the Valley, but I'm not sure of the precise moment between 1998 and 2000 when I became aware that I myself was suffering from a chronic case.

Once Beatnik grew to more than twenty-five employees, a lot of my time was taken up with what you might call people problems. Karen's abusive ex-boyfriend kept showing up at work. Paul was feeling increasingly isolated because the engineers thought I gave him preferential treatment. Jim missed a lot of workdays because of his health; it turned out he had a drinking problem. Tarq wanted his own office because he didn't like the way the guy in the next cubicle scrunched paper. Every day there seemed to be new fires to put out.

Beatnik was a mellow place to work, with a relaxed attitude to office hours, vacation time, personal projects, and so on. I would take people out for a beer or a meal; we'd go ten-pin bowling or for a company picnic in the park; we had a Ping-Pong table that was constantly in use. On Thursday evenings everyone would crowd round ChrisVR's cubicle to watch *The Simpsons*. I didn't need to crack the whip, because our little team enjoyed their work and thought nothing of putting in a twelve-hour workday if it was called for.

All Beatnik employees had stock options that would accrue over time, meaning that if they stuck around for a few years and we hit the big time, they might earn a six- or seven-figure bonus. So my usual reaction when someone came to me with a people problem was to say, "Come on, you guys, this is a cool gig and you're being well paid for it—can't you just figure it out?" I tried to remain approachable, but my employees probably found me quite distant. It didn't help that I was doing a ton of media and promotion. Every week they would see my photo in the paper or an interview on the local TV news. The press was fascinated by what was going on at backstreet tech start-ups in towns like San Mateo, and they liked the fact I was well known from my pop star days. "MTV icon hits it big in Silicon Valley," the headlines would read, and next to that would be my face, with a goatee, decked out in beret and shades in front of the Beatnik logo. Our employees probably heard from their friends, "Oh, you're working at Beatnik, that's Thomas Dolby's company, right?" It must have been hard for them to justify when their buddies were working for much bigger companies with better job security and a clear business plan.

After all, many of the hottest tech companies of the day had a prominent front man at the helm. Gates and Jobs, obviously; the billionaire CEOs Larry Ellison and Scott McNealy; sports franchise owners like Mark Cuban and Ted Leonsis. Steve Case at AOL. Music business upstarts like Michael Robertson at MP3.com and Sean Parker at Napster. Each of them used his notoriety to further his company's brand, and the press lapped it up. Although Beatnik was a tiny company, we got a disproportionate amount of publicity from the fact that I still had a modicum of celebrity left over from my rock music days. I was no longer putting out records, but I had something else to plug—a cool Web technology company with billion-dollar prospects.

We had a great logo, an elaborate *B* that, when printed large on a T-shirt, stuck out for miles. At tech conferences and in the crowded aisles of exhibit halls you could spot a Beatnik employee from miles away by their T-shirt and beret. Our sonified demos came over well on TV and on the radio. I hyped the company as if it were the greatest thing since sliced bread. I talked articulately, bridging the gap between tech and consumer jargon, and my longtime experience with journalists enabled me to shape the way their articles turned out. Big stages and TV cameras didn't faze me. But often in the middle of a radio interview or press conference my pager would beep with a Beatnik extension number, and I just knew it was another one of those pesky people problems for me to sort out when I got back to the office.

In principle, I was not against the idea of the board's hiring a proper CEO to replace me. The business aspect of running a company, though certainly stimulating, was not something I had a particular aptitude for, nor did I aspire to develop one. I knew there was a risk the board would try to install someone I didn't get on with. He or she would probably want to take the company in a new direction. But Lord knew we *needed* to change direction. Although everybody knew the Beatnik name, we were still running at a monthly deficit, and our new round of VC cash would not last forever.

Joe Rizzi warned me it might take months to find the right person. "I've been through this process before," he said. "You have to kiss a few frogs." We hired a headhunter at great expense. He brought us a frog or two. I tried to spend enough time with each CEO candidate to get a true sense of what they were like and how we interacted, but I found it hard to imagine relinquishing control to any one of them. Then we found out the headhunter himself was trying to poach one of our candidates to run his own dot-com venture, head-hunters.com. That was pretty much the way things worked in those days. As the dot-com boom gathered momentum, business ethics were falling by the wayside. We had to wait until the headhunter's six-month contract ran out to fire him. We'd drawn a blank.

One day my friend David Hoffman introduced me to Lorraine Hariton, a supersmart executive in her mid-forties, formerly a high-level manager at a much larger company. She was interested in the CEO job. I spent a lot of time with her, talking over Beatnik's products. She listened carefully and came back to me with her vision for the company going forward. I had a strong sense that her leadership style would work; we felt like a great fit. Lorraine reminded me of Kathleen and Mary in many ways—she had that feisty New

York way of calling it just like she saw it. "Yup, Lorraine's the one," I told Joe and Thampy. "I believe she can hit this company out of the park!" (I was really getting the hang of the lingo now, as you can tell.)

With Lorraine Hariton installed as our CEO, I changed the title on my business cards to "President and Chief Beatnik." I didn't object when the board told me it was typical for the CEO to have parity with the founder on salary and stock options. I wanted to make sure she understood my original vision for the company. Provided she kept sight of that, I was willing to let her run with it. I gave up my nice corner office for her, and she got to work. I built myself a small project studio and refocused on Beatnik's creative side, looking forward to the weight being off my shoulders. Over the next two months Lorraine set about the rapid expansion of the company. She spent a lot of time with our key managers in front of a whiteboard, mapping out our various lines of business, and I sat at the back, trying not to interfere.

The Beatnik Audio Engine was now in Java Virtual Machine, the WebTV set-top box, the BeOS used by many professional music and audio hardware manufacturers, and even (by some miracle) part of the Netscape Navigator installation. We'd streamlined the free Beatnik Web player so that it downloaded seamlessly in the background whenever a user hit a sonified Web page, and we had over a million registered users. We also had a $99 authoring tool called the Beatnik Editor so that musicians and programmers could sonify their pages. Millions of users had downloaded the Beatnik free plug-in. And we had negligible revenues.

At Lorraine's first quarterly board meeting she showed a PowerPoint presentation setting out our top priorities and paths to profitability. She hit the space bar and they scrolled down the screen:

1. Beatnik player ubiquity.
2. Fast and affordable editing tools.
3. Showcase sonified sites for Fortune 500 companies.
4. NRE fees from engineering contracts.
5. Beatnik Audio Engine licenses for multiple devices.

6. Sales of sound libraries and music.

7. Custom Web sound and "work for hire."

"Lorraine," said Thampy, "this is all very well, but how can a company with fifty-five employees have seven top priorities? What the hell kind of company is this?"

Lorraine and I looked at each other, then back at the screen. "I guess that's what I'm here to figure out, Thampy," she said.

"Too right," he replied. "Let's not go another quarter without you being able to answer that." After the meeting Joe Rizzi took Lorraine aside in the corridor. He said there was no need to swing for the fences; we just had to get on base. One look at Lorraine told me she was as bewildered as I was.

The right thing to do, obviously, was to move Beatnik Inc. to bigger premises and hire lots of top people, ramping up our "burn rate" and thereby shortening our "runway."

Office space in 1998 was becoming increasingly hard to find. New tech companies were starting up all over the peninsula, and landlords and real estate agents were having a field day, but if you were a new renter you had your work cut out. By the time a vacant office building made it into the commercial listings, it was already long gone. The corridor up and down the 101 freeway from San Francisco to San Jose was lit up with billboards and LED jumbo screens advertising the latest dot-com supernova. Even the salt marshes along the edge of the bay were being reclaimed and turned into landfill, and bulldozers, cranes, and steel girders moved into place to pave them over as yet another company broke ground on its gleaming new corporate HQ.

We finally settled for a former bank building on El Camino Real, about a mile south of our old office. It was covered in beige stucco and had almost zero personality, but it had 150 parking spaces and over twenty thousand square feet of office space on three floors, including a steel vault in the basement. This was to be Beatnik Inc.'s new home.

On a daily basis there was news of a new groundbreaking IPO or acquisition that affected people close to us. My friends at Marimba Inc. raised $80 million on the NASDAQ. Microsoft bought WebTV for $425 million. Yahoo bought Mark Cuban's Internet radio company for $5.7 billion.

But as the Internet revolution gathered pace, there was a mounting sense of agitation in the Valley. Every week new faces were pouring in from other parts of California, from the East Coast, and all across America. Brilliantly trained programmers from India and the Far East had to compete for work permits and green cards with newly arrived Brits and European nationals. At Beatnik we had around thirty job vacancies to fill. We had a director of human resources now, who would set Lorraine and me up to interview new hires. It was not unusual to finish an interview feeling as if we were the ones under consideration. One candidate talked briefly about the job he was applying for, which we'd advertised with a $92,000 salary plus stock; when I asked a question about his CV, he rapidly changed the subject to the stock option program: How many shares could he expect to earn in the first six months? Did we have plans for an IPO? Lorraine said that was something he should follow up with HR. He glanced at his watch and said he was sorry but he needed to beat the rush hour traffic, as he had another interview to get to in Redwood City.

So Lorraine and I were delighted when we got into serious discussions about the open position of VP of marketing with a man called Ian Powell. He was in his late thirties, super fit, with cropped hair and boy-genius spectacles. His résumé was compelling, and in person he was even more impressive. He'd been high up at Apple under the new Steve Jobs regime. He told us he'd played a major role in redefining Apple as the first choice for consumers who were bored stiff with the gray world of Windows computing. Those "Think Different" billboards on the 101 featuring the likes of John and Yoko and Albert Einstein? All his idea. Steve Jobs, he said, couldn't handle his high-energy presentations and constant suggestions for new features. To be in the inner circle, you had to agree with everything Steve said and be willing to have your ideas hijacked at short notice. We were bowled over with Ian, and excited when at the end of the week HR informed us he'd accepted the position, albeit at a salary that was not far below Lorraine's and my own.

Ian's insight into the Beatnik brand was invigorating. He felt that in the race to "sonify the Web" we had already lost out to Macromedia Flash. When I protested that Flash was a graphics animation plug-in, and its sound capabilities were massively inferior to Beatnik's, Ian said: "Ah, but sometimes, good enough is just that—*good enough*. All you need is a techno loop, a good fart sound effect, and the job's done. Who are the only people that care deeply about sound? Musicians. Like yourself. So that's who we sell Beatnik to. Professional musicians and labels—and all the legions of musician wannabes. They're willing to spend money to be on the Web. *That's* our market. Get the top names in pop music behind your brand, and the rest of the world will follow."

Out of all the sites and demos Beatnik had created, the one that intrigued Ian the most was my remix of David Bowie's "Fame." "Have you gotten permission from Bowie to use it?" Ian said. No, but I still had inroads to Bowie, of course, given my performance with him at Live Aid. I said I'd make the call.

"It's better if it comes from me," said Ian. "I can pitch him the whole Beatnik story, and he'll trust me because he's known you for years. Next thing you know he'll be wanting to invest in your company—just watch."

With Ian's help I persuaded Yahoo to feature our first three interactive remixes, or GrooveGrams, as I called them, on the Yahoo Music page. It was a diverse selection: Moby, Queen Latifah, and Britney Spears. Yahoo didn't want to pay us for the content, of course, but the respective record labels were very keen, granting us the rights and coughing up a small budget. If the campaign gathered pace I reckoned we'd be able to go to other labels and charge them as much for a GrooveGram as they paid for an MTV video, without the high production costs. This could be a profitable little sideline. And the association with top pop acts was helping drive awareness of Beatnik among the general public, especially young consumers. When you created a Groove-Gram remix you could click on the logo and e-mail it to all your friends, or enter it for a contest and win a prize.

Ian liked this approach, but he felt the way to make money from our remixes was to take them to the Madison Avenue advertising agencies. The ad agencies, he said, would be keen to use the power of "viral" Web content (this was a new word to me) to promote their clients' brands, via association with top music acts. Ian was well connected to several New York and Chicago ad agencies, as well as some of the big writers and thinkers of the day: he arranged brown-bag lunches in Beatnik's conference room with keynote talks by the likes of Malcolm Gladwell and Seth Godin.

But Ian didn't like the name GrooveGram. It had to go. He decided on a much better name: eMix. GrooveGram . . . eMix . . . I wasn't too bothered. I was just glad he was injecting some energy into the marketing department. He told me had already commissioned a new logo designed by a graphics firm he knew in San Francisco.

Lorraine and I agreed that the direction he was taking was exciting, and he needed reinforcements. There were other employees at Apple Ian said he could persuade to come over to Beatnik. He duly went out and poached several, including Shafath Syed, Stefan Schaefer, and a Web entertainment expert, Bahman Dara. Within the first few months he built his marketing group to twelve people, and they took occupation of a cluster of cubicles and offices in the southeast corner of our building. They would often flock to the conference room, where Ian would conduct lightning marketing meetings that were usually over in five minutes. They also shared a hobby: radio-controlled helicopters and cars. It was not uncommon to be tripped up in the corridors by a speeding model four-by-four, or to hear heavy footsteps on the roof of the building as they experimented with their remote-controlled choppers.

All aspects of Beatnik's Web site and brand image came under scrutiny. Ian's team created a fifteen-page document detailing the face-lift that we would undergo. The word soon went round the company that nothing, however small, could be decided or even discussed without your first talking to Ian Powell and his marketing team. They came to be known as the Apple Mafia.

Having a dynamic in-house marketing group freed up Lorraine and me to focus on bringing in new business. We traveled to meetings and presentations at East Coast–based companies like AOL and AT&T, trying to cook up agreements and partnerships, looking for any way to boost Beatnik's feeble revenues. We made a good double act: I would do my demos and make a fervent case for Beatnik-sonified Web sites, while Lorraine would take care of the follow-up and negotiations, all the little details that were never my strong point. She set about standardizing communications within the company, creating the infrastructure for performance reviews and pension plans. Lorraine was really settling into her role as Beatnik's CEO now, firmly on top of our finances, and well liked within the company and the boardroom. Mary Coller was mainly out of the picture, but still worked with me on music industry–related business.

In early 1999, music downloading and piracy were increasingly in the news. It was shaping up as a war of attrition between tech companies like Napster and recording artists such as Metallica and Garth Brooks. As someone who straddled both worlds, I was gaining a reputation as a joint spokesperson. Newspapers and talk radio shows would call me for a quote, and I was summoned to increasingly high-level meetings. On one trip to Washington, D.C., Mary and I attended an all-day copyright summit at the White House. In the morning we listened to an impassioned speech by Ted Kennedy about his family's love for music, and how it needed to be protected. An exclusive lunch was hosted by Vice President Al Gore, who had positioned himself as a tech guru. I spoke briefly to him, but with his glazed-over eyes it was as if the man had been replaced with a robot. (I met him again years later at TED, recovering from the failure of his presidential campaign. He had regained his humanity.) The White House event concluded with an early dinner on the back lawn along with the heads of the worldwide music-royalty-collection societies. They had come from Asia and South America, from Africa, Eastern Europe, and the former Soviet countries. With their warts and bushy eyebrows, these were the true dinosaurs of the music industry, the last relics of a dying breed. They ruled over organizations that were kept in business by obsolete copyright laws and questionable broadcast payment schemes. But this afternoon they were the special guests of the president of the United States, and many had brought their wives to America for the event. One group had come straight from a shopping spree and were laden with designer-branded clothes bags. It had been raining. As the lobster bisque was served, Bill Clinton took the stage with his saxophone to join Booker T. and the M.G.'s in a rousing rendition of "Green Onions"; and I enjoyed the comic display of several overweight women in Prada leopard-print dresses struggling to find their tables, stiletto heels sinking into the soft grass of the gently sloping White House lawn.

I saw many of the same characters the next day at a conference about the state of the music industry, where I was one of the keynote speakers. The thrust of my speech was that record labels, publishers, and collection societies needed to wake up to the reality of digital downloading. It was pointless to try to stamp out the pirate sites, and even more ridiculous that they were trying to sue individual music fans. It was time to license the catalogs of major artists to the new Web-based companies that knew how to create convenient, appealing download services, and to make music cheap enough so that the public would be happy to pay a small fee per song, instead of downloading it illegally. I explained how my own company, Beatnik Inc., was working in a field for which there was no current collection scheme in place. I was a paid-up member of ASCAP and PRS, but these organizations had no mechanism for collecting fees from the Web or game consoles or devices, and zero knowledge of technology or the behavior of early adopters.

As I spoke, I became aware of a reaction from the audience that in my forty-year career I have never encountered before or since. An audible hiss rippled around the room, and by the end of my speech it had morphed into a "booo." When I made my way through the foyer afterwards, the crowd parted like the Red Sea. Serbs and Estonians turned their back on me. ASCAP's president, Marilyn Bergman, expressed her condolences to Mary: she wasn't apologizing for the audience's reaction, she was sympathizing that Mary had to manage such a troublesome artist. I made an early departure from D.C., feeling angry and depressed about the music industry all over again.

I drove from SFO straight back to San Mateo. Beatnik's offices were buzzing: Ian Powell was about to debut his new corporate branding scheme, and in advance of the weekly company meeting everyone had been issued new business cards, coffee mugs, and mouse pads featuring the revitalized Beatnik corporate logo. Compared to the flowery B of the past, the new logo looked very official: it was a simple rectangle with a pair of intertwined wave forms, and the word Beatnik in plain letters. This, Ian said, would be better suited to a wide variety of uses, ranging from the top banner on our home page to small insignia on devices and appliances. Gone were the lively purple and yellow colors on the walls of the reception area. The new color scheme was to be navy blue. Ian spelled out his vision for Beatnik's outbound communications, which would announce to the world that we were a serious company to do business with, a solid and dependable brand. He spoke authoritatively and convincingly, walking us through his rationale in a strong, bold voice, leaving little room for debate. When he left the room to loud applause, a gaggle of his disciples filed out closely behind in his wake.

As my car wound through the hills on my way home that evening in a torrential downpour, there was a dull feeling in the pit in my stomach. It should have been a relief to get home and relax after three days away on yet another business trip, and to see my children; but as Kathleen and I sat on the couch and watched the kids playing together on the living room rug, a sense of nausea began to overtake me. I put it down to something I'd eaten, or perhaps a bug I'd picked up on the plane.

We lived in a sleepy coastal area, a dormitory town full of four-bedroom homes for middle-class Silicon Valley geek workers and their families. Our youngest child, Graham, was now nearly four, and he'd just started preschool. Kathleen relayed a story his teachers told her while I was away. Apparently the teacher had gone round the class and asked each of the kids what their dad did for a living. When it got to Graham, he said, "My daddy is in a computer company, but really he's a *magician*!"

You could understand Graham's mistake. I was the man who pulled pennies from behind his ear. He had never heard me sing or play music. These days the lid of the piano in the living room stayed firmly closed. Lily and Talia were a bit older than their brother, and though they'd yet to see me perform live, they always got excited when one of my songs came on KFOG radio, or over the speakers in Starbucks.

"Daddy," said Lily one day, "my friend John Bruno says you stole a song from the Backstreet Boys. Did you?"

I chuckled. The last time I'd released a record, the Backstreet Boys were still in grade school. "Which song?" I asked Lily.

"You know, the one where Mama's in the video, 'I Love You Goodbye.' He says you copied it from their big hit."

People often point out similarities between songs, and I'm not very good at noticing them. Mentally I flipped through the few Backstreet Boys songs I could think of. The one she was talking about had to be "I Want It That Way." I replayed it in my head. Okay—so the five-note melody of the hook was the same. No big deal, lots of famous motifs have five notes, there's a limit to the possible combinations. But actually, when I thought about it, it was more than five consecutive notes. The little passing notes singers add to the start and end of syllables, the inflections, were exactly the same as mine. They even repeated the hook line at the end, drawing out the penultimate syllable, exactly the way I'd done it in 1991. And then there was the lyrical structure of the choruses leading up to the hook. Each had four couplets, ending in a quote, sung to the same melody: I sang, "The hardest words I know are / 'I love you goodbye'"; they sang, "Don't ever let me hear you say / 'I want it that way.'"

The next morning I got on the phone to my bassist friend Matthew Seligman, who was now practicing as a lawyer in the UK, and asked his opinion. "Your song is beautiful," he said, "one of the best things you've ever written, and practically nobody heard it. That Backstreet Boys song is one of the biggest-selling singles of all time."

"I know, right?" I said. "It's been #1 in like twenty different countries. But it seems like such a blatant rip-off. Do you think I should sue the bastards?"

"Well, look at it this way," said Matthew. "Whether or not they consciously plagiarized you, the chances are they'd settle out of court, and even if they only gave you 10 percent of the royalties, you'd be a multimillionaire."

But I decided not to sue. Aside from anything else, the Backstreet Boys were on Jive Records, whose parent company, Zomba, had just invested $2.5 million in Beatnik. It wouldn't do to bite the hand that feeds. More important, did I really want to be known to the next generation of music fans as the guy that sued the Backstreet Boys? I was already on my way to becoming a very rich man once Beatnik hit pay dirt. Wouldn't I rather be thought of as a successful tech entrepreneur, with a precious musical past?

Suddenly the thought of my music, my chords and poetry, seemed a million miles away. To anybody under the age of thirty-five, it was ancient history. My kids barely knew me as a musician. They were going to grow up never having seen their dad do what he loved most. I thought of Beatnik and wondered if it was slowly draining me of that ability, now and forever. That night the thought gripped me like a fever.

The next morning was the day of the Hatch Elementary School concert. The whole school was taking part in the performance, celebrating the folk traditions of Central American cultures. The hall was packed with parents and grandparents, our friends and neighbors. I sat with Kathleen at the end of a row. Talia's class would be on around the middle of the show. I saw Talia sitting cross-legged, waiting with her classmates for their moment onstage, and she spotted us and waved excitedly. The little kids were adorable in their outfits, singing Spanish songs, clapping and dancing, to the delight of the audience. And all I could do was stare blankly. Their simple chants tore through my brain like a knife. I was knotted up inside. I told Kathleen I had to go to the men's room, but snuck out of an exit instead. Once in the open air I crumpled down against a wall and started poking aimlessly at my Black-Berry. I don't know how long I was there, maybe fifteen minutes. Rearranging old e-mails. Checking sports scores for teams I didn't care about. In the end, Kathleen came out and found me there, frantic with worry. "Sweetie, you're missing it!" she said, on the edge of tears.

I think that was probably the lowest moment of my life.

CHAPTER 14
BOWIE DOES BEATNIK

By the summer of 1999, Beatnik's office building was already near its capacity. It was sometimes hard to get a parking space in the garage, and Lorraine suggested she and I reserve a couple of spaces near the elevator with our names painted on the tarmac.

The last available cubicles were in the vault in the basement. Lorraine decided to offer them to a small start-up run by a guy named Tony Fadell. Tony had a strong background in handheld devices, and since leaving Philips he'd been doing paid consulting work for Beatnik. He was working on a digital jukebox, but his start-up was running out of money. Unlikely as it seemed that Apple would want to weigh in to the digital music fray at this late stage, Steve Jobs loved the idea of an Apple-branded music player. And so it came to be that Tony's prototype evolved into the Apple iPod, and he joined Apple and became the prime architect of the iTunes music service.

The music industry was a shambles. Following the drastic drop in CD sales during the 1990s and the widespread sharing of illegal MP3 files, the record labels had gone into a panic. First they tried to sue Napster and put the site out of business. Then they targeted individual music fans—their own customers. Finally, with a mob of litigators behind them, a consortium of major labels bought Napster out from under Sean Parker's nose and tried to launch their own music service. It was an utter failure. They spent two years squabbling among themselves, and with their own artists. I remember too well how EMI Records got into disputes with many of the major acts on their roster. EMI couldn't resist dipping its own hand into the tech cookie jar. They'd made a handy $50 million profit in six months by flipping the stock they'd demanded from a small tech start-up prior to its IPO. How much of that licensing revenue was credited back to bands like Queen and Pink Floyd and Duran Duran, whose music EMI had farmed out? Zero. Because that sort of revenue was never defined in the contracts we'd all signed decades earlier.

The labels had tentatively licensed small parts of their catalogs to tech start-ups like Liquid Audio and eMusic, but they were overly cautious about larger companies, reluctant to give away their power. So nothing could get done. The simple fact was, with the pressing plants and fleets of trucks taken out of the equation, there was no real reason for record companies to exist. They had no divine right to position themselves as musical tastemakers who would determine what the public got to hear. They were becoming little more than a roadblock between music fans and new music.

What the labels did have to fall back on was their long-term control of legacy catalogs. Their best and only weapons in the digital music wars were the binding agreements with the likes of Madonna and U2, the Rolling Stones and Bon Jovi. Their lawsuits against tech companies and music fans mostly ended in a stalemate, and their own efforts at digital music platforms were a flop. So by the time Apple came along and proposed a service that would link iPod users to the slick Web-based iTunes storefront, requiring an all-out license to each of the majors' entire catalogs, they met little resistance. Apple was the white knight; it had none of the sinister overtones of a Microsoft, nor the risk associated with early-stage start-ups. "Here," said the labels. "Take it all! We're too beat up."

Yet the history books will record that Steve Jobs single-handedly revolutionized the music industry. In the future, schoolchildren will be taught that Jobs was the innovator, the early bird, the fearless pioneer, who recognized the precise moment when music was ready to go virtual, and that the Internet was the place to buy it. In reality he was several years late to the party. I hope one day the iPod's true visionary will get his due recognition. Maybe then they will stick up a plaque on the side of Beatnik's old building on El Camino Real, proclaiming, "In 1999 the iPod was invented here by Anthony Michael Fadell."

Tony Fadell's iPod prototype was probably the only thing of real value to come out of our building during that period. It was right there under my nose, and I myself was oblivious, until the day he and his group moved out and went to work for Apple.

Day-to-day life at Beatnik was a frantic rush to create a real business, or at least to ally ourselves with companies who already had one. We had struck up a relationship with a small San Francisco outfit called Mixman, a group of DJs, musicians, and designers with a cool office near Chinatown. They made a plastic hardware console that looked a little like a scaled-down version of a DJ mixer and twin turntables. The parts didn't actually move, but you could load it up with multitrack song files and make your own mixes of songs by a variety of top artists. The Mixman box was on sale in a number of retail chains, including Circuit City and Walmart, and it was targeted at teenage males and tweens. In a way the product was the hardware equivalent of our own eMixes, but unlike Beatnik, Mixman actually had some revenues. In their best quarters they turned a small profit—a feat that was practically unheard of in the Web software sector. Beatnik's board was getting impatient with our lack of a solid revenue stream, and they were envious of Mixman's apparent success. One of our directors, Allen Morgan, who represented our largest VC investor, Mayfield Fund, had the bright idea that if we could merge with Mixman, we'd combine the fizz of an Internet start-up with a plausible revenue stream—and this might be enough for the combined company to file for an initial public offering on the NASDAQ.

While I was not a big fan of the Mixman product, Ian Powell was clearly very keen for this merger to take place. "In fact," insisted Ian, "the Mixman merger is the *only* way this company will survive." I wondered how on earth he planned to consolidate our two very different brands and types of customer. Mixman was all about consumer toy sales, whereas—thanks to Ian's recent efforts—Beatnik was making inroads into the corporate ad agency world. And what sort of logistical challenges would Lorraine face? A merger would mean twenty-five reluctant San Franciscan hipsters commuting down to our uncool San Mateo bank building every day, with their tattoos and piercings, and we'd have to find new job titles for them. I could sense the Mixman guys weren't really into it, either, but they recognized, as we did, that it was probably the best chance any of us had to make some money during the dot-com gold rush. My head began to spin. All these irons in the fire, and no clear sense of direction.

We pressed ahead with the merger plans, and tensions rose. While the contracts neared completion, the rest of the company was on a tight deadline: Ian was masterminding a major release party and product debut at the annual National Association of Broadcasters show in Las Vegas. We were announcing a suite of products that would enable music libraries and sound effects companies to license their music on the Web via a Beatnik-powered interface and e-commerce engine.

In times of crisis, I'd always put my faith in talent and creativity. I had the idea to approach two highly regarded audio industry figures to help spearhead the Vegas launch: the movie composer Hans Zimmer, a fellow Fairlight user I'd known since my London days, and Lucasfilm's Oscar-winning sound designer Gary Rydstrom. The plan was for me to conduct an armchair interview with the two of them onstage and discuss Beatnik's new products while showing off our demos on a giant screen. A small theater at the MGM Grand Hotel was booked for a private party, and the guest list was to be made up of top industry professionals.

Hans Zimmer and Gary Rydstrom agreed to take part for free as a favor to me, so I was quite surprised when Lorraine told me the marketing department's budget for Beatnik's Vegas party was over $85,000. I called Ian Powell from a pay phone at SFO to ask why it was costing so much.

"Well, there is the theater rental, the catering, and the band," he replied.

"There's a *band?*" I asked.

"Oh, I meant to tell you. We've booked Don Henley from the Eagles. But he's doing it really cheap."

"How cheap?"

"Only $60K, plus expenses," replied Ian.

I was flabbergasted. Why hadn't Ian asked me first? I have nothing against the Eagles per se—used to like them quite a lot back in the early seventies, actually—but surely I should have a say in what rock music act we chose to associate with the Beatnik brand? What sort of statement did it make that we were booking a middle-aged country rock star for our company party? Why not one of the cool current pop or hip-hop acts we were targeting with our eMixes?

I tried to stay calm, explaining that I needed to be consulted before he made a decision like that. I felt that the music business was my domain. But Ian cut me off, and he sounded pretty hot under the collar. "Look, I won't go into my reasons now. I have to get to a meeting. Gotta run." Then he hung up.

My next call was to Bahman Dara, Ian's second-in-command. Bahman said he was sure Ian had thought very carefully about the choice of Henley for the party. I should not worry. He'd known Ian for many years and was constantly amazed how he always seemed to make the right choices.

A few minutes later I got an e-mail from Ian on my BlackBerry. "I'd be grateful if you didn't talk to my team directly. They are busy preparing for Vegas and they need to stay focused. In future, please put everything through me."

That night, I barely slept. In fact, I was sleeping less and less. I was away on business trips a couple of times a week and working long hours at the office. Often after a full workday I couldn't face going straight home and plunging into domestic life, with paper bills to open and three small kids so eager to play with me. So I would stop off at a local Italian restaurant and have a couple of cocktails at the bar, chatting to the restaurateur, Pete. One night I confessed to him that I thought Beatnik was starting to affect my sanity, and I told him about my little problem with the VP of marketing.

"That's why I never put my own name on my restaurants," Pete said. "See, most restaurants will go down the tubes sooner or later, it's only a matter of time. You should never confuse your business with your own sense of self. Otherwise, when the business goes in the shitter, that's where your ego ends up, too."

Pete wandered off to tend to a table. As his words sank in, I caught sight of myself in the mirror behind the bar. I looked tired, frail, old. I hadn't been windsurfing in months and I was putting on weight. I couldn't remember the last time I'd fired up a synthesizer or written a song. And here I was hiding out in a bar, afraid to be at work to face my own employees and afraid to go home because I knew I couldn't be the dad my family needed. I thanked Pete for his sage words and downed the dregs of my whiskey sour.

I sat for a while in our driveway with the engine off, and I thought of Jim Clark in his darkened office at Healtheon, playing with his executive toys. He'd had the good sense to remove himself from his proud creation before the rot started to set in. He must have realized that Netscape's trajectory was set early on in the game, and there was little more he could do to affect its success or failure. When Netscape ultimately failed—selling itself off to the (by now irrelevant) AOL after suffering years of assault and battery from Microsoft—Jim was probably relaxing on the deck of his megayacht in some Mediterranean harbor.

Now Beatnik Inc. was hurtling perilously towards its IPO, with or without me. It was time to start building my escape pod. But unlike Jim Clark, I was still dependent on my monthly salary. I had a mortgage to pay off and three kids still in school. I decided I needed to occupy myself with some portion of the business where I could stay insulated from Ian and Lorraine and the belligerent Mixman employees.

Once Beatnik became a public company, I would be locked in for at least a couple of years. That was beginning to seem like a jail sentence. In private I confessed to Joe Rizzi that I was not sure I could go through with it. I was weighing the idea of getting out before my name got printed on the S1. "How strong is your desire for liquidity?" he asked me. "Because the board might agree to let you sell your shares privately for a few cents on the dollar."

Liquidity! What a concept. I was feeling more and more that the company I founded was nothing but vaporware. To survive this I had to return to solid matter, find a way to ground myself.

In a fog, I flew to Las Vegas and arrived in time for Ian's big product launch party at the MGM Grand. The drinks and hors d'oeuvres were flowing, and my onstage interview with Hans Zimmer and Gary Rydstrom went over well to a packed house. I could see Ian at the back by the bar, schmoozing his VIP ad agency guests. The time came for me to introduce the Don Henley band. As I stepped to the center of the stage and looked along the line of Henley's musicians, I spotted a familiar face: my former backing vocalist from Lost Toy People, Laura Creamer, whom I hadn't seen since the late eighties. I winked at her and she gave a little wave.

Don Henley played a slick one-hour set. He sounded great and looked very dapper with his blow-dried hair and light tan suit. I waited a few minutes at the end of the show, then headed backstage. In the wings I bumped into Don. I introduced myself and complimented him on his set, thanking him for coming to play at our company party, and I said I knew Laura and was she around? He motioned me up a staircase towards the greenroom. But when I got there, it was deserted aside from a lone janitor sweeping up.

"Where is the band?" I said.

"Oh, Don and his band came straight offstage and into a limo out in the back," he said. "I think they're catching a plane back to L.A. tonight."

"Well, that can't be right—I just saw Don downstairs in the wings!" I exclaimed.

"Christ, did that weirdo get in again?" said the janitor. "We had to kick him out during the sound check. He's a stalker. He follows the band everywhere, dressed exactly like Don. I'd better call casino security."

Sometimes I felt like a con artist myself, walking around Silicon Valley dressed exactly like Thomas Dolby.

Beatnik's board concluded several meetings with investment bankers to pick the firm that would take us public on the NASDAQ. At length we selected Robertson Stephens; or rather, Robertson Stephens selected us. All over Silicon Valley hopeful software companies were lining up for their IPOs.

The S1 form required by the Securities and Exchange Commission required an extensive analysis of our company's business prospects and a competitive risk assessment. I helped Lorraine Hariton write the corporate summary. I had to admit, as we listed our accomplishments and the deals we had concluded, I felt pretty good about what we had achieved. There was no need to overhype anything. Admittedly our revenues were sparse, and in our five-year existence we'd only ever had two profitable quarters. But the public was hungry for new tech investments, and compared to many of the wacky companies that were completing successful IPOs at the time, on paper Beatnik looked like a reasonably good bet.

What we could not disclose, though, was the warring that was going on behind closed doors. Many employees were getting bitchy in their quest for more elevated titles to print on their business cards. With promotion came an increase in stock options, and one day soon these would be worth a lot of money. In a company with 102 employees there were a dozen with the title of vice president or better. Lorraine Hariton's office door opened and closed with a constant flow of traffic as she played nursemaid and therapist to members of her senior staff. She had to listen to a torrent of suggestions and complaints from disgruntled employees. Rumors began to circulate in the corridors. Cryptic e-mails would make their way around the company, "accidentally" cc'd to key personnel. An anonymous posting showed up on a site called fuckedcompany.com purporting to be from a Beatnik employee, decrying our wasteful overspending on parties and press releases, and calling the company "just another get-rich-quick scam" by its founder.

Ian Powell was Beatnik's third-largest employee shareholder, and though he'd been at the company for under a year, the IPO would make him a multimillionaire. Yet every time he closed a deal, he would take Lorraine or me aside and complain about his compensation. He loved to remind me that he'd taken a major wage cut when he moved from Apple, and that given the value he was adding to the company he should be rewarded with more stock and his vesting period should be accelerated. I just sidestepped these demands. I'd fib that I was late for a recording session, or that I had to leave early to go to my step aerobics class over at 24 Hour Fitness. I told him I was trying to eat better and get in shape for the upcoming pre-IPO publicity tour.

"God, I hate that place," Ian said. "People always come up to me and say, 'How did you get *that* muscle, and *that* muscle?'" I'd never noticed before how when Ian clenched his jaw, the veins throbbed in his temples.

At the Beatnik board meeting, Ian proudly presented his latest campaign, "Bowie Does Beatnik." He'd persuaded David Bowie's management to adopt our technology for bowie.net, his state-of-the-art fan site. Ian projected a giant image of the proposed full-page and half-page ads. This was the first time Beatnik had invested in print advertising, and he explained that it was the logical next step in establishing our brand. The budget for the initial ad buy was $30,000, and the entire campaign was to cost us more than $75,000. Ian, in his persuasive style, was all hyperbole. The board members were clearly impressed, but one or two voiced some concerns. Allen Morgan commented that magazines and newspapers seemed a little "old hat." The bigger problem, for me, was the photo Ian proposed to use in the ads. It was by far the ugliest picture of David Bowie I'd ever seen. He looked old and haggard, and definitely underwhelmed by the product he was promoting. I worried that when the magazines hit the newsstands, this would be the main talking point. Did we really want people to associate the Beatnik brand with a sad, past-it rock star?

"What, like yourself?" said Ian. He immediately laughed, too loudly, as if to make light of his quip. There was a ripple of uncomfortable throat clearing around the room before Lorraine thanked Ian for his presentation and said we'd now proceed to other business.

"Before I go I'd just like to say what an honor it is to work with you guys, and how optimistic I am about Beatnik's success," said Ian as he stood up. "And I wonder if you would give some further thought to my request for an increase in my compensation. I've set out the key points here." At that he produced from his briefcase a one-page memo, duplicates of which he slid across the conference table to each of the external board members.

Ian left and Allen read out the memo. It called for a $20,000-per-year pay rise and an increase in Ian's original stock options by 440,000 shares. This seemed an arbitrary number. Until I remembered that, at the last count, it was the precise number of Beatnik shares I was due to vest myself during that period. Where had Ian come up with that number? The only people that knew the details of our share allocations were Lorraine and me, the board, and our director of human resources. In any case, the board was not thrilled.

"Lorraine, are you happy with Ian's work?" asked Joe Rizzi.

"Well, yes, he's doing an amazing job," said Lorraine. "I just wish he'd tell me about his plans before he commits money to them. Marketing accounted for over one-third of our expenditure in the last quarter."

Joe looked thoughtful. "A few thousand shares here or there is not going to change our lifestyle. Why don't you tell Ian we will revisit his comp situation in Q2, after the IPO quiet period . . ."

"But, Lorraine, you have to make it contingent on him falling in line with the priorities you and Thomas set for him," interjected Thampy. "We can't have Ian blowing through this company's cash for his own pet marketing schemes."

That Friday we threw a big party at a nightclub in San Francisco to celebrate our IPO filing. I stood in the line at the bar behind a Robertson Stephens investment banker chap and his tall blond trophy wife, and couldn't help eavesdropping. "And what do these ones do?" she asked him, shouting over the DJ's thumping trance beat. "They do music, darling. I told you," he said, "music on the Internet. You know, like those ones the other week, in Redwood City."

In the run-up to New Year's Eve 1999, Wall Street was getting nervous about what was known as the Y2K bug. Fanned by the media, there was a widespread panic that computers and networks would grind to a halt at the stroke of midnight on December 31 because their clocks were not programmed to deal with years that didn't start with the number nineteen. Yet in Silicon Valley, the race was on to see who could dream up the most elaborate millennium party. Chris Anderson invited a hundred of his closest friends to the ski resort of Whistler, British Columbia, and asked me to play for his guests. It was the first concert I'd done in many years, and it felt wonderful to get back to music—so effortless, so relaxing. Afterwards we all took the ski lift up to a mountaintop restaurant that Chris had booked privately for the evening. Out on the deck with a mug of mulled wine, Kathleen and I gazed at the Milky Way through a large telescope. The night sky was unpolluted and magnificent, and under the canopy of stars we talked about what we would do with all the money.

"We could get hold of an atlas," I joked, "and pick out our island in the Caribbean."

"Can it be in the Hebrides instead?" Kathleen said.

"Sure, why not? In a decade or two they'll be calling it the Scottish Riviera."

"The IRS will get most of the money, for starters," she reflected, "so the government can build more aircraft carriers. Can't we give some of it away ourselves instead?"

We decided to set up a revocable trust fund, distributing over half of our 2.5 million shares among our closest family and friends, as well as a number of Kathleen's favorite charities. Not only would this save a fortune in taxes, it would mean that those closest to us would be able to cash in their shares right after the IPO; whereas, as a director of the company, I would have a fiduciary responsibility to maintain my stake at a high level for several years to come. The taxman would get his dues, but we'd still have enough left over to retire and live comfortably for the rest of our lives. Most of all, I loved the idea of being able to make my music without any outside pressure.

For the first few months of the year 2000 I had butterflies in my stomach. I decided to keep my head down and leave the money matters to the experts. So I concentrated on my new obsession—making music for mobile phones.

Every time I traveled to Europe or Asia I saw that those cultures were far ahead of the USA in their adoption of mobile technology. On every street corner in Copenhagen and Singapore there was a teenager thumbing text messages into her cell phone. In Silicon Valley they had no idea. It was not a pedestrian culture—everyone drove a car, had a computer waiting for them at home and another at work. Venture capitalists were focused on the PC, and the gray corporate world they called "the enterprise." They didn't consider young people as a driving force for the economy: their sense of pop culture came from observing their own teenage kids, who attended private school in Atherton and got a Jeep as a sixteenth-birthday present.

So this gave me something to get my teeth into, something that would keep me out from under the feet of Lorraine and Ian and the board and the investment bankers. I saw it as vital that Beatnik reeducate itself, beginning with a small group, then the whole company. I put together a task force of the ten people most likely to understand and adjust to the mobile world, and we named our little stealth project Valhalla—after the Viking heaven. We met twice weekly, almost in secret, so as not to distract the rest of the employees until after the IPO.

Following the public announcement of our IPO, Beatnik suddenly had a lot of new friends. In March 2000, the board decided to open up a "mezzanine" round of investment. This was mainly for strategic partners and individuals who we believed could "bring something more to the table." Among the investors were MTV Networks; SoftBank, the Asian-backed VC fund; Kevin Wall, a top rock festival promoter; and Timothy Draper, from the prominent investment firm Draper Fisher Jurvetson. Lorraine Hariton did a marvelous job of pushing the investors to put pen to paper before our IPO window closed. On top of the new cash infusion, our IPO might raise $100 million more. I was aghast when I thought about the numbers; it seemed like something out of an Oliver Stone movie, with me in the Tom Cruise role. They were going to put me on the front cover of *Fortune* magazine, seated on a throne.

The mezzanine round brought in an astonishing $34 million of new cash. We put it in the bank. The very next day, Wall Street crashed, and Beatnik's IPO went up in smoke.

CHAPTER 15
DARK FIBER

We had a poker game on Thursday nights in Mark Gross's garage in Burlingame. Five or six guys, joking around, kicking back. We'd order pizza, drink some beers and a malt whiskey or two, smoke a joint. I was never that great at cards, but I found it enjoyably distracting. You couldn't win or lose more than a couple of hundred dollars in a night; mostly, the money just moved around the table. It was fascinating to look at our group of regulars and consider how each player's poker style matched their attitude to business and to life.

Mark Gross himself was a shrewd and conservative player. Dealt anything but the best starting hand, he would fold right away. He was happy to sit out the rest of the hand and observe. He would crack jokes, but you could tell he was watching closely. It was all a learning process. He would invariably finish up with a big pile of chips at the end of the night. He parachuted out of a career at imagine.com early on, and invented a brilliant way for parents to keep track of their kids' homework, called School Loop. It's been implemented in thousands of public schools in over thirty states.

Howard Bulka was a top San Francisco chef. He played cards for the fun of it and for the companionship, enjoying a surprise turn or a bad beat, even when it was at his own expense. He later turned his back on haute cuisine and opened Howie's Artisan Pizza in Palo Alto—and very good it is, too.

Rob Reid was an enthusiastic and attentive player. He calculated the odds and bet the percentages. He sold his music streaming company Rhapsody to RealNetworks the week before Apple announced iTunes, and married a beautiful TV presenter. He recently published his first sci-fi novel.

Bobby Levin was on the cautious side. A self-employed media consultant, he preferred it when the stakes were low. He would back off the moment the pot got too big to count. He rarely ended the evening a big winner, but he kept his losses manageable and had a great night out.

Stuart Illian made some smart moves. He would wait till he sensed he had the right hand, then back it to the hilt and make a killing. He had a rough time at xoom.com when the tech-homesteading balloon began to deflate. But his heart was never in it, so he switched to a business he loved: aviation. He left San Francisco before the height of the IPO mayhem and bought a jet charter company at a small airfield in Southern California.

When it was Chris Anderson's turn to deal, he would invent new games. He enjoyed the complexity of shifting probabilities and loved the thrill of a big pot. He always stayed in for the most exciting hands, where often his sheer self-belief paid off. He would get on a roll and win several hands running as a big pile of chips stacked up in front of him. On more than one occasion, though, I saw him stick around too long and end up doing the walk of shame to the nearest ATM. But Chris could afford it. He had built two massive publishing empires before the dot-com crash robbed him of a large part of his net worth. He put a big chunk of what he had left into his beloved TED conference—and over the next fifteen years he built his third global empire, one that will be treasured and remembered far longer than his magazine endeavors.

Why am I bothering to record this in such detail? Because there's an old saying in poker: if you don't know who the sucker is, the sucker is *you*.

After Beatnik withdrew its IPO in April 2000, I tumbled into a deep depression. My already sleepless nights were spent tossing and turning in a cold sweat. I lost interest in sailing, bicycling, reading, and sex. I lost interest in music. I didn't want to face my friends. I had no energy to play with the kids, and increasingly I needed to stop off at one of the local bars before heading home in the evenings. First thing the next morning I'd hit Starbucks for a couple of chocolate croissants and a triple cappuccino; halfway through my cappuccino, I needed a cappuccino. It took me a while to accept that I had to seek help. Eventually Kathleen persuaded me to see a psychiatrist, who said I was suffering from anxiety and depression, and put me on Prozac. I spent a night in the sleep lab at Stanford Hospital and they diagnosed me with chronic sleep apnea. The specialist was surprised I had been able to hold down a marriage or a job.

He recommended maxillofacial surgery to ease the pressure on my windpipe, but warned me that it could put my singing voice at risk. I took a deep breath and booked a date for the complicated procedure at SFSU Hospital, knowing that there might be no way back.

Round about that time, a brown padded envelope arrived in the mail. I glanced at the English stamps and watermark, and just looking at it made me feel homesick. I recognized the handwriting from years earlier. It was from Paddy McAloon of Prefab, and inside was a cassette tape, along with a nine-page letter. He wrote that the tape contained a home demo of a new solo composition called "I Trawl the Megahertz" that he wanted me to produce. It was a single track, nearly twenty-three minutes in duration. This time I was longing to hear it, but I needed to pick the right moment, when I had some peace and quiet. That moment arrived a few mornings later, when I got in my car and joined the slow commuter traffic of the early rush hour on highway 92 and popped in the cassette.

The piece began with a plaintive orchestral figure played on high strings and xylophone. Broad cellos and violas swelled in underneath, with that familiar sense of longing that all of Paddy's chords evoke in me. Then, a solitary female voice, an actress speaking a narrative:

> I am telling myself the story of my life,
> stranger than song or fiction.
> We start with the joyful mysteries,

before the appearance of ether,
trying to capture the elusive:
the farm where the crippled horses heal,
the woods where autumn is reversed,
and the longing for bliss in the arms
of some beloved from the past.
I said, "Your daddy loves you."
I said, "Your daddy loves you very much,
he just doesn't want to live with us anymore."

—From I *Trawl the Megahertz* © Paddy McAloon, 2003

By the time it got to the crippled horses I was already in floods of tears. I had to pull over on the gravel shoulder, with a line of angry commuters honking at me. I rolled to a stop in front of a boarded-up flower stall, restarted the tape, and buried my head in my hands. I stayed like that for the whole twenty-three minutes, and for a while after.

I felt that it was my name, my brand that had failed. I felt bad for the employees, guilty about the shareholders, embarrassed that the shares I've gifted to my family and friends would now be worthless. I kicked myself to think that I could have gotten out. With the approval of the boardroom, I probably could have resigned from Beatnik during the year before the planned IPO by selling my stake privately to one of the many greedy would-be investors. But despite my reservations about what we were doing, I'd hung in there. It wasn't even about the money—it was about the chance to score a massive hit versus the risk of looking the fool by cashing out too early. And I knew that I'd put it all ahead of my health and my family, and risked missing out on being a proper father to my children.

Lorraine was a good friend. She tried to console me with numbers and facts. Beatnik still had over $37 million in the bank, she reminded me, and although our annual revenues were only $1.5 million, they were getting ever closer to matching our outgoings. Perhaps it was a blessing in disguise that we could now focus on developing a real business without the scrutiny of public shareholders and the SEC. She set about reorganizing the company and looking for ways to trim our costs, maximize our runway, and give us a cushion to reach profitability.

I've never been great at tidying up behind myself, so I left Lorraine to it. Cash or no cash, I was convinced Beatnik was on its way to joining the long list of dot-com also-rans. I went to wander the corridors, hoping I'd have a brain wave that would rescue my company from the brink of oblivion.

It was sometimes soothing to hang out with the Beatnik engineers. They had a pragmatic approach to work problems, and although, like all of us, they all kept long office hours, their culture allowed them to take breaks and play video games, hang out at the water cooler, stage Nerf ball fights or Ping-Pong tournaments, and then return to the whiteboard to solve some programming puzzle or other.

I remember one morning—this was prior to our non-IPO and my ensuing nervous crisis—I was perched on the side of the desk in Muir's cubicle. He was twanging on his guitar. I noticed a pile of fading faxes and e-mail printouts, and I started thumbing through them. I stopped at one from a certain David Williams at Nokia. It was two months old and gathering dust. "What did Nokia want?" I asked Chris. "Oh yeah, that was from a few weeks back. They had some questions about the BAE. They're looking for a synth to put on their phones, to play ringtones."

I read the fax through. "Jeez, did you answer this?" I said. Nokia, based in Finland, was the biggest mobile phone company in the world, with a greater than 30 percent market share.

"Um—I think so, but I never heard back from the guy."

"For fuck's sake, Chris!" I said.

There was a phone number for a David Williams on the e-mail, with a UK prefix. It was already 7 p.m. in England, but I headed to my office to give it a try. To my relief, Williams answered in person.

"It's good you called. We're considering putting a sound chip in our phones," he said. "We've had simple ringtones for some time now, but some of these latest Japanese phones have got a Yamaha MIDI chip in them and they're playing proper music. I'd rather not have to license a chip if we can do it on our own CPU. There are some pretty good software synths like Propellerhead, but they use too many cycles. We've had a look at your synth running in Java, and it seems pretty efficient. We'd be interested to see if you can get it working on one of our handsets."

Muir and I set a date for David Williams to stop off in San Francisco on his way to Tokyo, where he was going to meet with Roland, which was offering a software alternative to Yamaha's chip. If it turned into a beauty contest between us and Roland, Muir said, we stood a good chance of winning. Beatnik had been designed from the ground up to have the smallest possible footprint for quick Web downloads and to be efficient enough to run on even the puniest processors. He reckoned he could get a stripped-down version of the BAE running on an old IBM 286 motherboard from the 1980s, which was roughly equivalent in power to the current Nokia mass-market handsets. When David Williams arrived on the date of the meeting, we surprised him with a demo, playing through the tiny speaker of a hacked Nokia handset. He said it already sounded as good as or better than the Japanese alternative, and he would recommend to his company that they enter into a proof-of-concept phase with us as a prelude to a possible licensing deal.

I used Valhalla to ease myself back into the swing of things. My semi-weekly workshop was up to fifteen people now, intently studying the emerging mobile market. We'd entered into an initial agreement with Nokia, and a couple of the engineers had jury-rigged a prototype phone so we could transmit content wirelessly to it. This was counter to FCC regulations governing the radio spectrum, so we kept the apparatus down in the bank vault. It all felt a little subversive. We made an experimental Web page that would allow users to select a tune from one of a library of custom ringtones and send it remotely to their phone number. If BAE were to become the audio engine embedded in every new Nokia handset, the Valhalla group speculated, there had to be ways we could gain an unfair advantage. We began to map out a blue-sky business plan that would wedge us in between the handset manufacturers, wireless carriers like Sprint and AT&T, and music producers. At weekly Wednesday morning general meetings I would present Valhalla's latest findings to the rest of the company, showing slides and demos in an effort to accelerate our collective understanding of the mobile marketplace.

So I was pretty shocked when, at the start of one Wednesday morning meeting, Ian Powell stood up and announced that he'd just returned from Chicago, where he'd concluded a co-marketing deal with Motorola, the largest U.S. manufacturer of mobile phones and devices.

Had Lorraine known about this? And if so, why hadn't I been told? As it turned out, she was as in the dark as I was. The deal Ian had agreed with Motorola apparently involved a commitment from Beatnik for technology, content, and work for hire, which Muir estimated would require an initial investment on our part of $40,000.

After the meeting I went right to Ian's office and interrupted him in mid-discussion with two of his cohorts. They both stayed to witness what happened next. I told Ian it was completely unacceptable for him to go out and make deals like this behind Lorraine's and my back. Quite aside from the fact we had to be more thrifty now that the IPO was abandoned, it was crucial that we all be united in our efforts to get Beatnik's business on track. As Ian knew, the mobile market was where I was now focusing all my energy, along with the fifteen participants in my Valhalla group; he knew we'd begun discussions with Nokia. We had plenty of valuable data to provide Ian in his approaches to companies like Motorola; that was the whole point. But it had to be a coordinated effort, and what he had done might have torpedoed the overall strategy.

As I told Ian this, I could see the blood start to pulse in his temples. For an instant he seemed to swell in size, like a bull toad preparing to strike out at a fly.

"I can't live like that!" he blurted out. "I can't work under a microscope! You don't understand—there's a way of doing things, and then there's the *Ian Powell* way. So fuck you, Thomas. You can stuff your company up your arse."

I turned and walked out, and Ian slammed the door behind me. It stayed shut for the rest of the afternoon. I passed him in the corridor once or twice over the next few days, but we made no eye contact. Nothing came in writing either. He seemed determined to carry on as if his outburst had never happened.

At the quarterly board meeting, Lorraine relayed the story of Ian's unauthorized trip to Motorola, and I told them about our subsequent confrontation. She said Ian had asked her once again that morning to bring up the question of his pay raise and stock options.

Joe Rizzi spoke up. "Lorraine, I want you to send for two security guards and frog-march Ian out of the building. Right now."

Lorraine laughed, but it was plain to see Joe was dead serious. Thampy just nodded gravely. Without a word, Lorraine stood up and went to tell Ian to clear out his desk. By the time the board meeting was concluded, Ian Powell was gone.

He was offered a severance package that included a noncompete agreement. A week later I was at a tech conference in Camden, Maine, and standing at a pay phone beside the harbor when Lorraine told me the news that Ian had signed the severance agreement and was out of my life for good. Oh, I punched the sky! I danced around on the cobblestones among the stacks of lobster pots like a drunken sailor.

Not only did Ian flout the noncompete agreement, he also poached away several of the more dewy-eyed Beatnik employees and formed a consulting company, hawking his services to most of Beatnik's customers in the process. But I wasn't bothered. Life is too short to worry about people like Ian Powell.

The final extravagance of the Ian era was a party in New York City to celebrate our partnership with David Bowie. Bowie wanted to do a free private gig for subscribers to his Web site, with his movie director son, Duncan, filming it for posterity. Ian had agreed that Beatnik would sponsor the show. Bowie booked the Roseland Ballroom, a modest venue with a standing audience capacity of twelve hundred and a nice balcony for VIP tables. I had barely seen Bowie since Live Aid, not even during our work on his Web site project, and it felt good to reconnect with a piece of my past. He had his whole backing band with him this time, including superstar session players Earl Slick, Carlos Alomar, and Gail Ann Dorsey. Bowie had to skip the sound check due to a severe cold, but sent me a personal message via his assistant asking if I'd like to join him onstage at the end for a couple of numbers, provided he had the energy to come back for an encore. I was immensely flattered, but he was sick and I wasn't holding my breath.

Showtime came around and Bowie managed to rip through a two-hour set of nonstop classic hits. I was seated with Kathleen and some of my in-laws at a table on the balcony. At the end of the set, the Roseland crowd went wild. They weren't going to let him go without an encore. Bowie returned to the stage, and shading his eyes, he pointed at me and beckoned. I grabbed a portable keyboard and rushed up onstage, in time to jam my way through "Let's Dance" and "Ziggy Stardust." And then we played "Heroes," which of course I remembered from that incredible afternoon at Wembley Stadium fifteen years earlier. I grinned out at the sea of happy fans in the semidarkness, many waving the green screens of their mobile phones.

It was just the jolt of adrenaline I needed.

I never said what kind of poker player I am. To me, it was always about the epic win. It wasn't enough just to pull down a big pot, or wow people with a straight flush. It had to be a *statement*, a work of art that would stick in the mind for years to come. I would wait all night for the perfect opportunity; sometimes several games would go by in Mark's garage, I'd lose a little each week, and the perfect opportunity would never arise.

Which is why I remember this one hand. The game was seven-card stud, nothing wild. I had two cards facedown and a five showing. The bet was to me, and I passed. Rob Reid had an ace up, and he raised to the max. When I matched his bet, the four other players looked at me quizzically. I could see Rob making a mental note that I maybe had another five down—possibly three to a straight or a flush—surely not a strong hidden pair or trips, or I would have bet initially. Three more players stayed in. After six cards had been dealt I was showing three fives and a king, and still banging it to the max. Everybody dropped out except Rob, who was showing three tens and an ace. Still I kept banging my hand.

"What makes you think I haven't got another ten under here, or a pair?" said Rob, studying my face, and he pushed in his maximum raise. "You better not have four fives, you bastard!"

247

I smiled and reraised him. He saw me. The dealer dealt us the final down card. We both peeked. I bet the limit, and Rob raised. "I don't think you've got a boat," I said, "and I reckon all the tens are gone." I threw in the maximum raise. Rob kept going, reraising me. I glanced at the pot and matched his final bet. There had to be $150 in the middle of the table now. Rob turned over his cards with a grin. Four tens. I turned over mine. Four kings.

When I got home that evening there was a FedEx package waiting for me, and I knew what was inside. It contained a brand-new Nokia 3510i, the first ever mass-market Nokia phone with my Beatnik synth embedded in it. Nokia's first manufacturing run of this model was thirty-five million units.

CHAPTER 16
THE NOKIA WALTZ

People seem to think all tech innovation happens in a blinding flash of inspiration—a lightbulb pops in some maverick genius's head in a Palo Alto garage. It's never really like that.

Back in 1999, when we signed our deal with Nokia, they controlled close to one-third of the global cell phone market. The company had become Finland's largest employer, with an annual turnover equal to 5 percent of the GDP for the entire country.

Only a few years previously, Nokia's main products had included tractor tires, rubber galoshes, and toilet paper. A member of Nokia's board, Tauno Matomäki, once famously stated he believed Finland would never successfully export products small enough that they didn't need to be bolted to the floor. He had no idea that this company, founded in 1865, would one day achieve world domination with a miniature device. Or that a big part of its brand appeal was that the average global consumer believed Nokia was a Japanese company.

Not to put too fine a point on it, ringtones were a complete and utter accident. Text messaging caught the world by surprise as well. Nokia stumbled unwittingly onto the "killer apps" for mobile phones, and Beatnik's lifesaving deal with them came about because I happened to pluck a fading fax out of a dusty pile on our chief engineer's desk.

David Williams explained why Nokia was so reluctant to license a hardware synthesizer chip. It wasn't just the price—though a licensing fee of a couple of dollars per unit soon adds up when you're selling a hundred million phones per quarter!—it was more about the liability of having a key component built in an Asian plant. One earthquake, tsunami, or bird flu epidemic, and the entire supply chain would be disrupted.

We told David that our synth was highly portable—it was already running on multiple operating systems and devices, ranging from computers to set-top boxes and handheld PDAs. On his return to Europe he asked us to send a small engineering team to Helsinki to attempt to "port" the Beatnik Audio Engine to run on their phones. We sent three of our best guys over, and after an intense ten days they managed to get a shrunk-down version of the BAE running pretty well. It was rudimentary, but it sounded a lot better than the bleeps Nokia's phones were making at the time.

A letter of intent was drawn up, and I was summoned to Nokia HQ in Helsinki to meet our potential new partners. They seemed pleased with their initial due diligence. We'd established a timeline for our engineers to port the Beatnik Audio Engine to run across their whole next generation of handsets, and the early indications were that we could get four notes of polyphonic music running simultaneously on their mass-market phones and sixteen notes on their high-end models—meaning an end to the simplistic bleepy tones they were currently saddled with, and no need for a dedicated MIDI audio chip from Yamaha.

This deal was brand-new territory for Beatnik, with real money attached. Beatnik's board and investors were pleased with the promise of added revenue. On the surface, it was just one more engineering contract, yet I sensed it had the potential to transform our business. The last time we were on the brink of a deal this significant, it was with Netscape—and I was still smarting from that one. So I was resolute that we should get this Nokia contract nailed down quickly, and not put the deal at risk by haggling over the terms. The tech license was just the beginning. I tried to explain the larger significance to the Beatnik board, and to get their guidance and support prior to my trip to Finland.

"We could be saving Nokia a billion dollars over time," said Allen Morgan. "We should be able to ask for a few million, even a small royalty."

"Yes, but shouldn't we look beyond the engineering fees?" I said. "I reckon there's about to be an explosion in music for cell phones. We have to work out how we siphon off a piece of that from the carriers, and maybe from the music industry."

"But, Thomas, why get involved with the music industry? It's a complete mess," said Thampy.

I could see his point. Piracy was rampant, with millions of MP3 files being freely downloaded every day and record companies in a state of panic. Lawsuits were flying around left, right, and center. There was no successful model you could point to for digital music sales. Who would want to invest in a music content company?

But if you never left Palo Alto, you wouldn't realize that most of the world was already a mobile culture. On the streets of Europe and Asia, young people were obsessed with their cell phones. They were ready to spend a fortune on plastic covers, wallpapers, and custom ringtones in the name of fashion. It had little to do with the "doomed" music business—it was a brand-new business altogether, and it was ours for the taking. Sadly, this lost on my Silicon Valley investors, who still saw Beatnik as an unsolvable riddle. I hoped to return from my first trip to Finland with some answers.

Exhausted after a long overnight flight from San Francisco via Frankfurt, I was met at Helsinki airport and driven straight to an industrial park in the suburb of Espoo. Finland's brief summer was over, and there was already an icy chill in the air. The instant I was in Nokia's front door, a secretary whisked me away into a small meeting room, where a pair of lawyers thrust a draft contract in front of me and immediately set about grilling me over some of the fine points. They weren't happy about the royalty we were demanding per unit sold. I'm not a lawyer, and I wasn't very familiar with the contract. It didn't seem fair that they were taking advantage of my jet-lagged state. I thought I was there to talk about youth trends and music, not source code escrow and force majeure! So I told them my specs were in my suitcase, and pushed the contract back across the table.

It was fascinating to be here in Nokia's inner sanctum. The Finnish business culture was very strange to me. They're not a talkative bunch. They sit in meetings for long periods and nobody says anything. You ask a simple yes-or-no question, and it falls into a cone of silence. You can almost hear the wind whistling across the tundra. Then, quietly, one of them replies, "Maybe . . ."

It is said that in Finland the difference between an extrovert and an introvert is that an extrovert Finn looks at *your* toes when he's talking to you.

In daylight, the corporate culture is somber. The more important the meeting, the longer the awkward silences. Yet when 5 p.m. comes around, they hit the saunas, and shortly thereafter the drinking begins in earnest. Wild vodka-quaffing sessions and hatchet-throwing games go long into the night. Then, early the next morning, there they are back in their meeting rooms, hungover, deep in contemplation.

After the second day of meetings, a dozen Nokians took me out to a restaurant to sample the local delicacies. The menu was saippuakala (soap fish) and reindeer carpaccio. They all spoke perfect English, the company's international business language of choice. At one point they reverted to their native tongue as a senior VP, Pekka Pohjakallio, told a joke in Finnish and everyone dissolved in fits of laughter.

I asked Pekka to share the joke. There were a few titters. "Well, I don't think this joke translates well into English," said Pekka, "but I will try if you like. Ten Swedes go into a cupboard to play hunting games. They turn out the lights, and each one throws his knife. The first one to squeal is called Sven."

More torrential laughter erupted around the table. Evidently the joke was just as funny in English.

The most senior and by far the most gregarious Nokian I met was Anssi Vanjoki, EVP of digital convergence. He looked suave in a pin-striped suit, but on weekends he rode a big motorbike around town sporting a red bandanna. In fact, he later earned the Guinness World Record for the highest-ever speeding fine—he had to cough up more than $119,000 after being clocked on his Harley-Davidson doing twenty miles per hour over the limit on the streets of Helsinki. (Speeding fines in Finland are proportional to the offender's income.)

Over a working lunch, Anssi told me how the idea for ringtones first came about.

"Late one evening back around 1992, in the days when our phone division was all in one building, I was in the corridor outside the engineering lab. I heard what I thought was music and poked my head around the door.

"'Ah, you've got them playing tunes now?' I asked.

"'No,' replied the lab technician, 'I'm just tuning the ringer to find the most annoying frequency.'

"'Well, could you program it to play a tune or two?'

"The lab technician thought for a long time, then he said, 'Maybe . . .'

"So I ordered up half a dozen tunes on a specially modified phone and had the lab technician bring it to a marketing meeting. Everybody loved the musical ringtones. 'Let's ship it!' they agreed. But a lawyer pipes up and says 'No no no—you can't just program some famous pop song into the phones, we'd have to pay a fortune to the music publishers and the songwriters.'

"'But what if the guy is dead? Then we would get away with it?' I say.

"Long pause. 'Maybe . . .'

"'We went through all this when we were choosing the music for the TV ad campaign,' says the lawyer. 'Are any of these tunes by dead people?' asks the lawyer.

"'Yes,' says the lab technician, 'there's this one that goes da-da-da, duh, da-da-da, duh, da-da-da, duh, duuuuh. It's from a guitar concerto by a guy called Francisco Tárrega. He's been dead for 150 years.'

"'Good,' I say. 'That's good branding. Let's ship the phone with that one!'"

And so "The Nokia Waltz" was born. Within a few years, it was to become the most-played musical jingle in history. It still goes off about fifty million times a day around the planet, annoying everybody within earshot.

The Nokia engineer programmed and transmitted the first ringtone using the text message protocol, SMS. But that, too, had very random origins. Back in the early 1980s, wireless field engineers were out and about in the

Scandinavian countryside installing the first cell phone transmission antennae. Some were up church towers, or disguised as pine trees, or even hidden in plastic reindeer by the side of the road. The engineers needed a way to send their reports back to HQ, so they created a back channel that allowed them to deliver up to a 160-character message. Clever teenage hackers managed to crack the protocol and began using it to send each other text messages on Nokia phones. Many years went by before the wireless industry standardized the protocol and made it available to the public.

The most primitive Nokia ringtones were created by punching numbers on the phone's keypad and sending the resulting tune as an SMS. Before long Nokia was using SMS to send ringtones, logos, and business cards, a process they called Smart Messaging. The adoption of Smart Messaging was so rapid that by Christmas 1999 more SMS messages were sent in a single day in Finland than there were people in the country.

When Lorraine Hariton arrived from California to wrap up the contract, I met her at the airport and told her that this was going to be a bigger deal than either of us imagined. Nokia needed a source code license to the BAE. As well as playing ringtones, they wanted BAE to trigger alarm sounds and key clicks, and mix them with the cellular voice signal. This would call for many man-months of custom engineering. After the initial development, we'd need to keep a small maintenance team constantly at the ready. They also wanted alternative sound libraries for the African, Asian, and Middle Eastern markets. I was to hire a group of musicians to compose and program a set of polyphonic ringtones for several quarters' worth of new phone models. We were required to assign all copyrights to the compositions over to Nokia, so that they effectively became their own music publishers. Last but not least, they wanted me to program a Beatnik-powered version of "The Nokia Waltz." If it all went according to plan, they expected BAE to ship in about ninety million phones in the first year.

Ninety *million* units. Lorraine had to sit down.

And that was just the number of physical devices. What they believed our technology would enable, on a huge scale, was ringtone personalization—that's to say, downloadable ringtones of pop hits from the latest Top 20 charts.

254

Nokia's studies had already shown that supplementary revenues for every phone they sold could average an additional ten euros in accessories, phone covers, ringtones, and screen savers. Teens and young adults were going nuts for personalization. Nokia was convinced there was a potential market for ringtones in the tens of millions of euros per year.

As it turned out, they underestimated that figure by a couple of decimal places.

I was in the Daly City Mall on a rainy Saturday afternoon close to the holiday season. The crowds, the tinsel, and the relentless Christmas Muzak were jarring my nerves, and I was pretty much at the end of my rope. Kathleen and the kids were off somewhere holiday shopping. I was sitting on a bench wishing I were anywhere but here. A cell phone ringtone echoed across the atrium. I recognized it as a feeble rendition of the synth riff from the latest Eminem hit, "The Real Slim Shady." It came from the direction of a gaggle of high school kids outside the window of a sporting goods store. A girl pulled her phone out of her purse and answered gleefully.

Eminem is a rapper, but the girl's ringtone had no vocals on it. It was just a synth riff, and this made me smile. She had probably paid $2.50 to download a vocal-less version of the song from a mobile service provider. This behavior was utterly bewildering to the major record labels, who were struggling to get their digital services off the ground. Why would a teenager spend $2.50 on a tinny ten-second ringtone of the song when she could have the whole track for a dollar? A series of beeps—merely hinting at the Eminem original—she was quite happy to pay for, yet she had no desire to pay a buck and own the full five-minute single?

Then the explanation hit me. This teenager didn't need to spend money to buy music, as she could get all the songs she wanted from Napster for free. Her pocket money was there to make her look good to her friends. Makeup, hair products, jewelry, clothes, shoes. She'd gladly spend $80 on a pair of Nike sneakers when she could have easily saved $35 for a cheap knock-off pair that were just as comfortable; but she'd pay the extra money for the Nike logo, because it said something about her. So when her cell phone went off as she was standing there in the mall with her mates, her choice of ringtone was crucial: it was a fashion statement. The $2.50 it cost to download from Verizon came out of her *fashion* budget, not her nonexistent music budget.

That was the moment I recognized that the U.S. ringtone market was about to go ballistic. Soon, once Nokia started shipping our technology, all those ringtones would be played back through the Beatnik synth. Surely there was a way we could cash in!

And if a consumer would pay $2.50 for a mere series of beeps, what would she pay for a clip of the original Eminem recording? For a while at least, only a BAE-equipped phone would be able to play that back.

I was intrigued by a small article in *National Geographic* magazine about how common or garden birds in Copenhagen had been heard singing the Nokia jingle. Strange, but true. For years, ornithologists have observed that birds are able to mimic common urban sounds, such as car alarms or trucks reversing. In the Indonesian rain forest, macaws have learned to reproduce the click-clack of an SLR camera shutter. Now it appeared that the ubiquitous "Nokia Waltz" had become the mating call of choice for the sparrows and starlings of northern Europe. While the businesspeople around me were licking their lips and calculating Beatnik's future profits, I was dreaming of saving the planet's endangered species.

By 2003, the global ringtone market reached a staggering $2 billion per year—representing about a quarter of overall recorded music sales, including CDs, vinyl, and tapes. And the majority of those annoying ringtones were played through the Beatnik synthesizer. Beatnik's revenue from the Nokia deal was in fixed fees and engineering maintenance. So, frustratingly, we were in no position to charge even the smallest levy on the billions of downloadable ringtones played back via our synth.

However, when Nokia committed to embed the BAE in every one of their new phone models, it was a nonexclusive license. That made Beatnik a must-have item for each of Nokia's competitors. In addition to extracting a healthy licensing fee from each manufacturer, we were able to demand a royalty of a few cents per phone shipped. So over the next few years, we successfully licensed the BAE technology to the likes of Samsung, Siemens, Sony

Ericsson, and Panasonic. The two biggest mobile chipmakers, Texas Instruments and ARM, each licensed code from Beatnik to embed in their chips. By 2004, BAE was in a staggering two-thirds of all new cell phones shipped around the world, making Beatnik the most-heard synthesizer in history.

In 2003 you could walk into a phone shop anywhere in the world and buy a handset with my little synth in it. But what was bugging me was, how could I make them *sound* good? With due deference to Leon Theremin, Robert Moog, and all the great synthesizer designers of the past, I know that ours was pretty simplistic and tinny sounding; it was only as good as the puny processors that ran on mass-market mobile phones at the time. Sitting on a trolley in San Francisco, walking through a shopping center, or waiting in an airport lounge at Heathrow, I'm constantly reminded of the corners the engineers had to cut to shoehorn BAE into those tiny gadgets.

Beatnik employed half a dozen musicians, and many of our programmers and engineers also played instruments. We were a company with a strong music pedigree, yet we were all secretly ashamed at the way the first Nokia phones sounded. I couldn't stand by and watch this happen. So I scheduled a series of meetings where we brainstormed ways to improve the sound quality.

Brainstorming sessions between Beatnik's musicians and engineers could be pretty amusing. They seldom took place in conference rooms surrounded by whiteboards: more often they were held over a burrito at Tres Amigos, or during a frantic round-the-table Ping-Pong session in the refectory. You could hear the engineers in there at all times of the day and night, smashing topspin forehands while arguing about Java subroutines. This is the way programmers think. They looked for ways to fine-tune the sound library, streamlining the source code and squeezing every last drop of performance from the phone's tiny microprocessor so the synth could operate more efficiently.

The sad reality was that Nokia didn't care. We'd begged them to support a file format we invented called RMF, or Rich Music Format. RMF was Beatnik's proprietary file type that encapsulated note information along with actual audio samples, meaning ringtones could sound "real" instead of synthesized. But Nokia's policy was to only support industry-standard formats, and they said they would remove the relevant lines of our code that allowed their phones to play RMF. Every bit and byte counted, they told us; and once again, "good enough" was just that—good enough. For a few more fiscal quarters, at least, the world would be cursed with tinny ringtones. This made me feel like a litterer, a vandal, a sound polluter.

When I was on the charts with "She Blinded Me with Science," I was known as a sonic innovator, the man who put warmth and humanity into synthesized music. I was embarrassed that now I was the guy people would blame for the global ringtone plague. Had I unleashed a monster? I couldn't wait for phone power and storage to increase so we could improve the way ringtones sounded. I badly needed Moore's Law to kick in.

In June 2002 I was excited to hear that Nokia had just come out with a new version of their high-end executive phone, the 9210i Communicator. It had BAE in it, as well as a decent loudspeaker, and they sent us one for testing. It was a high-end phone for executives, but I knew its innovations would eventually trickle down to mass-market phones.

The Communicator was a bricklike object with a screen that flipped open. It could send e-mails, surf the Web, and ward off muggers.

Significantly, the 9210i was the first phone that allowed you to include file attachments with an e-mail. So, on a whim, I set up an e-mail account and sent myself an RMF file. To my astonishment, the 9210i Communicator opened my RMF file and played it, in decent quality, through its high-quality mini stereo speakers. Now we're talking!

Did Nokia even know about their oversight? Probably not. Their engineers never got around to deleting the few lines of code that play RMF files. But now they'd unwittingly shipped several million phones that could play our proprietary files. Better yet, Nokia was including BAE in an operating system called Symbian OS that would be licensed to many other handset makers including the world's number-two and -three manufacturers, Sony Ericsson and Siemens. Before long, a huge swath of the world's mobile phones would be able to play a format of audio that could only be created using the Beatnik Editor, an app over which we had total control. For obvious reasons, I decided to keep quiet about this.

But I was thrilled. Authentic Eminem vocals coming out of a phone speaker! What's your poison—the Spice Girls in glorious five-part harmony? A Pavarotti aria, or maybe a John Bonham drum solo?

At the massive CeBIT trade fair in Hannover on March 19, 2002, Anssi Vanjoki—now touted by some as a future CEO—gave the opening keynote. There were dozens of journalists and analysts in the room, and the speech was being televised on business cable channels around Europe.

Anssi pulled out his 9210i Communicator. "This is my new phone," he said, "and it has a special custom ringtone that my friend Thomas Dolby made me." He pressed a button and it played the familiar "Nokia Waltz." A few notes in, we heard the sound of a Harley-Davidson revving up and peeling out, swiftly followed by the sound of a police siren wailing in pursuit.

This got a big laugh. Anssi had just given the world its first experience of an RMF "truetone" file, which, strictly speaking, was not supported by the new Nokia phones. In the next quarter they shipped more than a hundred million of them.

CHAPTER 17
WIND ACROSS THE TUNDRA

The Beatnik board meeting should have been a cheerful event. Q2 of 2002 was our first profitable quarter since 1996, and Beatnik was making good headway with handset manufacturers. We'd recently signed licensing deals with two more. Tech licensing prospects were looking pretty good.

The numbers on the music content side were less impressive. A relatively small percentage of our revenues was from content development. My production team made custom sound sets for our BAE licensees: a set of default ringtone choices for each model of phone, along with a library of small sounds tailored to the local market. These were not big earners, and they certainly didn't scale well. I was convinced Beatnik's future was in music content, leveraged by the tech licenses. I was just having a hard time convincing the board—notably Thampy Thomas, who never got his head around content and tended to think in purely technical terms. Allen Morgan from Mayfield Fund was equally skeptical.

And Joe Rizzi, it seemed to me, had simply had enough. He'd been coming to these Beatnik board meetings for over seven years, and he'd yet to recoup his original investment. Meanwhile some of his friends and colleagues had seen their stakes in companies like Yahoo and Google become worth billions of dollars. When Joe looked at me, he saw a man who lacked the killer instinct to turn Beatnik into a Fortune 500 company. Deep down, I knew it was the truth. At my core I'm a perfectionist who will choose great art over a pile of cash every time. My chief concern was how to make these gizmos sound better, while the rest of the board members were only interested in maximizing the return on their investments.

Lorraine also seemed to be running out of steam. I had a conversation with her in the corridor after the board meeting, and she told me she'd been thinking it was time to throw in the towel. Beatnik was finally profitable, but because of dilution, her ownership of the company (and ditto mine) had been reduced to single digit percentages. If Beatnik were to start earning a healthy profit—or even if we were acquired—it'd now be virtually impossible for either of us to make a fortune, because the last money in is the first money out.

The fact was, we were shell-shocked. We knew full well that a VC-funded start-up is like a time bomb on a short fuse, and our fuse was all burned out.

Lorraine Hariton decided to retire as Beatnik's CEO in mid-2002, to be succeeded by the CTO, Don Millers. Shortly afterwards I announced my intention to step down as president of the company I'd originally founded ten years earlier. I assembled the employees and made a rousing speech, spurring them on to great things. I said it was because I needed to get back to making music, but they could see I was tired. Beatnik had been a long struggle, with occasional massive highs but very many lows. We never completed a glorious IPO or spawned dozens of tech millionaires. In some ways it was astonishing we lasted as long as we did. I learned a lot and met some great people who will remain my friends for life. But the real payoff wouldn't become apparent for a while afterwards.

The board accepted my resignation, with a gradual phase-out. As part of my golden parachute, they asked me to sign a noncompete agreement; they had little objection when I requested that it should cover technology only, not content. This meant I was able to carry on consulting and making content for Beatnik's clients, using its proprietary software, but off the company's books.

In March 2003, as a free agent, I flew down to New Orleans to join a group of a dozen executives from Nokia who had planned a retreat at a small conference hotel in the French Quarter to talk about mobile music. I knew New Orleans pretty well, and my good friend Grant Morris was a local DJ and musicologist. After a day's brainstorming in front of a whiteboard, the Finns piled into a stretch limo and embarked on a tour of NOLA's historic bars, clubs, and music venues, with Grant as our deranged tour guide. There's nothing remotely like this in Scandinavia, and they were having a blast.

It turned out that this group of Nokia execs, as an escape from the frozen Finnish winters, regularly organized "think tank" retreats at their company's expense. On one such trip they all rented Harley-Davidsons, put on leathers and bandannas, and cruised down to Mexico like outlaws, their Nordic complexions turning lobster-colored and their white Viking hair flowing in the wind.

I was happy to be accepted into the group, and I made each of them a custom RMF truetone for their standard-issue 9210i Communicator smartphones. Some chose a Jimi Hendrix wah-wah guitar riff, others selected a blast of the Earth, Wind and Fire horn section. Some opted for a Chemical Brothers techno loop or a stuttering Fatboy Slim sample. These were all sound-alikes that I had recorded in my own studio. What set my truetones apart was that they utilized actual recorded samples, not just bleeps. In this way the Beatnik technology was secretly doing for the ringtone market what the Fairlight CMI did for professionals twenty years earlier: we were making music sound more human.

The group invited me to their next two events as an independent consultant. One was in a hilltop villa in Provence, where we interspersed our brainstorming with wine-tasting trips to local vineyards. The next was an elite conference at the Austrian ski resort of Zell am See, attended by top executives from all of Nokia's major mobile carrier customers—Vodafone, Orange, T-Mobile, Wind, Movistar, and O2.

My custom truetones were the hit of the conference. You could hear them ringing out around the ski lifts and pistes. All the carrier execs wanted to know how they could sell tones like these in their own countries.

One afternoon our group block-booked a mountaintop restaurant so we had it all to ourselves. As the sun went down over the ski slopes we were served jugs of vodka and Red Bull cocktails and trays of Schnapps shots on the deck by scantily clad Nordic models. We moved inside for dinner and more hard drinking. That night I learned to play various Scandinavian hunting games that involved tossing hatchets at wooden beer barrels. I strapped on a guitar and led a raucous sing-along. The lights went out and the laughter turned to sobs as everyone climbed up on the tables, linking arms and singing "Blowin' in the Wind" while they waved the little green LED screens of their phones in the air. Around two in the morning, under moonlight, we all piled drunkenly onto toboggans and raced down the precarious mountain road at impossible speeds. With my face inches above the snow and tears streaming from my eyes, it hit me that were I to run off the road at this moment and break my neck on a tree trunk, my body would not be found until the spring.

Somehow I don't think we'd have gotten away with a night like that in California.

I now saw an opportunity. Back in the United States, I rapidly formed a new virtual company, Retro Ringtones LLC. I managed to make smart deals with some of the new high-ranking mobile operator friends I'd made in Austria. Using my knowledge of the Beatnik Audio Engine, which now ran on three-quarters of the phones they sold, I codesigned RetroFolio, a system for rapid creation and management of RMF ringtones, with a brilliant German programmer called Till Toenshoff. We came up with a way for rights holders to feed their recordings into our system and have it automatically reformat and deliver them as ringtones to nearly sixty different wireless phones, on multiple European and U.S. networks. The RetroFolio server fed high-quality weekly ringtone content into the operators' mobile portals, giving users the most up-to-date access to the current pop charts. Every Sunday afternoon when the new Top 40 chart was published, my team of composers instantly began converting the new chart entries to ringtones; first thing Monday morning they were for sale on each carrier's portal. We paid an affordable statutory royalty to the respective music collection societies. While they maintained a production line for each week's new pop hits, I personally had a lot of fun producing quirky truetone libraries with names like *Sci-Fi Sound FX, Endan-*

gered Species Mating Calls, and *Great Lies of History*, which featured clips from famous politicians' speeches.

When the first royalty statement came through from one of my operator partners and I looked at the amount on the check, I thought there must be too many zeros on the end of it. The truetone market was bigger than I dreamed. Each of these partnerships began to generate tens of thousands of euros per week for my new company, and I had only seven employees, working from home part-time. I ran the team from a shed in my backyard in California.

My son, Graham, scribbled me a note: "Daddy I hop you ar happy in yur shed!" He slipped it under the door, and it made me smile. My family was very pleased to have me home for a change. And I was starting to feel a satisfaction I had not felt for years. I was back to being Booker T. Boffin the synth tinkerer once again. This time I made a promise to myself to not begin work until midafternoon each day, so as to spend more time with my wife and our wonderful children, or playing tennis and sailing on the San Francisco Bay. The money was pouring in, and with practically no overhead this time, I was able to put it straight into our savings account. Retro Ringtones LLC was my payoff for all the years struggling at Beatnik, and it would soon allow me to return to my first love.

As Retro was only a part-time commitment, it freed me up for a few months of the year to help with the development of the TED conference. My friend Chris Anderson had taken over TED in late 2000 after his magazine publishing empire Future Inc. was hit hard by the dot-com crash. He loved the atmosphere at TED and saw massive potential in the ideas that flowed from its dynamic community, and he set about converting it into a nonprofit organization under the auspices of his Sapling Foundation. His ambition was to share the TED Talks with a much wider audience than the elitist Silicon Valley crowd that its previous owner, Richard Wurman, had pandered to.

In 2001, the first year Chris Anderson ran the TED conference, we plotted out the show in his small rented office in Palo Alto, where he was working alone with a personal assistant. He appreciated that I had a background in live entertainment and that I could help flesh out the E part of the TED moniker (Technology, Entertainment, and Design). My role was to help select musicians to perform in between TED Talks and provide some relief from the intense intellectual stimulation of the four-day TED conference. Over the years we brought in established stars such as David Byrne, Paul Simon, and Herbie Hancock, along with YouTube phenoms like Jake Shimabukuro and Eric Whitacre. As a palate cleanser between the talks, their music helped the audiences process the powerful ideas contained in the sessions. I also composed short musical overtures for each of the twelve two-hour sessions, playing and singing from behind a rack of keyboards from the side of the stage. It was a breath of fresh air for me to get back to music after my helter-skelter life as an entrepreneur. I was scarcely in the same league as the highly educated, high-net-worth attendees, but I loved sprinkling some fairy dust on the TED proceedings.

By the time I stepped down from my role as music director twelve years later, Chris Anderson had expanded TED to a staff of over a hundred, and its online talks had been viewed by tens of millions of people all over the world. TED has become an influential platform for the dissemination of ideas and a true force for global good, unaffected by political or corporate agendas.

Like many of the phases of my career, I preferred TED when it was small. Small is beautiful. They ought to carve that on my tombstone.

CHAPTER 18
THE CROCUSES ARE STILL IN BLOOM

There's a fascinating online application called the Wayback Machine that lets you view any significant Web site as it was at any given point in its history. You pick a year and month, and it takes you back in time to see a snapshot of the site at that date. Sometime around 2005 I was up late one night in my shed and feeling nostalgic about my old company. On a whim I typed *www.beatnik.com* into the Wayback Machine and started to rewind through the years, beginning with the current date and ending up in January 1994. The result was an eye-opener. Viewing its evolution in reverse, Beatnik Inc. starts out as a bland, uninspired company with a boring logo, boasting a lot of tech-business lingo about its specifications, revenues, and licensing terms. Gradually Beatnik's graphics and branding become more interesting and its marketing messages more quirky. It adds new features and capabilities. Unusual interfaces materialize, with colorful buttons and dials encouraging users to experiment and have fun with music. Then the atmosphere gets more gamelike and imaginative. The buttons and dials disappear, and you are wafted into magical 3-D worlds where you can strum mythical instruments with your mouse, jam with other users online, and create ambient music from the orbits of planets. And all this is given away for free. It is like watching a company blossom!

This got me to thinking: What happens if you reverse the timeline of human progress over the last few centuries? It reads like the history of a highly evolved alien race. You could turn it into the script to an episode from the original *Star Trek*. Captain James T. Kirk beams down to an uncharted green planet and is amazed to encounter a tribe of ethereal beings living in a society without crime, weapons, or violence. Via telepathic projection, they show Kirk how they attained this state of perpetual peace: faced with the extinction of their planet, they felt the only way to save their species was to rapidly scale back technology and communications, unplug their computers, tear down their factories and power plants, dismantle their weapons, learn to work with their bare hands, and spend time with their families, sitting around the campfire telling stories and playing music.

"Ah, but that would not work on my planet," says Kirk. "The human gene is programmed for progress and advancement. We must double our computing power every eighteen months, we must consume and reproduce, we must boldly go . . ."

I spent the first thirty years of my career on a constant quest to explore new worlds. I was regarded as a musical maverick, a tech guru, an innovator, a futurist, someone who could effortlessly blend art and technology. But I reached a point in my life where I was forced to take a long hard look at myself. It wasn't making me happy. So many times, my restlessness drove me towards the next big thing, and I turned my back on the core of my being. After my long-drawn-out struggle in two industries—music and tech—I've come to accept that I have the soul of an artist and a tinkerer. I'm not a businessman or a politician. I'm Booker T. Boffin.

In 2006 Kathleen and I decided to move back to England, to the place where I had grown up. My family has visited the coast of Suffolk every year since our children were little. It is tranquil and unspoiled, a fertile marshland with flowing waterways and endless skies. The surrounding countryside is dotted with reminders of my ancestors, who built towns and factories here in Victorian times, but whose lineage I can trace back to the Middle Ages. There was no better place to rest, recuperate, and get back in touch with the artistry I'd lost.

The kids settled into the local comprehensive school, which we all felt was a vast improvement over the broken California educational system. It was a time of great change for my family. Talia was deeply involved in activism and school politics. Graham took up skateboarding and drumming. Our eldest child, Lily, came to be known as Harper, and began a new and much happier life, living as a male. Kathleen got a part-time job in a bookshop. As for me, I just took a deep, deep breath. It didn't take too long for the healing to begin. With the sound of the waves breaking on the beach outside our window, I was able to sleep through the night without waking to flip open some mobile device and check my messages. I unsubscribed from dozens of different newsletters and services. We cut down on paper mail sent to the house. We cooked family dinners and had actual conversations. We laughed a lot and went for walks through the fields. I rode a bicycle when I could and kept a small wooden sailboat on the river.

And the music started to come. Melodies and words began to take shape in my head, and when I sat at the piano, my fingers formed into long-forgotten chord sequences. I needed a "room of my own," but it made little sense to have a studio in a shed, the way I did in California, because our property is low-lying and at risk of flooding from the North Sea. So I had the idea of building it on a boat in the garden—something that would rise up when the floods came! I spent weeks and months researching different types of vessel, wandering around local harbors and boatyards, considering the relative virtues of boat designs from many different eras. I decided the right choice would be a classic fishing boat or lifeboat—broad, sturdy, with good visibility and not too much below the waterline.

I found her on eBay. She was a thirty-three-foot former ship's lifeboat, with seating for ninety-nine souls, the kind that the *Titanic* didn't have enough of. She was up on blocks in a farmyard near Reading, which is about as far away from the sea as England gets. Her owners had planned to keep her on the Thames as a weekend getaway, but she let in water like a sieve. The local council was hassling them to remove the boat from their farm, and they were on the point of burning her and selling her brass fittings as antiques. This gave me quite a good bargaining position, though of course the purchase price was just the tip of the iceberg. The lifeboat was transported to our village on a massive low-loader truck and craned into our garden, where she now rests on a row of railroad ties. I found two traditional boat builders from Lowestoft who agreed to undertake the restoration. They taught me a few simple wood-working skills and I rolled up my sleeves and joined them on the deck. I named her *The Nutmeg of Consolation,* after a novel in Patrick O'Brian's epic naval fiction series.

The *Nutmeg* had a rotten wheelhouse, which we dismantled and replaced with a new one made entirely from reclaimed timber, sourced from various local merchants. We raided a disused Victorian hotel, the locker rooms in a boys' boarding school, and even a Cold War nuclear bunker. We erected a wind turbine on the mast and solar panels on the deck. We removed the die-sel engine and replaced it with a bank of batteries. During the day the bat-teries charge up, so that if need be I can work through the night using nothing but renewable energy. I close the venetian blinds for privacy and open them for spectacular vistas. My new wheelhouse studio has a 360-degree view of seascape and marshlands, teeming with migrating birds and grazing sheep. I installed a periscope so I could scan my world. On the horizon I studied the massive container ships heading in and out of Felixstowe. When the light caught them just right, they looked almost like floating cities.

Friends visit me on the *Nutmeg* and typically say, "I don't know how you get any work done! I'd just be staring out the window all day."

And I reply, "Well, that's me working."

I composed and recorded an album in the *Nutmeg* over the first year and a half after we moved back to Suffolk. It was my first new recorded work in nearly fifteen years. In the music industry, a two-year recording hiatus is re-garded as risky to an artist's career, so this was truly like starting out from scratch. During my time away, many things had changed. For a start, computer-based recording software had advanced to a point where there wasn't any real advantage to spending hundreds of pounds per hour in a pro-fessional recording studio. There was no longer a music industry governed by the major record companies—two or three had survived, but they had lost their stranglehold on record sales. There were now hundreds of small independents, and tens of thousands of bands and artists were printing their own CDs or selling digital downloads online.

I relished this new business landscape. It was as if all my complaints and gripes about the music business had finally been heard, and my hopes and dreams of a level playing field had come to fruition. I was delighted to rejoin the fray with a new era already in full flow. I felt like Austin Powers emerging from two decades of cryogenic sleep, surrounded by sexy, shiny toys.

Before I first quit music in the early nineties, my relationship with the audience was limited to awkward interactions at the stage door, occasional fan mail exchanges, and the statistics my record company gave me about sales and radio play and chart positions. With the advent of the Internet, my fans were able to find each other via forums and newsgroups. They self-organized into a small but fanatical community. As I was no longer putting out records, they started to analyze my past work and reminisce about gigs they had attended. They would debate the meanings of the lyrics. Some wrote entire essays about individual songs. The musicians among them would notate the melodies and chord sequences, and they began sending me CDs of their own cover versions. Some even came up with fan fiction based on the characters and places within my songs. I would lurk in these forums, astonished by how seriously people were taking my work. I felt like one of those guys who dies and his music just gets bigger; now I was returning as a ghost. It was gratifying to read that my music had touched so many souls. It was not the hits they were writing about, or the better-known radio cuts, rather my more personal, atmospheric ones, songs like "Airwaves," "Screen Kiss," "Budapest by Blimp," and "I Love You Goodbye."

I wanted to embrace the new interest in my work, to give my online fans some new material to dissect and get creative with. As my new album neared completion, it occurred to me that while I'd been away, albums were something the public had stopped buying. They were too busy playing games, hanging out in social networks, friending and blogging and tweeting and taking

271

selfies. It would be one thing to reach out to my original devotees, but it would be another thing again to win over a new generation of fans too young to remember me from the first time around.

It struck me that there was no reason that my new work had to exist purely as an album, or an hour's worth of continuous music. Why couldn't it be a game as well, and a social network event to bring my older fans together, while welcoming younger people into the fold?

So over the next few years I released three EPs, an album, a multiuser online game, and a documentary film, as well as doing three concert tours, all under the umbrella of a single concept, *A Map of the Floating City*. I enlisted the artistic talents of my brilliant family: Kathleen drew the eponymous map, while our endlessly creative daughter Talia hand-sketched some graphics for the sleeve. Our elder son, Harper, now a university student, controlled some of the intricacies of the *Floating City* transmedia game.

I had no great expectation of commercial success. Radio play was now not a major factor, and I knew it was very unlikely I'd ever get back into the charts. I could press just enough CDs and T-shirts to meet the demand, and by keeping the production modest, I could make a small profit every time I went on tour. Yet I had something much more valuable than profit: the extreme luxury of working without external funding. I was not accountable to any label or manager or A&R man. There was no need to compromise artistically.

And in many ways, I believe the work I've created in the last few years is my best work ever. When you're a songwriter there's a lot to be said for a broken childhood, shattered love affairs, angry politics, and the path to substance abuse. But you can also make great music when you're happy and contented.

I have this fatal attraction to risky artistic endeavors. Synthesis, music videos, software, the Web, DIY filmmaking, mobile devices, online games: in all these pursuits, there was no user manual to read and no one around to teach me how to approach them, so I just dived in and taught myself by trial and error. Now I feel I have something to pass on to young people. Technology continues to evolve in leaps and bounds, but there's a creative mindset that will enable you to tackle any problem. This is something I can share with the next generation of musicians and artists, even as their skills surpass mine. So, in 2014, I accepted a professorial appointment at a top American university, and Kathleen and I now spend eight months of the year in Baltimore, Maryland, where I am teaching my students some of the things I've learned in a lifetime of breaking the sound barrier.

EPILOGUE

I live at the edge of the world. This is the tiny East Anglian village where I make my home. Population twenty-three. No shops. No pub. Time stands still here, but the sea has plans of its own.

This is a land of sightings and mirages, of vanishing sandbanks and deadly currents. It is an anxious coast. We count the days, waiting for an invasion that never comes. And slowly but surely, we're tipping into the North Sea.

> Cannonballs ricochet around the room
> I hurry home to lick my wounds
> I stumble home to Oceanea
>
> A nightingale sang above my mother's tomb
> Twilight in the afternoon
> I stumble home to Oceanea
>
> Not far from here
> In some other ecozone
> The crocuses are still in bloom
> I stumble home to Oceanea

And I'm free
I'm soaring on a thermal wind
I'm learning how to shed my skin
I made it home to Oceanea.

—From *The Invisible Lighthouse* © Thomas Dolby, 2013

ACKNOWLEDGMENTS

To verify names and dates, I sifted through dozens of old yellow pads, note-books, floppy disks, Filofaxes, PalmPilots, and Danger Hiptops in search of private journal entries and corporate meeting notes; many of which, knowing what I know now, were laughably naïve. Where possible, I have resisted the temptation to imbue my former self with the wisdom and perspective I lacked at the time. People recall things very differently: at the risk of offending everybody, I made a decision to tell it just as I remember it, and apologize later.

Several friends and associates have been invaluable in helping me recall facts and feelings that might otherwise have slipped through the cracks. In particular I need to thank David Hoffman, Andy Ferguson, Anssi Vanjoki, Chris Muir, Lorraine Hariton, Steve Hales, and Chris van Rensburg for their cooperation in my research for this book. In addition, *The Speed of Sound* would not have been possible without the help and encouragement of Peter Himberger, Merrilee Heifetz, Lisa DiMona, Mary and John James, Matthew Seligman, Athena Strutt, Meg Rosoff, Songmuang Greer, Bob Miller, James Melia, and Leslie Wells; my editor Colin Dickerman and my longtime art collaborator Paul Sizer; and of course my lifetime companion and moral compass, Kathleen Beller.